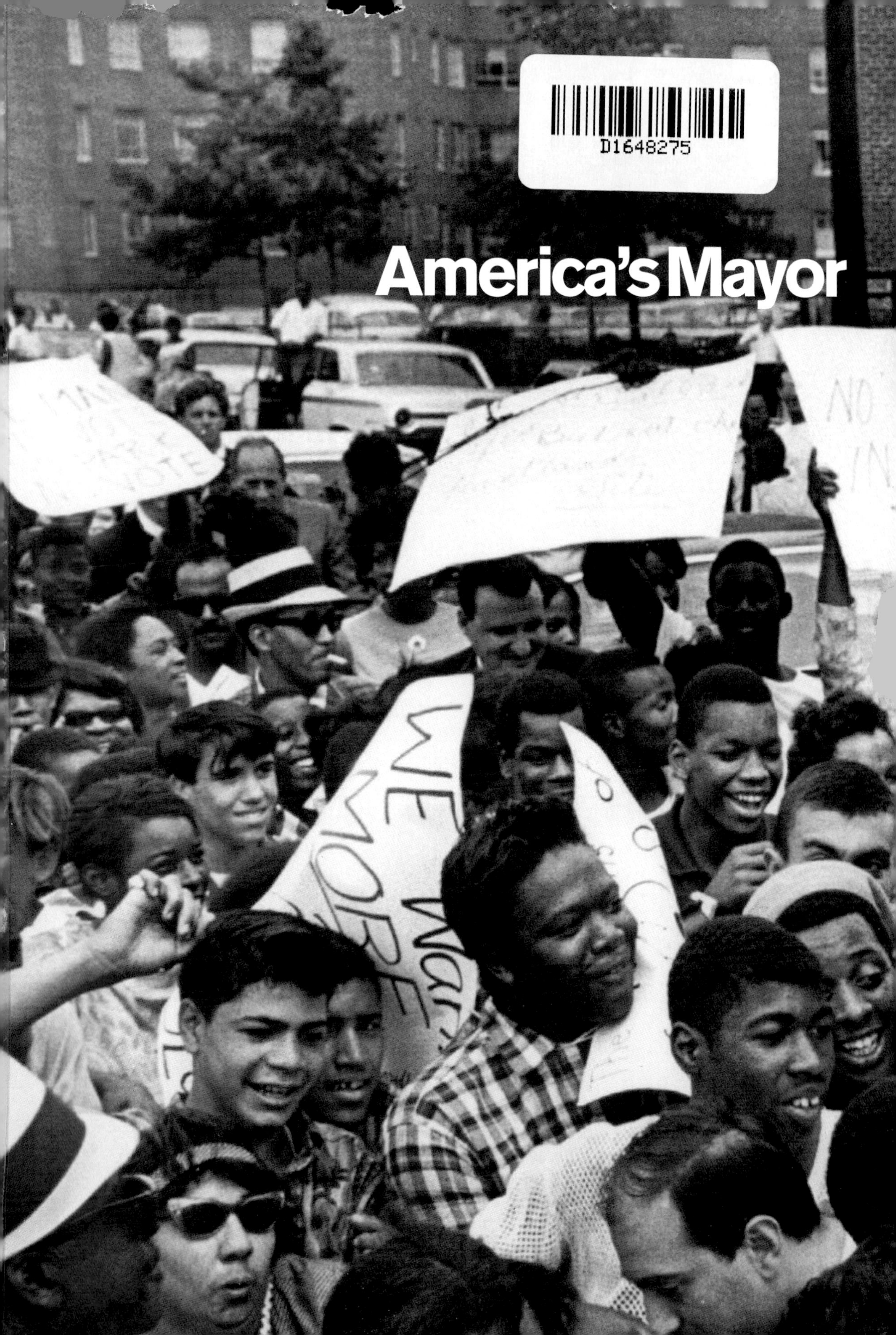
America's Mayor

America

Museum of the City of New York
Columbia University Press

Edited by Sam Roberts

’s Mayor

John V. Lindsay and the Reinvention of New York

Museum of the City of New York
New York

Columbia UniversityPress
New York

Design: Pure+Applied

TITLE PAGE IMAGE Mayor John Lindsay with demonstrators at the groundbreaking for Flatlands Industrial Park in Brooklyn, July 19, 1966. Black and Puerto Rican organizations had denounced the groundbreaking, shouting "Jim Crow Must Go," until Lindsay arrived and was cheered by the crowd.

The project to consider anew the years of the Lindsay administration is a collaboration among a number of organizations, including Thirteen, which has produced a documentary entitled *The Lindsay Years* in association with WNET.org, and the Museum of the City of New York, which has curated the exhibition *America's Mayor: John V. Lindsay and the Reinvention of New York*, created an interactive website, and co-published this companion book of the same name. The exhibition was presented with the cooperation of the Municipal Archives. Public programs were organized by the Museum and in conjunction with the John Jay College of Criminal Justice, the Paley Center for Media, and The Zicklin School of Business at Baruch College.

Key to this project are a group of individuals who provided invaluable assistance. At the top of this list is Jay Kriegel. Additionally, the project is indebted to Sally Bowles, Ambassador Walter J.P. Curley, William vanden Heuvel, Michele Cohn Tocci, and Stan Altman.

The generous donors are:

Arthur Ross Foundation*
The David Berg Foundation**

The Bodman Foundation*
Bloomberg
Charles Schwab Foundation*
Jeffrey Katzenberg

Robert D. Lindsay
Robert V. Lindsay
Margaret Lindsay and Michael Picotte
The Joan Tisch Family*
Robert Wilmers**

The ABNY Foundation*
Sunny and Dick Aurelio
Meyer S. and Floss Frucher*
Furthermore: a program of The J.M. Kaplan Fund
Lawrence M. Gelb Foundation
Ed Hamilton
Sandy and Linda Lindenbaum
George Lindsay Family

The New York Community Trust
William S. Paley Foundation, Inc.
Bob Price
Rudin Family Foundation*
The Howard Samuels Family
Constantine Sidamon-Eristoff
Pollock and Arthur Spiegel
John Zuccotti

Carter Bales
Barbaralee Diamonstein-Spielvogel
Don Elliott
David L. Garth
Roy Goodman

James Kagen
Eugene Keilin and Joanne Witty
Wynn Kramarsky
Joan and Leonard Leiman
Norman and Tina Levy
Stephen McDonald

Charles Moerdler
Fred and Fran Nathan
Victor Palmieri
Ken Patton**
Hal and Judy Prince
Norman Redlich

Gordon Stewart*
Bob Sweet
William Golden Foundation*

Bill Bardel
Robert and Marti Dinerstein
Herb Elish and Eloise Hirsch
Lew Feldstein
Barbara Fife*
Lew Frankfort
Marilyn Friedman

Robert and Amy Heller
Lyndsay Howard
Lew Kaden
Christopher Kennan
John Koskinen
Jay L. Kriegel/The Tides Foundation

Edgar Lampert
The Leonard Friedland Charitable Foundation/Sid Davidoff and Robert J. Malito
Nathan Leventhal
Robert J. Newman

Chuck Ortner
Marilyn Shapiro
Gina Sharpe
Herb Sturz
Joan Tilney
Martha Wallau
Harriet Higgins Warren

Stephen R. Aiello
Judith Areen
Querube Arias
Mimi Barker
Carol Bellamy
Samuel Berger
Norborne Berkeley Jr.
Stan Brezenoff
Leonard Chazen
Ann and Elias Clark
Brian Conboy
Alex Cooper
Evan A. Davis
Peggy Cooper and Gordon J. Davis
William Diamond
Murray and Mary Drabkin
June Margolin Eisland
Ethan Eldon
Ronnie Eldridge
Paul Elston
Justin Feldman
Susan B. Fisher
Joy Manhoff and Stanley Flink
Joseph Forstadt
Patsy Glazer

Peter Goldmark
Betsy Gotbaum
Herb Halberg
Jane Havemeyer
Robert Hazen
Stephen Heard
Susan Heilbron and Andrew Goldman
Marian S. Heiskell
Michael S. Helfer
George Hirsch
Elizabeth Holtzman
Steven Isenberg
Anthony Japha
William Josephson
George Kalkines
John Keker
Allan Kennedy
Andrew Kerr
Arthur Klebanoff
Jerome Kretchmer
Michael Lacher
Philip Allen Lacovara
Dale M. Landi
Michael J. Lazar

Lance Liebman
Stan Litow
Linda Lynn in Memory of Ted Lynn
William Maloney
Teddy and Peggy Mastroianni
David and Barbara McGregor
Ronay and Richard L. Menschel
William Miller and Lynn McGuire
Milton Mollen
Charles Morris
Jason R. Nathan
James Nespole
Basil A. Paterson
Elizabeth B. Patterson
Peter Piscitelli
Charles Raymond
Fergus Reid
Suzie Rentschler
Alice Richmond
Jaque Robertson
Mitchell Rosenthal
Bill Roskin
Laura Ross
Jerold Ruderman

Bob Ruskin
Heather and Jim Ruth
Stephen Salup
Norman Samnick
Marvin Schick
Anthony and Marion Scotto
Robert Selsam
Robert Shrum
Lester Shulklapper
Alan M. and Carol Silberstein
Joel Silver
Hildy Simmons
Anthony Smith
Micho Spring
Peter Stangl
Norman Steisel
Thomas D. "Toby" Thacher
Franklin Thomas
Katrina Thomas
Carlisle Towery
Carl Weisbrod
Alan Wiener
Joan and Peter Wynn
Joanne Jablow Yunich

---

* Donor to WNET.org

** Donor to WNET.org and the Museum of the City of New York.

In addition to those listed above, the Museum is most grateful to the 89 additional donors whose gifts of up to $1,000 also helped to make the project possible.

Important in-kind contributions have been gratefully received from the *Daily News* and *The New York Times*.

Contributors as of February 22, 2010

CONTENTS

THE KILLERS

TWU
ON
STRIKE
MABSTOA
NO CONTRACT
NO WORK

CONTENTS

FOREWORD

My first job in New York City—the second job of my life—was in the Lindsay administration. I was hired as the cultural affairs assistant in the Mayor's Office of Lower Manhattan Development, working with Richard Weinstein and Terry Williams, the Director and Deputy Director, and with John West and many other colleagues.

I was swept up in a swirl of what seemed to me radical thinking—architects, planners, and lawyers who saw urban design as a new approach for the preservation and growth of the city—really, as a way to save the city. The challenges were many—deteriorated districts, crumbling landmarks slated for demolition, private developers focused on bottom lines, burgeoning suburbs that drained wealth from the city. Within a short period of time, I, too, believed that our urban experience could and should be reshaped by a variety of interventions, including special zoning districts, landmarks designations, new parks, and more.

We worked hard on the creation of the South Street Seaport Historic District—developers were threatening Schermerhorn Row, a block front of intact early 19th century buildings from the days when Manhattan was a seaport. The solution was a public/private initiative and a bold plan that scooped up the development rights over the block and banked them—to land at some future point on designated receiver sites. This was a strategy used earlier by the Lindsay administration for Grand Central Station—a strategy that in part enabled the U. S. Supreme Court to find that no undue "taking" of private property rights had occurred.

We were committed to combining commercial, cultural, and residential uses to create a 24-hour community in Lower Manhattan. We worked hard on the Special Greenwich Street Development District, the Nassau Street Pedestrian Mall, and Manhattan Landing, and we planned and rewrote the zoning for Battery Park City, preserving visual corridors to the Hudson River and mapping the promenade along the water. All this was part of the implementation phase of the 1966 Lower Manhattan Master Plan.

We worked to ensure the preservation and re-use of the Custom House on Bowling Green, which was left empty when the U. S. Customs Service moved to 7 World Trade Center. We rezoned TriBeCa to enable residential use of the area, paving the way for its future designation as a landmark district.

We closed the Brooklyn Bridge to traffic on the occasion of its 75th birthday, and Mayor Lindsay led a parade of people across it, with a fireworks display that evening.

Along with those who worked in improving administration, public health, community relations, public safety, transportation, poverty, civil rights, and a host of other issues, we were filled with optimism about the future of the city—even as times grew bleaker.

I, for one, have changed very little in the ensuing decades. The Lindsay years were a platform for my development, and while I have learned more over the years I think no less of those lessons about urbanism, which apply not only to the city's built environment, but also to its culture, economy, people, and politics. Today, at the Museum of the City of New York, we trumpet our urban values of diversity, opportunity, and perpetual transformation, ideals that resonated strongly in those Lindsay years.

So many people have come together to make the exhibition, website, and book possible. John Lindsay's children, Anne Lindsay, John V. Lindsay Jr., Katharine Lindsay Lake, and Margaret Lindsay Picotte, generously provided access to their family archives, including those on deposit at Yale University. Dr. Steven H. Jaffe, the guest curator, has done a terrific job and has mastered the complexity of the Lindsay era. Sam Roberts, the editor of this book, we salute with huzzahs for being a gracious and wise colleague, a superb organizer of the book's content, and an uncommonly dexterous editor. Paul Carlos, Urshula Barbour, and Virginia Chow of Pure+Applied have created a wonderful design for the book and the exhibition, and Vivian Ducat of Ducat Media has produced a lively companion website. Our own Deputy Director and Chief Curator, Dr. Sarah Henry, has held all the many pieces of this project together, moving forward on all fronts with equanimity, vision, and a firm intellectual grasp. Special thanks to John Thorn, for introducing us to our partners at Columbia University Press, who have done such a splendid job with this book.

The Museum was aided by a dedicated advisory team, including Dick Aurelio, Sid Davidoff, Gordon Davis, Ronnie Eldridge, Don Elliott, Peter Goldmark, Betsy Gotbaum, Steve Isenberg, Jay Kriegel, Bob Laird, Nat Leventhal, Ken Patton, and Gordon Stewart, as well as Warren Wechsler, who also assisted immensely with acquiring content for the website. Jonathan Barnett (who helped plan a compelling design and planning symposium), Marilyn Friedman, Jaquelin Robertson, Richard Weinstein, Myles Weintraub, John West, and Terry Williams gave our curators valuable lessons about urban design; and Ray Horton shed light on issues of budget and labor relations. Historians Joshua B. Freeman, Robert W. Snyder, and Clarence Taylor provided invaluable scholarly guidance. And finally, we must single out Jay Kriegel, who has been tenacious and focused, and it is he who is the force behind this multifaceted project. Our great gratitude to him!

SUSAN HENSHAW JONES
Ronay Menschel Director
Museum of the City of New York

EDITOR'S ACKNOWLEDGMENTS

America's Mayor was very much a collaborative endeavor.

Thanks especially to all of the essayists—Richard Reeves, Charlayne Hunter-Gault, Pete Hamill, Nicholas Pileggi, James Sanders, John Mollenkopf, Joshua Freeman, Hilary Ballon, Jeff Greenfield, Charles Morris, Steven Weisman, Kenneth T. Jackson—for their expertise, professionalism, and grace in making this book possible.

Thanks, also, to the other contributors—including Stan Altman, Jimmy Breslin, David Burnham, Robert A. Caro, Mario M. Cuomo, Robert Curvin, Barbarlee Diamonstein-Spielvogel, Lew Feldstein, Juan Gonzalez, Ada Louise Huxtable, Ed Koch, Charles Rangel, Jim Sleeper, Clarence Taylor, and Frank Thomas—for their generosity in providing valuable personal insights that brought the 1960s and 1970s in New York back to life and for granting permission to reproduce their earlier observations. Vincent J. Cannato, author of *The Ungovernable City*, the major and most recent study of the Lindsay administration, unselfishly offered his advice.

Thanks, too, to all the Lindsay alumni—among them, Richard Aurelio, Stan Brezenoff, Gordon Davis, Ronnie Eldridge, Peter Goldmark, Betsy Gotbaum, Ed Hamilton, Steve Isenberg, Nat Leventhal, Victor Marrero, Bob Shrum, John Zuccotti—who graciously offered their reflections for this book, for interviews with Michael Epstein and Tom Casciato for a documentary by Thirteen for WNET.org, and for the concurrent exhibition at the Museum of the City of New York being curated by Steven H. Jaffe.

The entire project would not have been possible without the unsparing efforts and meticulous attention to detail of the indefatigable Jay Kriegel.

The officials and staff of the Museum of the City of New York were, as usual, generous and good-humored in offering their magnanimous support and wise counsel. Special thanks to Susan Henshaw Jones, the savvy president and Ronay Menschel Director of the Museum; Sarah M. Henry, the ingenious deputy director and chief curator; Kathleen Benson, the discerning project director for exhibitions and publications, who tirelessly, tactfully, and conscientiously shepherded all the participants; Autumn Nyiri, the adroit senior curatorial associate, and Anne Lebleu, project associate, who so diligently found and secured permissions to reproduce the vivid illustrations that bring the Lindsay era alive.

The designers, Paul Carlos and Virginia Chow of Pure+Applied, made a major undertaking look effortless as they transformed disparate and sometimes disjointed words, titles, and images into a handsome and accessible book.

Thanks to Philip Leventhal, associate editor of Columbia University Press, for his faith in this project.

Countless other people contributed, but a few deserve to be singled out for special praise for their time and magnanimity, including Phyllis Collazo and Jeff Roth of *The New York Times*; Sheelagh McNeill, a former *Times* researcher; Arthur Browne, Martin Dunn, and Marie McGovern of the *Daily News*; the photo archive staffs of *The Times*, the *Daily News*, and *Life* magazine; Charles Brecher; the staffs of the New York City Department of Records and Information Services/Municipal Archives; the photographers whose vivid images are included; and the manuscripts and archives division of the Yale University Library.—SR

Sam Roberts

Introduction

On November 22, 1965, three weeks after John V. Lindsay was elected New York City's 103rd mayor, *Man of La Mancha* opened at the ANTA Theater in Washington Square. As Mitch Leigh, the show's composer, would recall years later, the emotional appeal of its theme song "The Impossible Dream" was universal: disaffected blacks, Puerto Ricans, feminists, gay-rights advocates, and antiwar protesters all appropriated it as their singularly personal anthem. The show would run for 2,328 performances, nearly as many days as Lindsay would serve as mayor.

Many New Yorkers agreed with Lindsay that in post-World War II New York "change was associated chiefly with decline." To them, the mayor-elect himself embodied a dream—not necessarily an expectation, but the hope that had been ignited a few years earlier in Washington by John F. Kennedy's New Frontier and rekindled by Lyndon Johnson's Great Society—that achieving change for the better might still be possible.

This book is about John V. Lindsay's dream to reinvent New York. It is not just a history book, though revisiting his mayoralty would, in itself, be justified, since some previous accounts were freighted with ideological baggage, or they insufficiently assessed the administration's controvertible record in the context of those turbulent times. Moreover, half of today's New Yorkers weren't even born, much less lived in the city, during Lindsay's eight years as mayor. But even beyond history's claim, fully a half-century since Lindsay was elected to public office, the aftershocks of his record still reverberate as a society grappling with the consequences of immigration, income inequality, a health care crisis, and environmental adversity confronts the legacy of the 1960s.

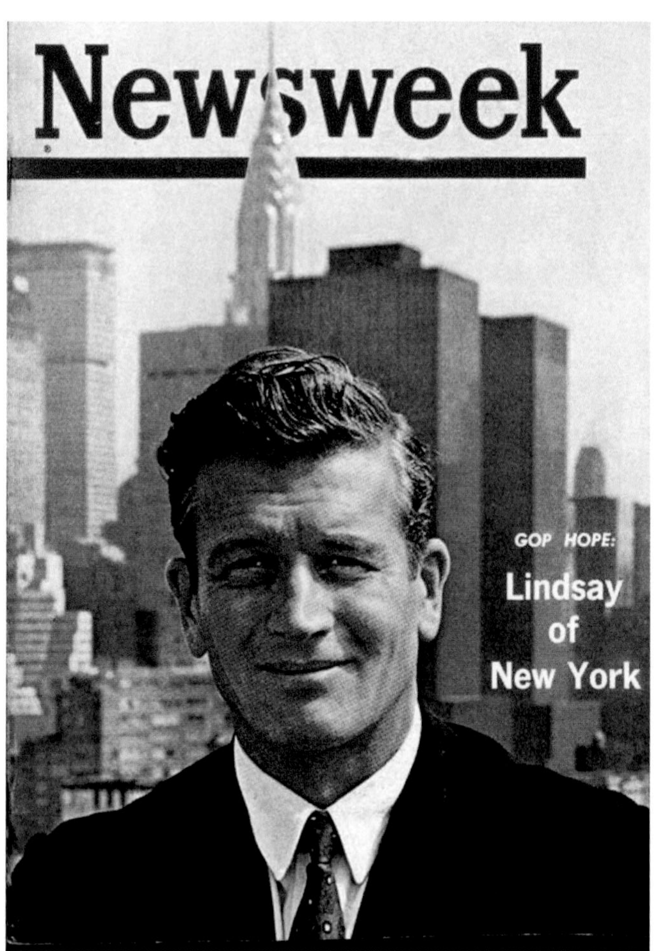

Newsweek, May 31, 1965

A generation before Rudy Giuliani usurped the title, Lindsay was America's Mayor. While he came to personify the decade's explosive problems, he also exemplified bold potential solutions that were advanced as a national urban agenda, one that resonates today as states and municipalities struggle to avoid bankruptcy. Galvanizing fellow mayors across the country, Lindsay became a telegenic spokesman for the always-suspect cities just as residents of megalopolises of over a million people were verging on becoming a majority of America's population. He was the first media mayor, innovatively exploiting free and paid TV marketing to win higher office and retain it. His very election projected him onto the covers of national newsmagazines.

Even before he was credited with keeping New York from boiling over in the racial cauldron that exploded in other cities, Lindsay was being hailed as America's great hope. As a Manhattan congressman, he not only survived the avalanche that buried Barry Goldwater and so many other Republicans in 1964, but was re-elected in a landslide. The following year, as a mayoral candidate, the mythology he generated began the very first day. That May 13, as Lindsay declared his candidacy, Oliver Pilat, his press secretary, wrote in his diary: "John Lindsay began running today for president by way of New York's City Hall." Pilat's prediction was followed by *Time* magazine's gushing observation that "far beyond New York, there was wistful talk of Lindsay among Republicans hungry for a dynamic presidential candidate." The day after Lindsay was inaugurated, *The New York Times* reported: "The ceremony marked a major transfer of political power in the city that could have national repercussions....[and] his assumption of the mayoralty of the country's largest city made him a potential candidate for the presidency." But when Lindsay visited his City Hall office for the first time, he was jolted back to the present by an ominous totem that he discovered on his desk. It was a tiny metal shamrock, a reminder, as if he needed one, that his fate, at least in the first few days, rested in the hands of a blustery Irish-born labor leader to whom he had taken an instant dislike, and vice versa.

Most of the authors of the self-contained essays in *America's Mayor: John V. Lindsay and the Reinvention of New York* witnessed the Lindsay era for themselves, but as outsiders without the baggage of having to second-guess their own record. In this book, they explore whether Lindsay's dream to reinvent the city—to bridge the income and affordability gap, bring racial minorities into government, integrate neighborhoods, empower communities through decentralization, impose strategic urban planning to spare the environment, and make cities more livable—was realistic to begin with in what Vincent Cannato's book called *The Ungovernable City*. Was Lindsay's the right dream at the right time? Was his promise *The Dream That Failed*—as his first press secretary, Woody Klein, wrote in a premature verdict? Was *The Cost of Good Intentions*, as Charles Morris's book described it, prohibitively high? To what extent did he achieve his agenda? And, perhaps most fundamentally, would any other mayor have done a demonstrably better job juggling the seismic political, social, economic, and cultural revolutions that defined the anarchic decade and were by no means unique to New York? That hypothetical question is integral to judging an administration that succeeded magnificently at some things, but failed miserably at others.

"What produced Lindsay's record of failures: the leader or his times?" Joyce Purnick asked in *The Times*. "That question is central to understanding today's urban policies."

"Working on John Lindsay's mayoral campaign in 1965 changed my life.... There were lots of lively, funny, intelligent, and committed people determined to get Lindsay elected and give New York a fresh start. This was a great tribute to the candidate himself. He was a brilliant campaigner. I don't think it's entirely unfair to say that he was probably better at campaigning than at governing, though obviously as jobs go governing New York was in those days almost in a class of its own...Anyway, thanks to John Lindsay I spent my life in politics, which as he demonstrated can be an honorable adventure, and I have never regretted it."

—Christopher Patten
was a member of the British Parliament and the governor of Hong Kong. Lord Patten is chancellor of the University of Oxford

Lord Bryce, the British historian, wrote in the 1880s that municipal government in the United States was the most conspicuous failure of American life, which may be one of the reasons that no former mayor of any city has been elected president since Calvin Coolidge, of Northampton, Mass., in 1924. There is a reason, too, that since the 19th century the mayoralty of New York has been a political dead end. The presidency can elevate the most mediocre of men, Wallace Sayre and Herbert Kaufman wrote in their seminal *Governing New York City*, but, they warned, "the mayoralty is the highly vulnerable symbol of all the defects in the city and its government." When H.L. Mencken learned that Representative Fiorello H. La Guardia had been elected mayor in 1933, he expressed the hope that La Guardia ,"if he is well-advised he will make his

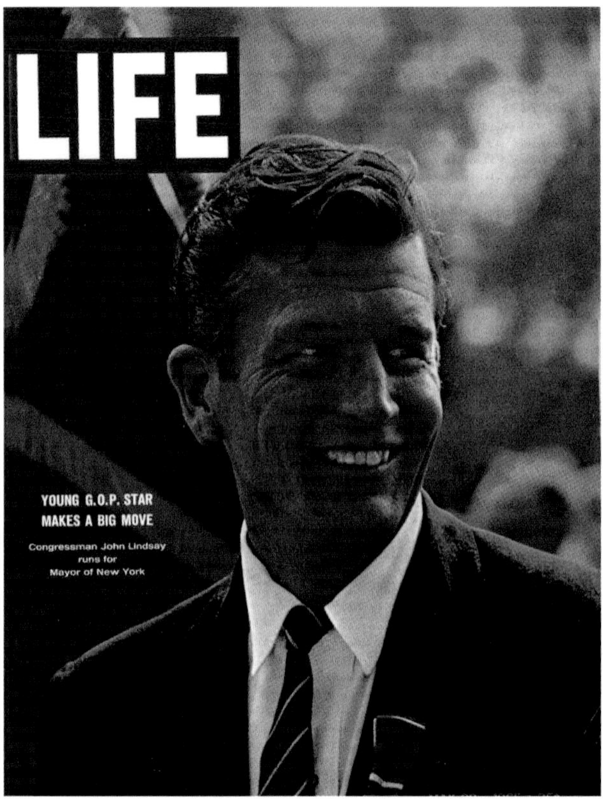
LIFE
YOUNG G.O.P. STAR
MAKES A BIG MOVE
Congressman John Lindsay
runs for
Mayor of New York

Life, May 28, 1965

will, get a shave and haircut, burn all the letters that he has ever received from women" and jump from the tallest building.

In 1965, the challenges facing the city seemed so overwhelming that New Yorkers were willing to gamble again on a maverick Republican, as they had with La Guardia three decades earlier. When the year began, a *Times* editorial raised the "sickly hope" among some Republicans that in that off-year for federal elections, one of the city's few phenomenal Republican vote-getters—maybe Senator Jacob K. Javits or, perhaps, that young East Side congressman, John V. Lindsay—might be induced to go down what was admittedly "suicide road toward City Hall."

In 1965 and again in 1969, as Richard Reeves and Jeff Greenfield recount, Lindsay was blessed with being the only liberal in the mayoral race. The import of the second campaign was that he managed to harness progressive New Yorkers' fury over a faraway war to overcome the handicaps he had placed in his path to re-election at home. The significance of his first election, in retrospect, was that the campaign presaged the governmental reinvention that would mark his administration. He recruited hundreds of volunteers to staff local storefronts, which suggested his commitment to decentralization and democratization and to modern management and which, coupled with prodigious fund-raising and imaginative television tactics, would, as John Mollenkopf writes, circumvent and undermine the Democratic Party machine. His very first mayoral campaign speech—proposing the creation of a civilian board to review complaints of police abuse—signaled his willingness (or confrontational compulsion) to challenge old guard power brokers and, as Charlayne Hunter-Gault recalls, to embrace disenfranchised black and Hispanic New Yorkers.

As a democratic urbanist mayor, he cared enormously not only about how the city looked, how creative urban design could be encouraged by City Hall, as Hilary Ballon writes, but also about how New York could be made more livable. He turned the city into an adventureland, as James Sanders calls it, a film capital and a stage for street and park spectacles that capitalized on the vitality that New York epitomized.

"If New York is ungovernable, then we're all doomed," Lindsay bluntly warned even before he began to govern. Mario Cuomo, one of the many great talents whom Lindsay tapped, would later say that campaigning is poetry (with more rhyme than reason sometimes) while governing is prose. In Lindsay's case, however high-minded his prose, it was sometimes overwhelmed by the viral sloganeering that resounded in the echo chamber of New York's Agora. Lindsay governed when New York was ground zero in the 1960s culture wars, when every interest group was discovering its voice and demanding not only a seat at the table, but also a piece of the proverbial pie. As Pete Hamill writes, in promising to deliver power to the people—to *those* other people, not to the discontented white middle class outside Manhattan—Lindsay stood tall as an inviting lightning rod. And, as Steven Weisman explains, he hastened the city's spiral into fiscal crisis not only by providing generous welfare benefits that, as it turned out, helped perpetuate dependency, but, as Joshua Freeman recalls, also by delivering liberal wages and fringes to municipal employees that delivered them, too, from near-poverty.

By the time the second term was over, the accumulated political and social breakage from confronting the city's permanent government would obscure much of what Lindsay had accomplished. But, as Kenneth T. Jackson concludes in ranking him and his legacy in the pantheon of Greater New York's 20 mayors since 1898, Lindsay is beginning to look better with time.

Time, November 12, 1965

When he began, though, it was different. The dream was still very much alive, perhaps even possible. It was a time, after all, when, as Donald H. Elliott, the chairman of Lindsay's City Planning Commission put it, "government was expected to make society better and everybody believed it could do so." That was the underlying conceit of the Lindsay administration's 1969 futuristic strategic plan for New York. For all the administration's naiveté, its utopian illusions, and its reputation for taking itself too seriously, the commission's master plan was paradoxical and prescient in defining Lindsay's constituency and in rendering its verdict on his mayoralty. "We are, in sum, optimistic," the planners wrote. "But we are also New Yorkers. We cannot see utopia. Even if all of these recommendations were carried out, if all the money were somehow raised, 10 years from now all sorts of new problems will have arisen, and New Yorkers will be talking of the crisis of the city, what a near-hopeless place it is, and why doesn't somebody do something."

Sam Roberts

City in Crisis I

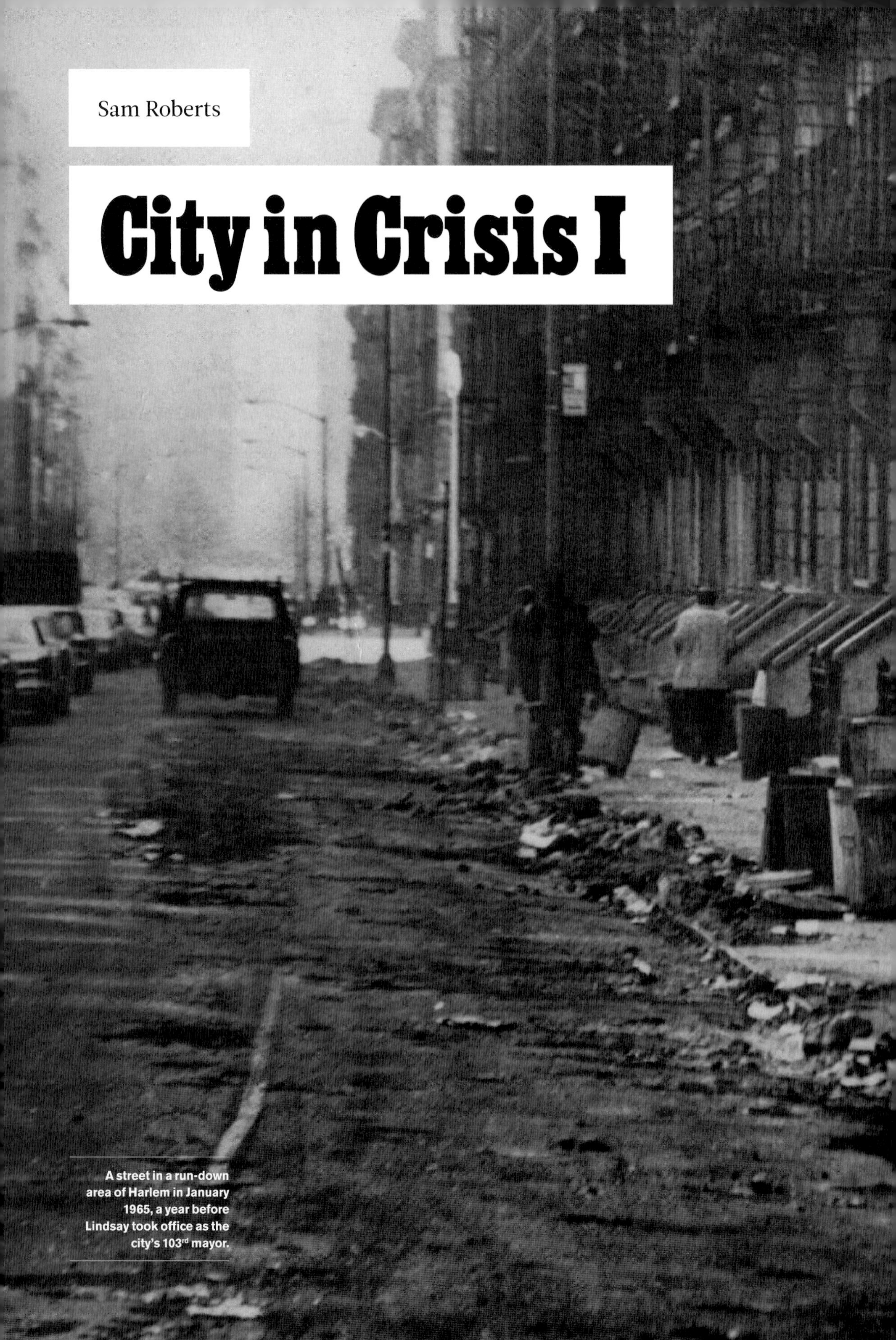

A street in a run-down area of Harlem in January 1965, a year before Lindsay took office as the city's 103rd mayor.

"New York, Greatest City in the World," the headline on the front page of *The New York Herald Tribune* declared on January 25, 1965, "And Everything Is Wrong With It." So many things seemed wrong that most New Yorkers had given up on the city's governability. All but the most chauvinistic were beginning to doubt even its greatness.

SAM ROBERTS is the urban affairs correspondent of *The New York Times* and the host of *The New York Times Close Up*, *The Times's* weekly television program on NY1 News. Before joining *The Times* in 1983, he was a reporter, columnist, and city editor of *The Daily News* in New York. He is the author of the books *Only in New York*, *A Kind of Genius*, *The Brother*, *Who We Are*, and *Who We Are Now*.

When the year began, Robert F. Wagner was wearily finishing his third term as mayor, but he still seemed destined to pursue an unprecedented fourth. He had "contributed 12 honest and reasonably efficient years as mayor," Richard Reeves wrote in *The New York Times*, "and he left us convinced the town couldn't be governed."

When the year ended, John V. Lindsay would inherit what was, as *The Trib's* series dubbed it, a "City in Crisis."

What did New York look like in 1965? In January, welfare workers struck for 28 days, disrupting relief to 500,000 New Yorkers. A vast array of anti-poverty programs was being administered by 12 separate agencies with what outside auditors concluded was "little or no coordination, sometimes at cross purposes, and often puzzling and frustrating the people whom they are designed to serve." Transit policy was so chaotic that Robert Moses's Triborough Bridge and Tunnel Authority announced plans to renovate the West Side Highway without consulting either the City Planning Commission or the Traffic Department.

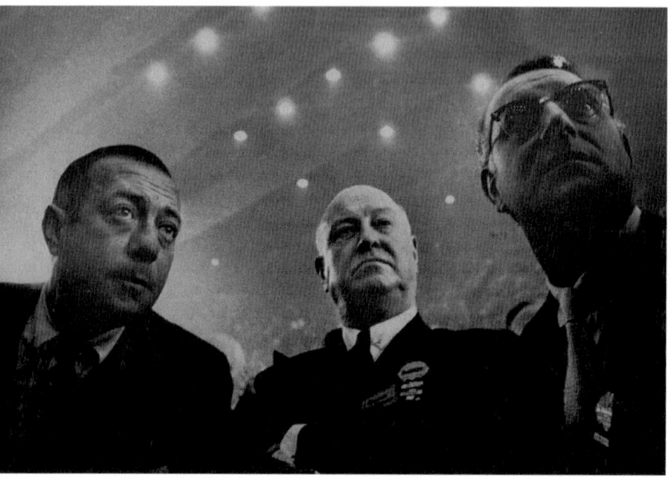

Former Mayor Wagner (left) with Tammany Hall leader Carmine De Sapio (right) at the Democratic Convention in 1956. In 1961, Wagner ran against the Tammany bosses and won.

Factories, which employed one in four New Yorkers, were hemorrhaging 18,000 jobs a year. One third of the city's schoolchildren were testing below the norm in reading and arithmetic. Ancient garbage trucks were out of service 40 percent of the time. During a drought that summer, a mayoral candidate made front page news when he discovered a broken sluice gate in Central Park that was leaking hundreds of thousands of gallons of water a day.

Standard and Poor's lowered the city's credit rating and comptroller Abraham D. Beame, whom one Lindsay supporter, Democratic Socialist Michael Harrington, dismissed as having "accountancy as a political philosophy," was warning about "the treacherous fiscal path being followed by our city."

By 1965, the social and cultural turbulence that would define the decade was already being visited upon the city. But the era's other transcendent emotion—an improbably romantic sense of possibilities—was still awaiting some enkindling spark.

New York was also reeling from riots that erupted in Harlem and Bedford-Stuyvesant the year before, after a 15-year-old black youth was shot to death by a white police officer on the Upper East Side. (Mayor Wagner promised more summer jobs and vowed to assign more black cops to Harlem, but he refused a request from the Reverend Martin Luther King Jr. to name an independent police review board).

Major crime, meanwhile, had soared by nearly 15 percent in the past year alone. During the campaign, Lindsay visited the site in Kew Gardens, Queens, where 38 neighbors failed to respond to the screams of Kitty Genovese, a 28-year-old woman who was being attacked. Their silence stunned a city inured to apathy. What the murder "tells us," Lindsay said, "is that something has gone out of the heart and soul of New York City." (The murder of a young woman in a quiet residential neighborhood was originally considered so routine—before the apathy element emerged—that the first account was relegated to four paragraphs on page 26 of *The Times*.)

Today, New Yorkers may reflect nostalgically on the city of 1965, proudly pointing to levels of crime that have plunged to lows unseen since then. But, by 1965, many New Yorkers were figuring that the city's greatest days were behind it. And while they were dissatisfied with the status quo, they regarded change even more warily. After all, so many of the changes that had occurred since what were considered the city's glory days seemed to have been for the worse.

The Greatest Mayor

Fiorello H. La Guardia is still widely considered New York's greatest mayor, in part because of the Depression-sized hardships he found himself facing. In the 1930s, New Deal resources from Washington harnessed to local political will proved to be up to the task. By the mid-1960s, in contrast, the promise of a Great Society was already competing with the cost of a faraway war. Moreover, the challenges—not just political ones, but the search for practical solutions to an influx of poor people and of heroin—seemed more intractable.

Consider this grim assessment by *Time* magazine in 1965:

> *New York seemed a shiftless slattern, mired in problems that had been allowed to proliferate for decades. Its air was foul, and so were its surrounding waters—and there was barely enough water to drink. Its slums rotted away undisturbed, its new apartment buildings and public housing were as shoddy as rapacity and bureaucracy could make them. The city was deep in hock and going deeper; interest on its debt alone was $1.4 million daily—more than the cost of police, fire and sanitation services combined. More and more, it was a place where only the rich and the welfare-dependent poor could afford to live. Its crime rate was rising as inexorably as its traffic slowed down. East Side, West Side, male and female prostitutes seemed like shades of prewar Berlin. Even the fabled skyline had lost much of its old majesty. As Architect Edward Durrell Stone lamented: "If you look around and you give a damn, it makes you want to commit suicide."*

For years, Jason Epstein, the book editor and publisher, would write later, New York seemed to have been run by "a kind of anarchic common sense," a formula, if you could call it that, which Wagner had honed to an art. But, Epstein continued,

> *by the middle 1960s you could see the city changing all around you. New construction was going up everywhere, herding the old residents and their*

New York is the world's financial and cultural center, the nation's tastemaker and the home of the power elite, but to many of its eight million citizens, it is no longer the greatest place to live.

Discontent has always been a distinctive quality of the New Yorker—restlessly unwilling to accept the status quo—and in the past this discontent has been channeled into the tremendous creative energy which has given the city its dynamic character. But in the complex years since the end of World War II the creative channels have clogged up. The city's simple problems require complex answers. And the complex problems seem to have no solutions at all. With responsible outlets denied, the citizen's discontent has turned inward to bewilderment, frustration, rage, and, finally, fear or indifference.

It is a city in which:

Nearly one-fifth of the city's people now live in poverty conditions—families earning less than $3,000 a year and individuals earning less than $2,000 a year—many in cramped, inadequately heated, insanitary, rat-infested apartments.

More than 70,000 youths now roam the streets, out-of-work and out of school, untrained and uncaring.

The mayor and city officials have done little to keep the middle-class whites from leaving.

Half a million people, more than the number living in the states of Alaska, Delaware, Nevada, Vermont, or Wyoming, are now receiving welfare with no solution in sight.

At the rate that public housing has been constructed over the last two years, it would take someone more than 10 years to gain admission to a public-housing project if he applied today.

To many New Yorkers, urban renewal has come to mean Negro or human renewal, the shifting of a minority group from one slum to another.

An 84-year-old woman, rushed by ambulance to a hospital after suffering a stroke recently, had to wait eight hours and be transferred to three different hospitals before a bed could be found for her.

The police force has added more than 7,000 men in the past decade yet the narcotics rate in New York City has skyrocketed (half of the narcotics addicts in the U.S. now live in New York) and gambling, the numbers, and prostitution continue to flourish. The court backlog has become so bad that it takes four years to get many cases

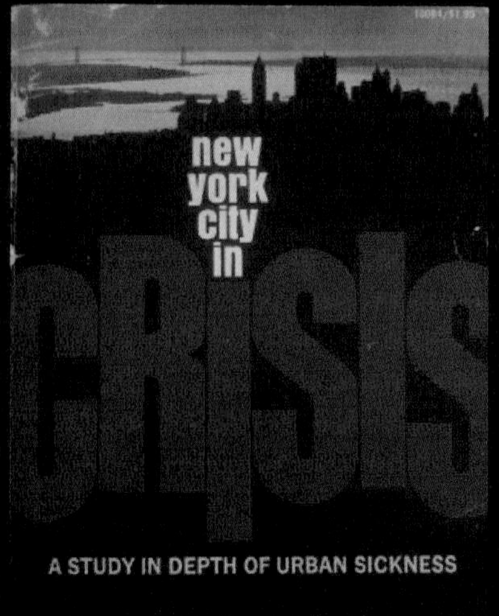

new
york
city
in
CRISIS
A STUDY IN DEPTH OF URBAN SICKNESS
By the staff of the New York Herald Tribune
Prepared under the direction of Barry Gottehrer

The *Herald Tribune*'s 1965 series, *New York City in Crisis*, was also published in book form. Written by the *Tribune* staff, the book was prepared under the direction of Barry Gottehrer, who later served as special assistant to Mayor Lindsay.

Lindsay the candidate inspects a Harlem tenement. He said, "I, for one. cannot stand by while the decline and fall

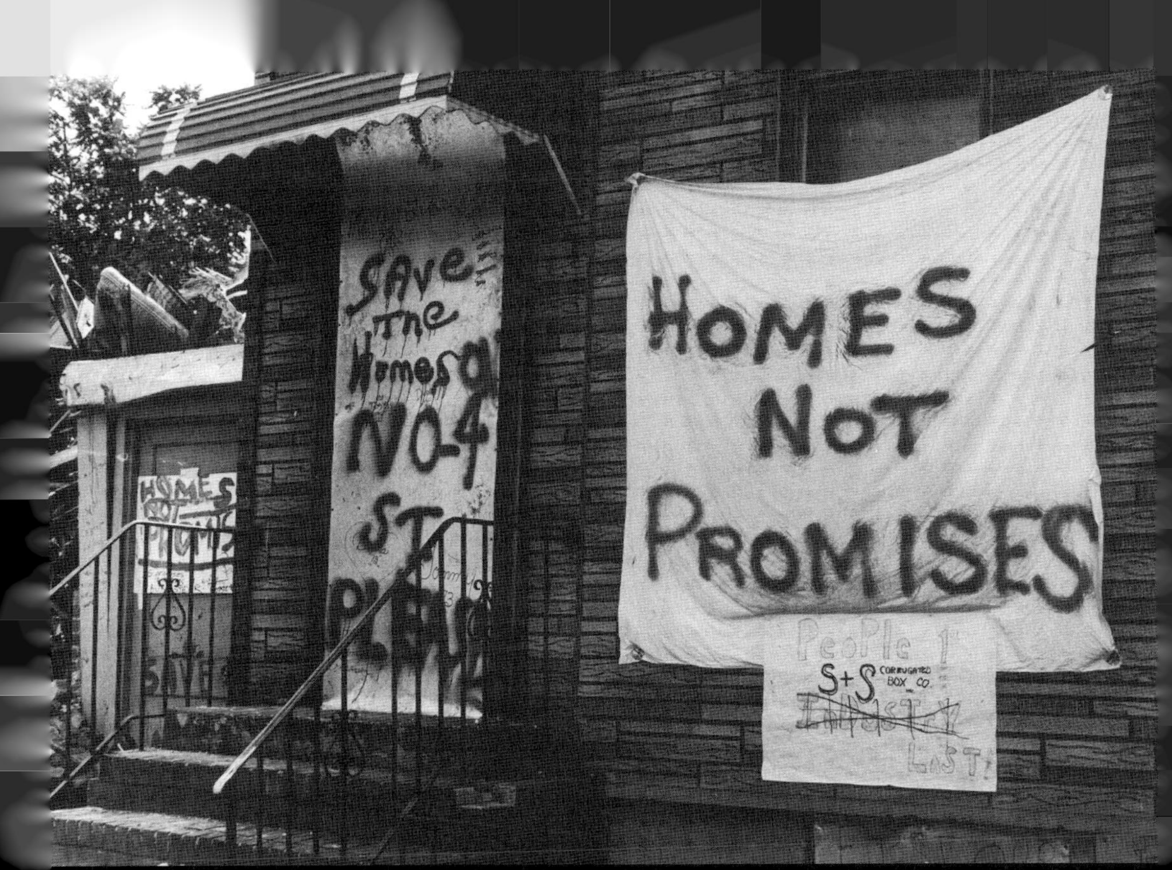

A protest against proposed demolition of housing in Williamsburg, Brooklyn in 1972.

A gigantic school system is torn by overcrowding and substandard teaching, particularly in slum areas, and has become a political football for the mayor, the Board of Education, civil rights groups and racists. Though the city has built more schools and classrooms under the present administration than it had in all of the previous administrations, the vocational schools have been allowed to become woefully outdated (more students drop out than graduate) and almost nothing has been done to prepare for an elementary school population in the Bronx and Manhattan that is now more than 55 percent Negro and Puerto Rican.

The financial needs grow increasingly critical every day and the source of possible revenue increasingly difficult to find. It has now reached the point where 14 percent of each year's expense budget—nearly $1.3 million a day—must go to pay debt service.

Representative John V. Lindsay, a young Republican mentioned increasingly as a candidate for mayor, suggests: "I think that under Mayor Wagner New York has lost its will power, its great energy, and its great leadership. You hear a lot of people say that the city is too big to be governed by one man. I don't agree with that at all. It's just a cliché. But to run this city properly and get it going again, the mayor has to be very tough. He's got to ask for the moon and he's got to convince the people to make sacrifices. It will take a man who loves the city and a man who loves its people. If we don't get going again soon, New York will become a second class city."

A separate article by Barry Gottehrer in the same issue of *The Trib* on the proposed Lower Manhattan Expressway quoted Wagner aide Julius C.C. Edelstein:

> *There is no easy solution here. It's one instance where you can't please everyone involved. But by doing what he has done, the mayor has left himself room to maneuver, to work out an effective compromise. That's the only way to govern New York. You can't go around stepping on toes. You'd have chaos and you wouldn't be mayor long enough to get anything accomplished.*

businesses into ever narrower enclaves, or driving them out of the city altogether. Meanwhile, the expanding ghettos were overflowing with refugees driven here by the mechanization of Southern agriculture and by Southern welfare practices that made Northern cities seem deceptively generous by contrast. Southern legislators joked that the meager welfare programs which they diligently enforced provided one-way bus tickets north for their unwanted blacks. Between 1960 and 1970, the proportion of blacks in the city had risen from 14 percent to 21 percent, most of them trapped here by a city that didn't need their labor and that had, in fact, begun to export its menial and routine work to less costly labor markets, often to the same areas which these new arrivals had recently abandoned.

The 1960 census was the first ever in which New York City registered a decline in population—the result of an exodus of mostly white middle-class taxpayers to suburbia. And what those New Yorkers left behind were slums and ghettoes that rivaled the tenements that Jacob Riis exposed in the late 19th century; so-called changing neighborhoods—a euphemism for places that were being exploited by blockbusting real estate agents and were poised on the brink of tipping into a precipitous decline—and a shrinking number of communities whose ordinarily pliant residents, fiercely resistant to any change, were preparing to man the ramparts.

By 1965, exactly 100 years since the Civil War had ended, black impatience with the fruits of emancipation was coupled with another phenomenon, a profoundly divisive one, which Daniel Patrick Moynihan and Nathan Glazer astutely described in the preface to their updated edition of *Beyond the Melting Pot* in 1970: "The Protestants and better-off Jews determined that the Negroes and Puerto Ricans were deserving and in need and, on those grounds, further determined that those needs would be met by concessions of various kinds from the Italians and the Irish…and the worse-off Jews." (By 1969, Andy Logan wrote in *The New Yorker*: "there is no doubt, of course, that in New York, as elsewhere in the country, an all-out segregationist would draw larger and friendlier crowds in many neighborhoods than he would have drawn a few years back, when the blacks were still being quite patient and many Americans could view the complaints of their nonwhite fellow citizens with indifference, and even benevolence.")

Easy to Underestimate

Wagner would recite his third-term accomplishments—overhauling housing and building codes (earlier, he had shepherded legislation that banned housing discrimination), imposing a landmarks-preservation law, and fluoridation of the city's water supply (before it was depleted by a drought that left the reservoirs at less than 42 percent of capacity). He would also insist—as Lindsay himself would do later—that New York, like the rest of urban America, was being plagued by problems that "are the result of nationwide forces and

In 1964, tactical police were deployed to a protest over the police shooting of a black teenager on the Upper East Side, precipitating what became known as the "Harlem Riot of 1964."

Mayor-elect John V. Lindsay and his wife, Mary (left), meet the press at Gracie Mansion, with Mayor Robert F. Wagner and his wife, Barbara, in November 1965.

factors" that required national solutions and were beyond the capacity of any one city to solve.

While Wagner reminded one reporter of "an unloved Airedale," he was, like Lindsay, a Yale man (a graduate of Yale and Yale Law School). He was also, as the political scientist Wallace Sayre wrote, "the easiest man around to underestimate."

Still, the government that Wagner was running (even the verb suggests more energy than was apparent to the public) was creaky and seemed inadequate to a 24/7 city. As one report explained, at City Hall "two girls answer the main number on weekdays from 8 a.m. to 5 p.m." By the time Lindsay took office, nobody could find written contracts for police officers and firefighters. The duplicative process to approve capital construction had grown to 49 steps. The city was manufacturing asphalt for road paving at a higher cost than private vendors were charging. The proposed new Police Headquarters was in its 17th year of site selection. And transit officials had all but given up on air conditioning the subways. The municipal mindset was summed up by this story, however apocryphal, that nonetheless resonated: When the mayor's limousine got stuck in gridlock near a subway construction site on Sixth Avenue, he demanded to know how long the perpetual traffic jam there had been going on.

"Two years, sir," an aide replied. "Should we do something about it?"

"We certainly should," Wagner supposedly replied. "Turn right at the next corner."

When Wagner formally bowed out of the race on June 10, 1965, after John V. Lindsay declared his candidacy, the mayor himself acknowledged that "much of the pleasure and satisfaction I have always derived from even the day-to-day work schedule had been drained from me," adding, "I feared I might go stale." Laurence Siegel, an 11-year-old from Brooklyn, captured the contrast between the mayor and his potential challenger in verse:

John V. Lindsay
He is for New York
We want Lindsay's action
Not Robert Wagner's talk

That the immediate challenges Lindsay inherited—"the city is on the brink of financial disaster," he declared during the campaign—were prodigious was evident in this ambivalent election night congratulatory telegram he received from the journalist Jerry Tallmer: "God bless you and God save you."

The fact is, whatever fiscal crisis he would leave eight years later to his successor, Lindsay inherited a fiscal crisis, too.

"John Lindsay Begins"

MURRAY KEMPTON

New York World-Telegram, May 14, 1965

Many New Yorkers recall a single sentence in the closing paragraph of a Murray Kempton column. Representative John Lindsay adopted it as a campaign slogan. Here is the column in full:

There is a certain absence of electricity to any mayoralty campaign observed in the month of May; and it has been said that the voyage of John and Mary Lindsay and their four children about the five boroughs yesterday had its dreary and unattended sides.

Congressman Lindsay went to the Grand Concourse, Brooklyn Heights, Forest Hills, Richmond Hill, and the midtown East Side, reading in each the announcement of his candidacy and answering what questions there were.

The effect was odd. In Staten Island, Lindsay came to rest in a setting for all the world the way lower Bergen County used to be before the auto dealers accomplished its ruination, and read aloud lines like: "in our city our streets are dirty and unsafe…crime, brutality, and narcotics are rampant…the vicious cycle of slum living continues."

The journey had been a discovery of how immense New York is, and how complicated. Manhattan is, after all, the only one of its boroughs where the middle class and the poor generally live in one another's sight, and whose residents have that sense of wandering in a jungle which we have come to assume is the New York feeling. Forest Hills is the site of the West Side Tennis Club; Brooklyn Heights is intactly charming, and Staten Island at least transiently rural.

There are places in the city which are almost villages; and, standing in them, it is hard to remember the Manhattan experience of hourly combat with the urban catastrophe. Congressman Lindsay was well-advised to have begun early; he has undertaken nothing less than the discovery and pacification of an empire.

He was a little awkward yesterday; and his voice and his rhetoric just a shade stilted and artificial. But he will walk more easily when he knows the terrain better; before long what he sees will instruct him to cease talking about this magnificent city as a ruin and begin to describe it in those real terms upon which his essential appeal rests, as a community whose failure is in not having achieved its proper greatness.

At the moment, he is a little unformed. He is marvelously humorous, and detached, very much St. Paul's and Yale, and unused to the despair and the revolt which he describes and depends upon as the New York mood.

He has serious handicaps. There are few professional Republicans in New York City, and many of such as there are have small hope for any candidate and no enthusiasm either for Lindsay's youth or his notions. The Republican leader of Bronx County, assuming there is one, did not even bother to show up at the Concourse yesterday.

It is, moreover, hard to believe that Governor Rockefeller, as commander of the successful Republicans, is totally committed to Lindsay's campaign. The governor likes Mayor Wagner and the mayor so compounds that affection in return that he would do almost anything to help Rockefeller's re-election up to the point of running against himself if nothing else will work. If Wagner is defeated, control of the Democratic party is certain to move to the hands of hungrier men more dangerous to the governor.

Lindsay said yesterday that some of his most devoted campaign contributors had begged off this time. Lindsay, they argued, could not win this election and, even if he could, his career would be blighted because he would be bound to fail at governing a city which cannot be governed. He is, then, the candidate of a party whose leaders despair both as politicians and as citizens.

Still he must be made the favorite, if only on hunch. He is fresh and everyone else is tired. He has the face that could make New Yorkers hope again. You looked at him yesterday, awkward as so many of the great candidates are when they begin, and there was one thing which could not be overlooked. You can beat ability. You can beat experience. You can beat dedication. Lord knows, you can always beat honesty. But the one thing you're never safe in running against is simply charm.

"He is fresh and everyone else is tired."
Murray Kempton / World-Telegram & Sun
VOTE FOR
JOHN LINDSA
FOR MAYOR
Paid for by Committee to Elect John Lindsay as Mayor
MAC NAUGHTON LITHOGRAPH COMPANY, INC.

1965 poster from Lindsay's first mayoral campaign, featuring the famous Murray Kempton quote.

The Slippery Slope

Wagner's credo that "a bad loan is better than a good tax" was epitomized by his decision to issue nearly $256 million in short-term notes to balance the 1965–66 budget of $43.9 billion—"borrow now, pay later," the mayor explained. In effect, the city was taking out a loan against a property tax increase that had neither been imposed nor even approved. It was the first step on a slippery slope that would bring New York to the brink of default a decade later.

Wagner argued that the 1965–66 budget was legally balanced. No gap would develop in the first six months of the Lindsay administration, he insisted, unless the new mayor began delivering on his expensive promises without raising revenue (although Wagner acknowledged that the following fiscal year's budget would be out of whack by $140 million). He complained that his successor was playing the latest version of a familiar political game, "pin the tail on Mayor Wagner," to inoculate himself against a backlash from New Yorkers disappointed that the dollars needed to deliver the changes for which they voted didn't exist. Lindsay, Wagner said of the incoming mayor, "must find a way of postponing the fulfillment of them until public memories begin to fade a little."

In fact, many of the "good intentions" that ultimately got the city into trouble for overspending began under Wagner. After he broke with the Democratic Party bosses in 1961, Wagner's progressive instincts were galvanized by his new alliance with reformers and their social agenda and with municipal unions, to which he had already granted the power to bargain collectively. His dependence on these "expenditure-demanding political forces," Martin Shefter, the political scientist, wrote, "helps explain why locally financed municipal expenditures rose twice as rapidly during Wagner's third term as during his first and second terms." From 1962 to 1966, municipal expenditures relative to total income in the city rose from 8 percent to 9.5 percent—more than in the previous 10 years. "Human needs are greater than budgetary needs," Wagner said. "I do not propose to permit our fiscal problems to set the limits of our commitments to meet the essential needs of the city." (Assessing Lindsay's first term several years later, his former chief of staff and special counsel, Jay Kriegel, would advise Lindsay: "Don't be too rough on the fact of the fiscal squeeze—that's no one's fault; it's the choice of solutions that deserves criticism.")

Short-term debt during Wagner's third term soared by what Ester Fuchs, the Columbia University political scientist, wrote was an "alarming" 79 percent, adding: "The city was saved from fiscal crisis during this period by new revenue in the form of inter-governmental aid, and a prosperous national economy."

"It is not to be overlooked," Robert A.M. Stern, the architectural historian, once recalled, "that Wagner's social commitment and his consensus approach to governance was in no small way responsible for the city's ultimate

"Mayor Wagner's Gift"

The New York Times, Editorial, February 13, 1991

On the occasion of Robert F. Wagner's death, the editorial staff of *The New York Times* paid tribute to the former mayor:

Hard as it is to imagine now, there was a time when New York City was in an uproar over a plan to add fluoride to the water supply. Mayor Robert F. Wagner supported the proposal but kept refusing to bring it to a vote. "Trust me," he said for months to his frustrated Health Commissioner. Then he finally relented—and the Board of Estimate duly approved fluoridization.

Some people probably said the mayor had been trying to avoid controversy. Those who knew him knew better. He waited for two reasons: to see if the dispute would cool down (it didn't), and to see if some heavy politicking could line up the votes (it did). Had he moved sooner, he would have lost.

The episode captures the essence of Mr. Wagner, who died yesterday at the age of 80. He wasn't a compelling public figure who could hold an audience or inspire a crowd. He was, instead, a wise, dedicated public figure who cared more about results than appearances. He had an innate understanding of the politics and people of his city, so much so that he won three terms in office.

Critics often accused him of ducking decisions by naming task forces or study commissions, and sometimes they were right. But more often he was motivated by a gift for conciliation, and a belief that in public life, delay could allay.

He inherited that approach. His father, the famous U.S. Senator Robert Wagner, once said to his son, "When in doubt, don't." It's the kind of advice Mayor Wagner may well have given one of his sons, Robert, who has also served the city with distinction in one capacity after another.

Mayor Wagner's phlegmatic style masked 12 years of integrity and achievement. He cleared slums and built public housing, established the right of collective bargaining for all city employees and created the city university system by uniting separate public colleges. He was the first mayor to bring significant numbers of blacks and Hispanics into government, and at his urging, New York adopted the first city code of ethics.

Robert Wagner made mistakes. During his troubled third term, he was blamed for growing social, racial, and fiscal problems, and was disappointed that he couldn't do more to rebuild slums. Mr. Wagner earned some of the criticism. But his 12-year record earned him New York's gratitude and respect for his old-fashioned belief in the power of government to do public good—and for doing it.

downfall." As Roger Starr, an urban planner, would put it: the Lindsay administration entered office "following headlong the course marked out for it by Wagner and the Manhattan elites."

If Wagner was right that Lindsay's estimate of a $500 million gap through the next fiscal year was protective overstatement, then Wagner's assurances were, at best, wishful thinking and, at worst, bald-faced baloney. An independent commission—appointed by Wagner—was projecting a deficit of more than $315 million in 1965–66. And, after scolding Wagner's borrowing scheme as "so reckless that it invites repudiation," on the eve of the new administration a *New York Times* editorial rendered this unequivocal verdict on New York's fiscal pickle: "The city is living on a credit card." That verdict was validated just a few weeks later: On January 27, 1966, just under four weeks into Lindsay's first term, the city borrowed $253 million, the largest financing in the history of the municipal bond market, and was forced to pay the highest interest rate since 1932. Beame's successor as comptroller, Mario A. Procaccino, would blame the lenders' skittishness, in part, on an assessment by the mayor-elect himself: "I'll be acting as a receiver in bankruptcy when I take over at City Hall," Lindsay said.

"More Adults"

The transition from Wagner to Lindsay would last 58 days. Both sides made appointments to an informal coordinating panel and at Lindsay's request, Wagner ordered his commissioners to prepare memos advising the new mayor of what to expect (Lindsay smugly asked that they be kept to a maximum of 10 pages). As Milton Mollen, a Wagner administration alumnus who was Lindsay's running mate in 1965 for comptroller, remembers, "If there was a functioning transition committee, I don't recall it. There should have been."

But most of whatever transition occurred was one-sided. In keeping with mayoral tradition, Wagner sought to lock in his legacy and reward loyal employees with midnight appointments (including one to the Triborough Bridge and Tunnel Authority board, whose vote would help ensure Robert Moses's dominion). Lindsay, meanwhile, fleshed out policy initiatives (mapping plans, for instance, to reorganize 99 city departments and agencies into 11 general groupings and paring the estimated 235 committees he inherited from Wagner) and recruited loyal supporters and outside experts to his administration.

Those appointments were the most visible manifestation of the new administration's cavalier rejection of government veterans whose savvy was not the stuff of transition memos. Jack Lutsky, a legal aide to every mayor since 1947, was never recruited by Lindsay (Wagner named him to the Family Court), prompting Lindsay aide Jay Kriegel, to lament candidly years later, "We needed more adults." Meanwhile, the new administration enlisted gutsy acolytes with good intentions and youthful exuberance, but no experience. Sid Davidoff recalls that after being named an assistant buildings commissioner at

Transport Workers Union president Michael J. Quill tears up a strike-barring injunction issued by the New York State Supreme Court and declares: "The strike is on." Quill's action was taken at a hastily called press conference 10 minutes after John Lindsay became mayor of New York at midnight on December 31, 1965.

the start of the Lindsay era (he later became the mayor's administrative assistant), "I came into my office, and a civil servant said, 'Can I help you, sonny?' 'Yes,' I said. 'You're sitting at my desk.'" When a reporter asked Davidoff what qualified him for the job, he deadpanned: "I've lived in buildings all my life."

The distrust wasn't limited to city employees. Lindsay was of the establishment, but considered himself an outsider. He would enter office facing a Board of Estimate on which he could count on only six of 22 votes and a City Council controlled 30 to 7 by Democrats. In a veiled warning of what was in store for the next mayor, coupled with a jab at Lindsay's inexperience, a Wagner confidant, Julius C.C. Edelstein, drafted a campaign speech for Paul R. Screvane, the mayor's anointed successor, to be delivered a few months before the Democratic primary in September 1965. "Yes, New York City has problems,"

Edelstein wrote, "more problems than Mr. Lindsay knows about. He hasn't caught up with a good many of them. But he'll learn as he goes along."

Seeking Change

With all the challenges Wagner was leaving the new mayor, the most immediate was a New Year's Day strike deadline by the city's subway and bus workers, and Lindsay was ill-prepared and ill-advised in his unsophisticated efforts to avert it. The strike would dramatize the fledgling mayor's disdain for the city's power brokers ("they know who they are," Lindsay said, without mentioning the first whom he would confront, the Transport Workers Union's Michael J. Quill) and would define his often destructive relationship with organized labor.

"John Lindsay looked at Quill and he saw the past," the columnist Jimmy Breslin wrote. "Mike Quill looked at Lindsay and he saw the Church of England." When Quill denounced Lindsay's telegraphed refusal to directly negotiate until he had evidence of good-faith bargaining, the mayor-elect replied that he stood on his telegram, to which Quill retorted: "He can stand on the telegram, sit on it, or do anything else with it that is handy." Wagner's negotiators figured a contract agreement would cost the city less than $40 million. By the time Lindsay got through, according to a mayoral commission, the bill for the transit strike and settlement had more than doubled, to $100 million, and the 15-cent fare was raised by 33 percent.

On December 31, 1965, 14 hours before his term would expire, Wagner left New York City for Mexico. "This is Lindsay's show now," he said. The audacious mayor-elect, his untarnished armor gleaming, girded for battle before a world of hyperbolized hope. "John Lindsay," said Deb Myers, Wagner's former press secretary, "is the only man I've ever heard of who is already the greatest mayor in history before he took office." At 6:10 that evening, after a six-minute ceremony, the new mayor was off to an inauspicious start. Carl Cusanelli, administrator in the mayor's office, placed before him the heavy ledger in which Lindsay signed his name to record that he had taken a loyalty oath to the Constitution. Cusanelli asked the mayor for the 15-cent fee required by the city's Administrative Code from officials who complete the oath-taking form.

The mayor who promised change cheerfully searched his pockets, but came up empty-handed.

Street campaigning in the summer of 1965 when he was fresh.

Richard Reeves

The Making of the Mayor

John Lindsay finished his studies at Yale a year early, as did many of his classmates. It was May of 1943 and there was a war on. Lindsay's war, he told me one day, was not unusual—long periods of boredom punctuated by short bursts of adrenalin and fear. A gunnery officer in the Navy, he won five battle stars, in the invasion of Sicily and then in the island-hopping campaign in the Pacific. He spent a lot of time on watch, he said, looking into the darkness from the bridge of a destroyer and thinking about what he should do when it was over.

RICHARD REEVES, who was the City Hall bureau chief and chief political correspondent for *The New York Times* during the Lindsay years, is the author of 15 books and a syndicated columnist. He is a Senior Lecturer at the Annenberg School for Communication and Journalism of the University of Southern California.

He knew he could go to law school, but after that it would be a choice between money and politics. He needed money; he only looked rich. His father was a lawyer, but not a wealthy one, and it cost a lot to send his five children to New England prep schools and Ivy League colleges. If John Lindsay was going to live the Episcopalian upper-class life, worthy of his middle name, Vliet, he would have to earn his own way. He also thought about acting: he was a loner who loved performing.

He chose politics. First he went back to Yale for law school and then performed as a trial lawyer for five years at Webster, Sheffield, Fleischmann, Hitchcock, and Christie. But he was spending his nights at the New York Young Republican Club, quickly becoming president of that group, mostly young veterans yearning to overthrow—or even just dent—the political power structure of a city with fewer than 670,000 voters enrolled as Republicans, compared with more than 2.4 million Democrats.

He founded Youth for Eisenhower in 1951 and threw himself into Dwight D. Eisenhower's 1952 presidential campaign, catching the eye of Ike's campaign manager, another Manhattan lawyer, Herbert Brownell. When Brownell became Eisenhower's attorney general, Lindsay followed him to Washington, serving as his executive assistant for three years. He came back to New York determined to run for Congress in 1958 in the one Manhattan district held by a

(left) Young John (second from left) with his siblings, twin brother David, Robert, Eleanor, and George around 1926.

(middle) John Lindsay aboard the *U.S.S. Swanson* around 1944. He served as a gunnery officer in the U.S. Navy during World War II.

(right) Lindsay with President Dwight D. Eisenhower in the 1950s.

Republican, Frederic Coudert Jr.—the 17th, covering midtown, the Upper East Side, and Greenwich Village. Coudert, 60, who had retained the seat by only 374 votes in 1956, dropped out rather than face Lindsay, who was an energetic and stubborn 36-year-old who looked like a young god, or, as Warren Weaver of *The New York Times* wrote:

> *Lindsay looks remarkably like his past: Yale, Yale Law, a top New York law firm, a significant Eisenhower Administration job. Politically, however, he has been an upstream swimmer, challenging the regular Republican organization, converting his variegated district from a close political proposition to a personal fan club.*

True to form, the regular organization endorsed someone else in 1958, but Lindsay, going door to door with help from the Young Republicans—particularly a 32-year old lawyer named Robert Price—won easily and then won the general election over a formidable young Democrat, Anthony Akers.

A family portrait in Washington D.C., 1963, when Lindsay was a United States congressman.

The 17th in those days was called "The Silk Stocking District," home to the rich and powerful. Lindsay was in office for only three weeks when he first challenged the Old Guard with his confrontational outspokenness (courage, too, though these words would play well back home). Under the headline, "Freshman in House Breaks Old Rule," it was reported that Lindsay had defended the liberal Warren Court: "Young Mr. Lindsay squirmed but kept quiet as Representative Noah M. Mason, Republican of Illinois, attacked the Supreme Court as a tribunal that 'casts aside' cherished precedents and substitutes 'socialist doctrines.'

"When several other members complimented Mr. Mason on his speech and none defended the court, Mr. Lindsay got to his feet.

"'I will defend as long as I have voice in my body the jurisdiction of the Supreme Court in every area involving personal rights and liberties of our people, including in the area of national security. In my view history will show, and historians will write, that this Supreme Court is one of the great courts of our history.'"

Lindsay for Mayor

Campaign ads, 1965

Fiorello La Guardia was famous for reading the comics on the radio during a newspaper strike, but John Lindsay was truly the city's first media mayor. Lindsay was made for television. He had dipped his toe into television advertising to win re-election to Congress and went all out in a mayoral media campaign (and later, as mayor, in a weekly television program that allowed him to bypass reporters and speak directly to his constituents) designed by David Garth. Four years later, deftly produced TV ads were vital to his re-election.

• I'm John Lindsay. I was born in New York City and I've lived here all my life. And I'm running for mayor because I know that our city is in a crisis. Everyone knows the facts—about crime, schools, safety, air pollution, water pollution, transportation, and all the rest. But the worst thing of all is the feeling of apathy and indifference that exists among our people, the shrug of the shoulders as if it doesn't make any difference if we can't do better. New York *can* do better. New York can be a great city. We've seen what Beame's experience amounts to. He's not going to change and you know it. Think about *that* on November 2nd. I say that New York City *can* do a job. I say that our city can lead the country, and I'm prepared to do the job if you'll give me a chance. We need a change, and we need it now. I ask you to join me. I tell you that I will do a job, and I will tell you the truth.

VOICE-OVER

Vote the Lindsay team—Lindsay, Mollen, Costello. Elect John Lindsay Mayor. Something *can* be done about New York.

OICE-OVER

n a mismanaged city of eight million, here's what happened to one man, Milton Lippman, Bronx truck driver:

ILTON LIPPMAN

've just gone through a frightful experience in connection with the horrible situation we now have in the city hospitals—my grandmother lying for 37 days in critical condition, and these are some of the things that I witnessed as I went to the hospital: Cockroaches crawl all over the walls. If a person is incapable of feeding themselves, the food is just left there. If a person is dirty in their bed, they just lay there. This is the way we were notified that my grandmother had died: They sent a telegram. "Your grandmother died. Come and make the last arrangements."

JOHN V. LINDSAY

Milton Lippman's tragedy is not an isolated example. I happens every day of the year in the city hospitals o New York. An administration that cannot do better thar this must be replaced.

VOICE-OVER

Elect John Lindsay Mayor. Something *can* be done about the city hospitals of New York

ELECT
JOHN
LINDSAY
MAYOR

This is John V. Lindsay. Some loud voices from City Hall are telling us that New York City, every day in every way, s getting better and better. And yet, before this day is over, someone will be murdered. Children will be bitten by rats. Negroes will be denied jobs because of their race. Fifty-thousand drug addicts will need another fix. Fifty jobs will leave the city. Countless families will be without water, without heat. And all of us will breathe the deadly air that is the same as smoking two packs

They tell us everything is fine and getting better all the time. We have drifted to the edge of disaster, and this is the truth, whether they like it or not. The men at City Hall have let it happen because they have no ideas and no hope. I ask you to join me. I *will* do a job and I will tell you the truth.

VOICE OVER

Vote the Lindsay team: Lindsay, Mollen, Costello

Lindsay's 1965 campaign attracted energetic future voters, further adding to the allure of Lindsay being "fresh" and everybody else being "tired."

On Two Stages

A couple of years later, while the young congressman was appearing off-Broadway as the narrator of a revival of Stephen Vincent Benet's *John Brown's Body*, he introduced legislation to abolish the 10 percent federal tax on Broadway tickets. That earned him a longer piece in *The Times*, in which he said, "I am the greatest ham in the world....If the voters throw me out in November, I know where I'm going—on stage."

On the national stage, Lindsay was endeavoring to reconcile an emerging brand of liberalism with Eisenhower Republicanism. Both, he argued—in a philosophic foundation for his support of civil rights and antipoverty programs—recognize that individual worth includes "creation or protection of basic conditions of living that will not permit any person, who cannot help himself, to live below a minimum standard of decency in a civilized nation." Defining liberal Republicanism, he argued in 1964 that the national party's platform committee "should reject the anti-individual, anti-libertarian forces that stem from every organized power group, whether that power group be the Central Government, the industrial-military complex, the big city machine or the local constabulary." The planks Lindsay embraced were internationalism, affirmation of the 1964 Civil Rights Act, and federal urban aid.

At the convention, after Governor Nelson A. Rockefeller of New York was booed by the delegates for his rejection of the Republican right, Lindsay was among the first to congratulate him for his speech.

That year, he refused to support his party's candidate for president, Senator Barry Goldwater, the Arizona conservative, against President Lyndon B. Johnson. Both *The Times* and *The Herald Tribune* reacted to all that by pushing Lindsay to run for mayor against the three-term incumbent Democrat, Robert F. Wagner, sad-faced after 12 long years in office.

A Republican mayor? It did not seem the likeliest of ideas. Representative Lindsay was a liberal Republican, a WASP lost in the ethnic mosaic of the city.

And his upward political mobility was blocked by Rockefeller, a Republican colossus, and two senators who could not be moved, the Republican Jacob Javits and the new Democrat in town, Robert F. Kennedy.

An Uphill Battle

History, too, was not on his side. Since Greater New York had been created with the incorporation of what became the other four boroughs into New York City in 1898, only two Republicans had been elected mayor. Both benefited from waves of Democratic scandals and neither one was exactly a 24-carat member of the Grand Old Party: John Purroy Mitchell, "The Boy Mayor," elected at the age of 34 in 1913, was actually a Democrat; Fiorello H. La Guardia, elected in 1933, was a maverick Republican who won almost half his votes on the "City Fusion" line.

So, Lindsay said no way—for a while. Finally, after weeks of uncomfortable talks with Rockefeller—the two Republicans neither liked nor trusted each other—about how to finance a $2.5 million campaign, Lindsay announced his candidacy on May 13:

"Cities are for people and for living and yet under its present tired management, New York City has become a place that is no longer for people or for living. In these long years of one-party leadership, we have witnessed the decline and fall....I for one cannot stand by while the decline and fall continues headlong."

Abraham D. Beame, John V. Lindsay, and William F. Buckley Jr. debate in 1965. Could Buckley win? "No," he replied.

Both *The Times* and *The Herald Tribune* printed the full text of Lindsay's speech, a signal of where they stood. They, not the party, were the young congressman's real constituency. *The Trib*, owned by a Republican senior statesman, John Hay Whitney, had for months been running a series, "City in Crisis," which was really a white paper trail of the Lindsay candidacy.

Politically, the city was energized. Within two weeks, *The Times* headlined across four columns:

Wagner Asserts He May Not Run,
Citing Family Duties And Strain;
Denies Maneuver To Unite Party

On June 10, Wagner announced he would not run for re-election. The mayor's quiet departure opened up the chance for Lindsay to win the endorsement of the Liberal Party, which had 62,794 enrolled members, but far more influence than that—particularly in a city where many Democrats were reluctant to actually pull a lever marked "Republican."

While the Liberal Party debated the Lindsay candidacy, the city was amazed by the emergence of an even more unlikely candidate. William F. Buckley Jr., the 39-year-old founder and editor of *The National Review*, a Yale man like

Lindsay's walks in black and Hispanic neighborhoods sometimes attracted celebrities, like Marlon Brando (center right) on this Harlem visit in 1968. At far right is Ted Gross, who was a member of the mayor's Urban Action Task Force.

Lindsay, announced that he would run for mayor as the candidate of the four-year-old Conservative Party, which had only 8,700 enrolled members. If any was needed, that was taken as confirmation of just how much Goldwater-loyal Republicans disliked the congressman from the fashionable addresses of the Upper East Side and the heart of left-wing America, the West Side and Greenwich Village.

Buckley said he was running to represent "the New York that seethes with frustration while the politicians conduct their quadrennial charade." Charades, it seemed, was not Buckley's game. Appearing at the Overseas Press Club, standing in front of a painting titled "The Merry Men," Buckley merrily took questions.

"Do you have any chance of winning?"

"No."

"Do you want to be Mayor?"

"I've never considered it."

(top) He may not have been the sexiest man alive, but he was probably the sexiest mayor. Lindsay wowed the crowd at the Brighton Beach Baths in Brooklyn during his 1965 campaign.

(bottom) Lindsay campaigning with Liza Minelli in Coney Island. If the rhetoric wasn't always memorable, the tactics were.

Democrats Are Fractured

Meanwhile Democrats who did want to be mayor scrambled for position after Wagner's withdrawal. They were the usual suspects, led by the City Council president, Paul R. Screvane, and the city comptroller, Abraham D. Beame, and two more liberal candidates: Representative William F. Ryan and Paul O'Dwyer. Beame, who was 59 years old and claimed a height of 5-foot-2, more than a foot shorter than Lindsay, easily won the Democratic nomination. Buckley, who did not campaign on the streets—he took advantage of television's equal-time provisions to quip away at the two major candidates—offered: "The differences between Mr. Beame and Mr. Lindsay are biological, not political."

There was, however, at least one more difference between Beame and Lindsay. The Democrat talked about nothing but party. The Republican never mentioned his.

Here is Beame: "I ask you to help keep this city a Democratic city. Only the Democratic Party is interested in the masses. It is the party of Roosevelt, of Truman, of Kennedy, Stevenson, Humphrey and Johnson. Remember Medicare, remember Social Security. Let's not take a chance to give that up."

Lindsay wanted people to remember only him. Billboards featured his handsome face and the legend, "This man can get New York going again." The campaign slogan was lifted from Murray Kempton, the erudite columnist, who wrote of Lindsay: "He is fresh and everyone else is tired."

It was not a memorable campaign rhetorically. Lindsay, who could be snappish and confrontational—and more than a little self-righteous—looked better than he sounded. "What do I have to know all this for?" he cut off a briefing by an assistant one day. "All I want to know is what I have to say." In a bit of foreshadowing, the patrician Republican was occasionally booed or ignored in the working-class Catholic neighborhoods of Queens, but, surprisingly, cheered in Harlem and other black neighborhoods.

Beame sounded as dull as he looked and mangled language a bit, thanking a campaign manager for "the great façade which he gave my candidacy." He had worked for the party all his life but had never really campaigned—and it showed. He would stop to speak at empty halls and then have to find a pay phone to find out where he was supposed to be next. But there were still those overwhelming Democratic numbers favoring him.

And if the rhetoric wasn't memorable, some of the campaign tactics were. Lindsay opened 123 neighborhood storefronts, which were a precursor to his creation of a personal political organization that would endure for eight years, and to his decentralization of government. Television advertising extended his reach beyond the power of the Democratic machine. Detailed position papers had the heft to appeal to his intellectual base and also the proper catch phrases—preserving rent control, the 15-cent subway fare, free tuition at the City University—to win over the middle class. From his very first speech as a candidate, his call for a Civilian Complaint Review Board for the police demonstrated both his willingness to challenge powerful institutions and to support the aspirations of the city's growing black and Puerto Rican population. And the campaign wooed influential Democrats, including a city councilman from Greenwich Village, Edward I. Koch, whose endorsement was considered crucial. (Lindsay's later failure to reciprocate when Koch ran for Congress created a legacy of bitterness.)

Election Night, November 2, 1965. Many happy returns at Lindsay headquarters in the Roosevelt Hotel. Robert Price, Lindsay's campaign manager and soon to be deputy mayor, is behind the desk; Lindsay is on the phone. Senator Javits is at end of desk. Future City Hall aides Barry Gottehrer and Jay Kriegel are at far right.

The Results Are In

The greatest excitement of the campaign, in the end, was in the ending. Voter turnout jumped by almost 10 percent over the 1961 totals to 81 percent, the third highest in the city's history to that point. On November 2, 1965, John V. Lindsay was elected the 103rd mayor of New York City with 1,165,915 votes (43.3 percent) to 1,030,771 (39.5 percent) for Abraham Beame. William F. Buckley won 339,127 (12.9 percent) votes.

"The politically incredible has come to pass," said *The Times* in a post-election editorial. "This city weary of 20 long years of plodding one-party rule has cast its vote for a better future. The people have made it plain they want a change. They will get it in Lindsay...."

November 3, 1965: The day after the election, Lindsay returns to the streets to thank the voters and is mobbed by well wishers in Bedford-Stuyvesant, Brooklyn.

Peter Kihss, analyzing the vote for *The Times*, wrote a day later that Lindsay won "by cutting across the board into traditional Democratic Jewish, Catholic, Negro and Puerto Rican strength." A pollster, Oliver Quayle, estimated that the voters were 48 percent Catholic, 35 percent Jewish, 17 percent Protestant, many of them among blacks, who accounted for about 8 percent of the vote. In general, Quayle estimated, Beame ran roughly 5 to 10 percent below Wagner four years earlier. One surprise he recorded was that Lindsay, a strong civil rights advocate in Congress, won about 40 percent of the Negro vote, compared with 5 percent for Barry Goldwater the year before. Lindsay also received about 40 percent of the Jewish vote and fared well in traditionally Republican Queens and Staten Island. One in four of his votes—amounting to twice his victory margin—were recorded on the Liberal Party line. And Buckley? "He did very well at the expense of Beame among Catholic Democratic voters," said pollster John Kraft.

Sure enough, Mayor-elect Lindsay did find the city in crisis. The Transport Workers Union and the Transit Authority were deadlocked in negotiations over a new contract to take effect on New Year's Day, 1966. The T.W.U. president, Michael J. Quill, spent weeks goading Lindsay, calling him "a juvenile" and a "pipsqueak"—and the strike began at 5 a.m. New Year's Day. Five hours after Lindsay took office the men and women running the city's buses and subways, serving five million people each workday, walked off their jobs.

Still, it was hard to hold down the spirits of the New Yorkers and others who had worked to put the fresh mayor into City Hall. One of the others, the entertainer Sammy Davis Jr., warmed up the 4,000 invited guests at Lindsay's inaugural ball New Year's night by saying, "What a mayor, eliminating crime in the subways after only 24 hours on the job."

First Inaugural Address

January 1, 1965

January 1, 1966: The inauguration of New York's 103rd mayor, John Vliet Lindsay.

My fellow New Yorkers:

New York City represents all that is exciting about our cities and everything that threatens to destroy them.

New York symbolizes the traditional aspirations of man—power, fame and wealth. Yet it magnifies every adversity of city living—the crowds, the noise, the dirt; the innumerable accommodations and sacrifices exacted from those who live in an urban society.

It is a city in which individuals have been characterized by vigor and affluence; New Yorkers have always sought out the newest and best in their own lives. As citizens, however, they collectively tolerated a government possessing neither attribute.

Until now.

Last Nov. 2, the people of New York decided that their government was not good enough; that it must do better. They voted for a change in leadership, one which would promise to restore to this city the imprimatur of pride.

In keeping with this mandate, I affirm a dedication to a simple, perhaps old-fashioned concept, drawn from the finest of American political traditions. It is that the public interest must prevail over special interests; the good of the community over the desires of any group. This is the credo of responsible conservatism no less than of modern progressivism; it was the spirit of Theodore Roosevelt and Franklin Roosevelt, of William Gaynor and Fiorello La Guardia.

It is the spirit of men who cared.

They cared about the malignant effects of injustice, intolerance, and indifference. And they dared to believe that men could rise above the claims of party or class; that public service could offer the largest satisfaction in life. They dared to assert that men could find new answers to old questions.

The question now before us is whether men of conscience and conviction can reject ignoble partisan intrigue and join in a massive effort to make real our dreams for New York.

If we fail, the implications of our defeat will be assessed throughout the nation, to be proclaimed by the cynics as proof that great cities are no longer governable.

(Continued on next page)

If we succeed, we shall have demonstrated that ndependent government, free of the irrelevant dic-ates of party politics, can overcome the sickness and hame of our cities.

Divided, we can do little to meet the powerful chal-enges facing the city.

United, there is little we cannot do.

Together, we can open direct lines of communication etween the people and their government. My plan to pen Little City Halls in the neighborhoods of our city, nanned by the people in those neighborhoods, will stim-late a new citizen involvement in the life of the city.

Their function will be in keeping with the oath taken by he young men of ancient Athens to "strive unceasingly o quicken the public sense of civic duty."

In this pursuit, a major objective is to destroy the ssumption that those who serve their city are somehow ompromised or demeaned.

I have undertaken to attack that premise by selecting nen and women of known ability and stature to assist ne in City Hall.

I hope that my appointments and reappointments will ive tangible credence to my resolve to regard merit as he only test of service.

There will be tolerance for honest disagreement and uman error within the offices of our government.

But there will be no protection for indolence, incompe-ence, or graft.

My hope is that the highest level of this administration vill establish a moral and ethical tone which will per-ade every department and agency with an unshakable espect for decency and honesty.

In this way we shall lay the foundation of "The Proud City."

My vision of "The Proud City" encompasses far more han self-esteem; the phrase describes the kind of city ve hope to achieve for ourselves and our sons and aughters—a city in which each individual can fulfill imself in dignity and freedom.

The New Yorkers of today will decide the destiny of he New Yorkers of tomorrow—by proving their readi-ess to accept the inconveniences and irritations, the ardships and responsibilities, that must accompany ny transition.

I cannot predict whether—at the end of four years -this administration will be beloved by many. But I hope will be respected by all.

As I speak, our city is crippled by a strike against the us and subway system. It is an unlawful strike against he public interest, called even before the collective bargaining process had run its course.

It is an act of defiance against eight million people. I shall not permit the public interest to be flaunted, no matter how severe the stress.

The oath of office I have just taken requires me to uphold the law of the land. That I shall do—in the name of those eight million people.

I say to the parties to this dispute that theirs is the immediate responsibility for arriving at a swift and equitable settlement and I insist that they discharge that responsibility.

This is a time for reason; a time to serve the common interests of this city.

The current crisis is but one of the many which afflict New York. Let us move against each of them—now.

Let those who compile riches from the misery of slums hear this message as their eviction notice: There will be no compromise with the profiteers of poverty.

Let those who exploit human addiction hear me clearly; New York will no longer be your marketplace.

Those who would do business as usual may be dis-tressed. Those wise enough to see the need for change will find that a city in rebirth will provide the healthiest climate for business and every other sector of the city.

We will combat terror in the streets. And we will do so with full respect for the rights and privileges of every citizen.

We will have the rule of law—and that means rigorous, diligent, corruption-free law enforcement. It also means that although wrong will be fought night and day, the Bill of Rights will remain a shield for all.

And so, my fellow citizens, I summon you to enlist in the fight for a better New York:

The fight to revive the hopes of the downtrodden, the sick, the exploited.

The fight for new and better employment.

The fight against wretched slums, poisoned air, stifling traffic, and congested subways.

The fight for excellence and equality in our educa-tion—and for the integrity of our historic system of inde-pendent free city colleges.

The fight for new parks and recreation facilities.

The New York for which we are fighting is as old as the vision of brotherhood. It is a city in which there will be new light in tired eyes, and the sound of laughter in homes. Our enemies in this battle are greed, ignorance, bureaucracy, prejudices, and defeatism—in high places and low.

But no mayor and no city can go it alone. The rebuilding of New York will necessitate a close—and I hope fruit-ful—partnership with state and Federal governments.

ELECTION FINAL
DAILY NEWS
NEW YORK'S PICTURE NEWSPAPER
ELECTION FINAL
'MR. MAYOR'
THE WINNER! JOHN V. LINDSAY, THE REPUBLICAN-LIBERAL CANDIDATE
Lindsay Victor in a Hot Finish

Daily News **cover, "Mr. Mayor" on November 3, 1965: He was still fresh, after edging out his two rivals.**

I am confident that our governor, our senators, and our legislators will help, realizing that our needs are in many ways the needs of the state and the nation.

My administration will be a visible government. No longer will New Yorkers be obliged to seek out the distant, unfamiliar offices of their city; from this day on, their city will go to them.

Your mayor and his associates will be seen in this city. We will visit the slums and the waterfront. We will go into the schools, hospitals, and prisons.

We shall go forth with the selfless perspective—with the knowledge that what we do here may gain us neither gratitude nor glory except in the judgment of a later age.

Our commitment to New York is timeless; to our city we cheerfully devote our spirit and our hands, our energies and our skills.

We have faith that we can build what must be built…

Preserve what must be preserved…

Change what must be changed.

The fulfillment of that faith begins today.

Charlayne Hunter-Gault

Black and White

As one of Mayor Lindsay's signature approaches to governing, he often walked the streets without a visible police presence and informally listened to residents.

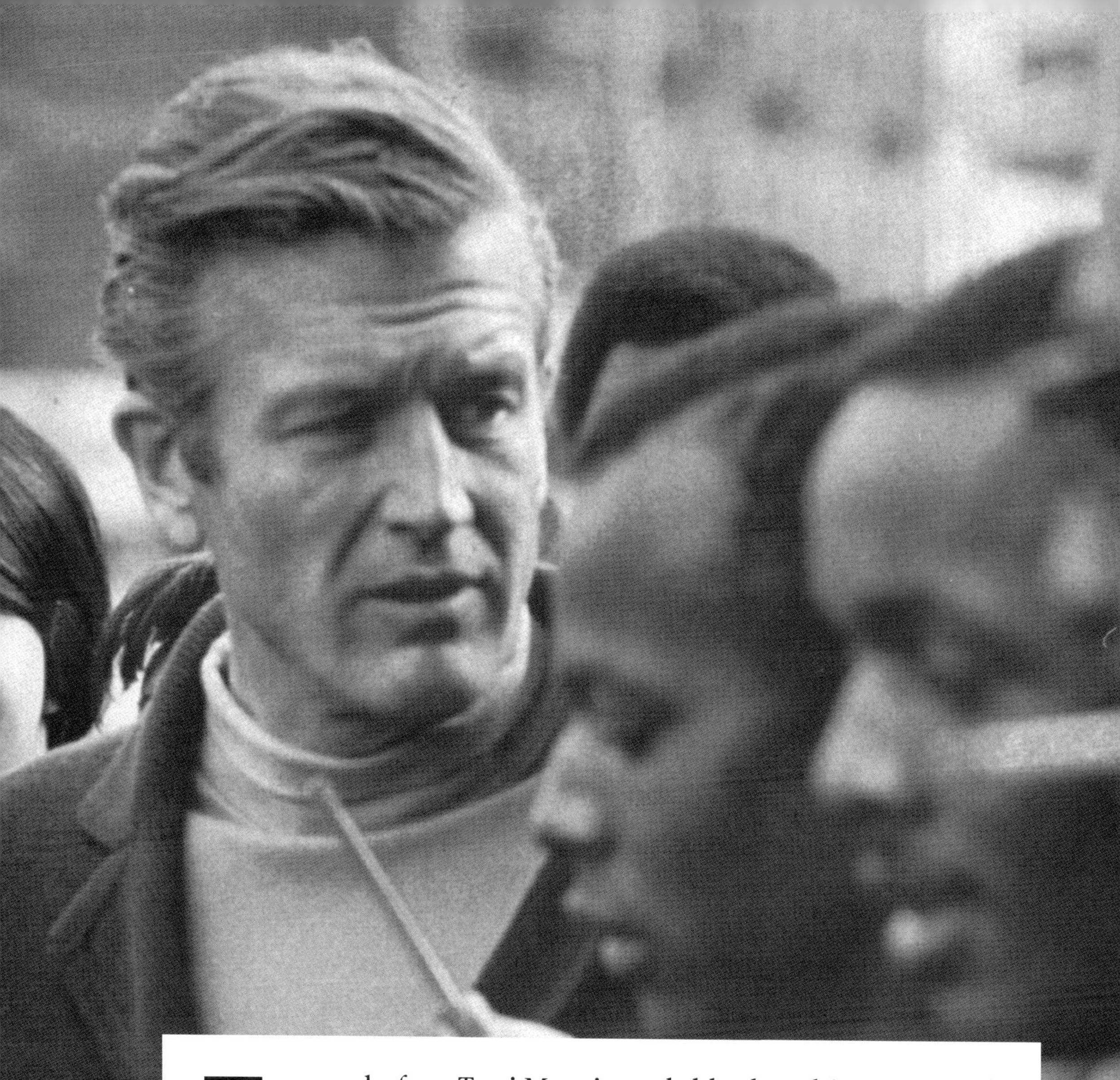

Long before Toni Morrison dubbed a white man—Bill Clinton—the First Black President, John V. Lindsay was known in black neighborhoods of New York City as the Black Mayor—an otherwise-odd title for a square-jawed Yale-educated, tennis-and squash-playing W.A.S.P. from a well-connected family, a Republican, who entered politics representing "The Silk Stocking District" of New York to boot.

CHARLAYNE HUNTER-GAULT is an Emmy and Peabody award-winning journalist and author. In 2005, she returned to NPR as a Special Correspondent after six years as CNN's Johannesburg bureau chief and correspondent. Hunter-Gault joined NPR in 1997 after 20 years with PBS, where she worked as a national correspondent for *The NewsHour with Jim Lehrer*. She began her journalism career as a reporter for *The New Yorker*; then worked as a local news anchor for WRC-TV in Washington, D.C., and as the Harlem bureau chief for *The New York Times*. Her latest book is *New News Out of Africa: Uncovering the African Renaissance*, Oxford University Press.

"Lindsay was the quintessential urbanist of his time. He will surely be remembered for holding New York City together when mayors, especially white mayors, faltered in responding to the emergence of both black power and black problems in cities....He walked the streets of Harlem with greater ease than any white man before him. History will always remind New York that the city had the right mayor for the right time in history."

–Eleanor Holmes Norton, *who was chairwoman of the city's Human Rights Commission, became the District of Columbia's representative in Congress.*

John Lindsay may not have been black or poor, but he seems to have possessed an instinctive understanding of the issues, the unmet needs and yes, even the emotions, of black and poor people—qualities that got him into trouble with other groups but that saved New York City from the fate of many other urban areas during the mid to late 1960s, when simmering rage in poor black neighborhoods boiled over into outrage that ignited cities from Newark to Los Angeles.

It was not as if New York City was immune from simmering tensions. Indeed, the mid to late 1960s landscape in the city was dotted with race-related eruptions and fissures. Many predated Lindsay's mayoral tenure as manufacturing jobs disappeared and as the black and immigrant populations grew—mostly with arrivals from the South and from the Caribbean Islands, accelerating white flight to the suburbs. But the effect fell on Lindsay in his first two years in office as the welfare rolls soared.

Undaunted, Lindsay raised taxes to help provide needed services for the poor, but he also used funds coming in from President Johnson's War on Poverty to help empower them. Lindsay created jobs and made it possible for community people without traditional experience to fill them, producing possibly the largest ever pool of black and Hispanic New Yorkers who learned for the first time about the inner workings and administration of government. Lindsay's very first cabinet appointment was imbued with powerful symbolism: Robert Lowery as the first black commissioner of the whitest of all agencies, the Fire Department. Lindsay elevated blacks to senior positions in the Police Department, beginning with Lloyd Sealy as an assistant chief inspector with line authority over a borough command. Major Owens, a Brooklyn librarian and community activist later elected to Congress, where he would serve for more than two decades, was named community development commissioner.

These appointments were also unusual in that Lindsay reached beyond the traditional entrenched black political clubs and found new people without baggage who were talented and open to doing things differently. For example, Lindsay demonstrated a rare quality in a politician when he hired Eleanor Holmes Norton, a young civil rights activist and an up-and-coming human rights lawyer, to head his Commission on Human Rights. What made the appointment highly unusual was that, as a lawyer for the American Civil Liberties Union, Norton had sued the Lindsay Administration in 1968 over its resistance to allowing segregationist presidential candidate George Wallace to hold a rally at city-owned Shea Stadium. Norton had no brief for Wallace, but was committed to the constitutional guarantee of freedom of speech. And though she won the case—on constitutional grounds—Lindsay respected her mind, didn't hold a grudge, and appointed her to her first political post.

Norton joined the administration in 1970 and set as its major priority fighting job discrimination, the first such agency in the country to pursue such a mandate. She went on to win more than $20 million in jobs for minorities and women, as I wrote in *The New York Times*, by forcing companies to correct their discriminatory practices.

In 1972, Human Rights Commission Chairwoman Eleanor Holmes Norton, joined by John D. Rockefeller III, announced the formation of a Citizen's Committee on Population and the American Future. The purpose of the committee was to increase public awareness of a presidential report on population growth.

Norton, who went on to become the District of Columbia's representative in Congress, says that what was refreshing about Lindsay was that he sought advice. "He really wanted to pick up on what he didn't already know and was not embarrassed to ask. Going to cabinet meetings—often at Gracie Mansion—was a pleasure." Says Norton about the way in which Lindsay created a committed multiracial, multi-generational talent pool: "It was a miracle."

Among other politically unencumbered blacks to whom Lindsay reached out was H. Carl McCall, a minister transplanted from Boston whom Lindsay stole from the New York City Mission Society. In his early 30s, McCall was put in charge of the Council Against Poverty, a creation enabled by Johnson's War on Poverty. The C.A.P., as it was called, was given the task of fighting the war on poverty in New York on many fronts, including employment, as well as providing a broad range of services to poor minority communities. It also served as a political training ground for many blacks. McCall, who would later be elected state comptroller, remembers that Lindsay attempted to respond to, rather than condemn, black rage, a policy fraught with complexities:

Lindsay "believed their outrage was legitimate and had to be channeled. And he saw that these people had leadership qualities that had to be developed in a constructive way," McCall said. "I think he clearly understood that the way to respond was to bring in people who obviously felt left out and therefore were acting out and getting involved in a lot of negative behavior. A lot of people got hired who used to riot. And now they were getting a paycheck and involved in activities [as] most ended up working in their own communities, getting services redirected in a positive way."

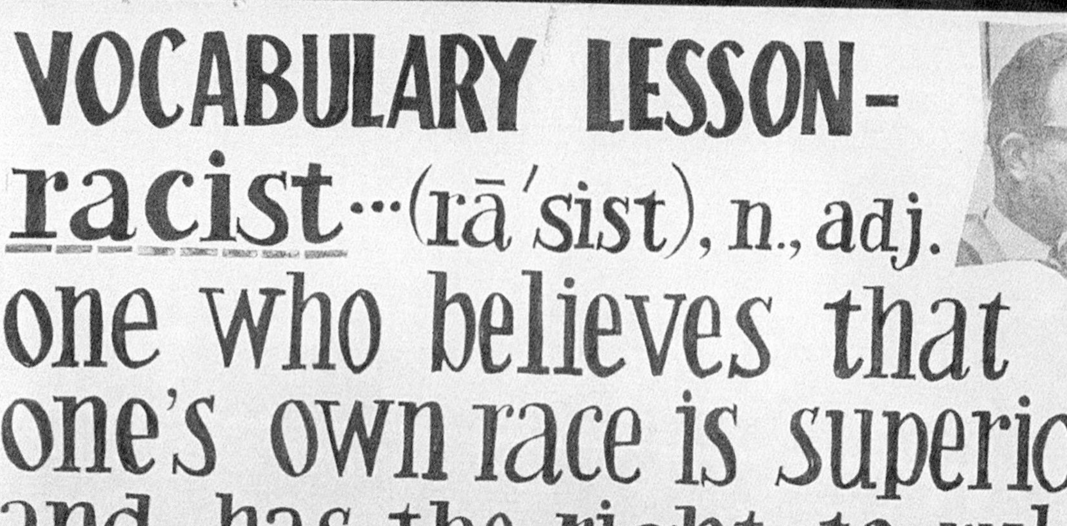

VOCABULARY LESSON-
racist...(rā'sist), n., adj.
one who believes that one's own race is superior and has the right to rule others.
bastard...(bas'terd), n., slang-
a vicious, despicable person

The Ocean Hill-Brownsville school decentralization experiment produced lasting racial divisions. Here, a demonstrator at P.S. 39 in Brooklyn in December 1968.

Hearing Other Voices

Lindsay drew on the urban expertise of men like Mike Sviridoff from New Haven, who later went to the Ford Foundation, and Ed Logue, both of whom had creative ideas about new ways of salvaging the inner city and its people, based on their successful model in New Haven. Lindsay also assembled a team of people, including Barry Gottehrer, Sid Davidoff, and Teddy Gross, whose job it was to work the streets, to get to know all the players—including the black militants who had their own fiefdoms and could loudly make demands and create chaos when those demands weren't met. They ranged from the Congress of Racial Equality to Allah and the Five Percenters, a Black Muslim offshoot that was in its prime, and Black Panthers who were trying to shed their West Coast incarnation as violent revolutionaries.

But they weren't the easiest group for the Establishment to get along with. In Harlem, the Panthers established a free breakfast program for children. At the time, I was a *New York Times* reporter and was initially denied access to the launching of the program "because you work for The Man and The Man ain't gonna let you tell the truth about us," as one of the Panthers told me. After a long exchange, in which I challenged his assumptions about my integrity and invited him to read the piece I would write and feel free to deny me access in the future if it weren't a true reflection of the meeting, he agreed to let me in, provided I "come in right."

Rather than dismiss the street militants or arrest them when they disturbed the peace, Lindsay's team—through Gottehrer's Urban Action Task Forces—got to know them, courted them, hired them, and in some cases made friends among them. When Neil Armstrong became the first human to walk on the moon in 1969, one of most vocal of the street agitators watched it in Teddy Gross's apartment.

Part of the Lindsay approach was to set up neighborhood City Halls that brought government to the people. But Lindsay also went to the people, a familiar figure in shirtsleeves, walking the sometimes mean streets of black and Hispanic neighborhoods, talking to the people who lived there.

Earl Caldwell, then a *Times* reporter, often accompanied the mayor to those neighborhoods and recalled:

> *He was ahead of his time in how you deal with people. When we would stop the car and get out, the thing that struck me about this white boy was he had a comfort level with black people. Its one thing to go walking up to a stoop in Brooklyn, but people can tell. Your body language gives you away. He wasn't afraid. He saw black people as human beings. Lindsay had this way that people gravitated to him. He had a very realness about him, the way he'd go onto these porches and talk to people and they could talk about anything they wanted to talk about. I think that makes a difference. They respected and cared for him.*

Summer in the city in 1966: Spray caps, like this one in Harlem, soothed tempers and also saved water.

On the Street

Lindsay walked the streets in the best of times and the worst of times, sometime at his peril, such as the tense night in April 1968 when Martin Luther King Jr. was assassinated. All over America, hurt was turning to explosive anger. Lindsay had been at the theater when he got the news. He left immediately, and after setting up a command post at Gracie Mansion, he sped to Harlem. Crowds of sorrowful and angry black mourners poured into the streets and Lindsay leapt from his car and walked among them, expressing his condolences to the growing throng. But some were in no mood for sympathy and made threatening moves towards him. At the moment, he was just another white man, probably like the one who had killed King.

As hostile residents threw bottles and bricks from rooftops and were admonished by the gathering police to "Go home," the response that produced a bold-faced headline in the next day's paper was "We are home!"

Undaunted, Lindsay remained in the street until the Manhattan borough president, Percy Sutton, a black man, who earlier that evening had advised Lindsay against coming to Harlem and was now sensing that the crowd was turning ugly, literally pushed the mayor into his car, driving him away from potential danger. The mayor returned to Gracie Mansion but went back to Harlem in the wee hours of the morning, walking now-calmer streets. Still, as inner cities across America burned, Lindsay and his team of urban warriors kept the lid on New York's anger and, among other things, channeled it into Harlem's churches.

"John got out of the car, spread his arms and said, 'I'm terribly sorry, I'm terribly sorry.' Everyone including me thought we were going to be killed by the mob. Instead, the only fight that developed was which group wanted to protect John Lindsay first. I will never forget the look on his face as he spread his arms like the Messiah. John had that half smile on his face and he went from potential victim to obvious hero in an instant. I did not know what John was feeling inside, but he never blinked!"

—David Garth *Lindsay's media adviser, who notified Lindsay, who was at the theater that night, that Martin Luther King Jr. had been assassinated and then walked with him in Harlem.*

And, there were times when Lindsay, too, went to church, despite being admonished by some of the more militant blacks to "stay outta Harlem." Another black political neophyte hired by Lindsay was Gordon Davis, who recalled that during Lindsay's re-election campaign in 1969, Lindsay went to Harlem to the Convent Avenue Baptist Church at 145th Street and Convent Avenue.

"The Congress of Racial Equality, and its leader, Roy Innis, had thrown down a verbal gauntlet—Lindsay is not welcome in Harlem and if he tries to walk our streets we will keep him out," Davis remembered, continuing:

"But as Lindsay was emerging from the church, a black Harlem guy in his 20s wearing a leather trench coat who had been helped by Lindsay's administration prevented Innis from using the loudspeaker he had hooked up to denounce Lindsay by chopping its power cable in two with a hatchet that he took out of his briefcase."

Members of the Young Lords at a Puerto Rican Day parade in 1971.

Davis, a lawyer who became the president of Lincoln Center for the Performing Arts, remembers that after Lindsay emerged from the church, he and his entourage—cops and street guys working with Barry Gottehrer and Sid Davidoff—walked to 145th Street and down the hill into Central Harlem, pushing Innis and the CORE group right down the street and in the process attracting a larger and larger crowd of cheering black people shouting their support for Lindsay and calling Innis and his entourage a bunch of Uncle Toms working for the Republicans, who had rejected Lindsay in their primary.

The Kerner Commission

"The city where I was born–the District of Columbia–the capital of the United States is still recovering from the urban riots, and I don't think anyone will cast a doubt on the assertion that John Lindsay had everything to do with why New York remained intact, and other big cities just went aflame.... He could not have saved New York from decline, but New York could have been torn asunder on his watch, and it was not, and it was in no small part because New York had a strong mayoral government. Much depended on who was the leader. Who was the leader? John Lindsay."

–Eleanor Holmes Norton, *the District of Columbia's representative in Congress, in an interview conducted by Tom Casciato for the film* The Lindsay Years, *produced by Thirteen for WNET.org*

Two years earlier, Lindsay had played a pivotal role in dissecting the causes of the stunning urban rebellions in other cities, having learned much from the laboratory he set up in his own boiling cauldron of a city. He had been tapped to serve on the National Advisory Commission on Civil Disorders set up by President Johnson to look into the causes of the unrest that had plagued America's inner cities since the mid 60s. The 11-member commission was headed by Otto Kerner, the former governor of Illinois, and became widely known as the Kerner Commission. Lindsay was made vice chairman. He would be instrumental in producing one of the most profound documents of our time, the Kerner Commission report, which bore Lindsay's mark in its declaration that "our nation is moving toward two societies, one black, one white—separate and unequal." And it blamed an uncaring white society for the problem and warned that unless drastic remedial steps were taken, America was spiraling potentially into "urban apartheid."

It was a stunning wake-up call to the nation, and, by validating the Lindsay administration's pioneering policy of police restraint (both on the streets and in prison unrest in New York City), it had a powerful impact on riot-control practices across the country. Its recommendations had other far-reaching consequences, not only in New York City, where Lindsay used federal money that flowed in from Johnson's War on Poverty to give summer jobs to the young and restless, which kept them off the streets, but also nationally. For the suffering cities all over America, the commission recommended greater investment in programs dealing with training and jobs, housing, welfare, community action, and education. It was in the wake of the Kerner Commission report that black students in New York demanded that the predominantly white City University open its doors to them. And it did in 1969, allowing entrance to any high school graduate. Minority enrollment immediately tripled and remedial courses were provided for many of the minorities with poor high school preparation.

One of the Kerner Commission's strongest indictments was leveled against the predominantly white media, which, the Commission said, bore significant responsibility for the rebellions because of its failure to cover the inner cities. As a result, they and their readers and listeners were surprised by the rebellions that tore through the country's inner cities. And the commission indicted the media for not having anyone on their staffs who looked like and lived among those who exploded. It was a recommendation that media companies quickly took to heart, establishing a summer program at Columbia

From the Kerner Commission Report

1968

As the Kerner Commission moved to complete its work, the White House worked to ensure that the report would neither criticize federal efforts under President Johnson nor call for expensive federal programs. When the staff presented its 27-page summary, John Lindsay, the vice chairman, found it so bland and stilted that it diluted the urgency of the commission's conclusions.

But revising the draft at the end of the surprisingly harmonious deliberations would foment a divisive political conflict and Lindsay was convinced that only a unanimous summary would have a significant public impact. So he conceived an alternative approach. On the night before the commission's final meeting, he and his aides, Jay Kriegel and Peter Goldmark Jr., culled the full report for the most forceful conclusions and boiled them down to two pages.

The next day, Lindsay reminded his fellow commissioners of why a unanimous report would be so valuable—a veiled warning that he might consider dissenting if they rejected his revised summary. They were stunned that it merely synopsized what they had already adopted. Here are excerpts:

January 10, 1968: A meeting of the National Advisory Commission on Civil Disorders, known as the Kerner Commission. From left to right: Mayor Lindsay, vice chairman; Governor Otto Kerner of Illinois, chairman; staff director David Ginsberg; and deputy director Victor Palmieri.

The summer of 1967 again brought racial disorders to American cities, and with them shock, fear, and bewilderment to the nation.

On July 28, 1967, the president of the United States established this commission and directed us to answer three basic questions. What happened? Why did it happen? What can be done to prevent it from happening again?

This is our basic conclusion: Our Nation is moving toward two societies, one black, one white—separate and unequal.

Reaction to last summer's disorders has quickened the movement and deepened the division. Discrimination and segregation have long permeated much of American life; they now threaten the future of every American.

This deepening racial division is not inevitable. The movement apart can be reversed. Choice is still possible. Our principal task is to define that choice and to press for a national resolution.

To pursue our present course will involve the continuing polarization of the American community and, ultimately, the destruction of basic democratic values.

The alternative is not blind repression or capitulation to lawlessness. It is the realization of common opportunities for all within a single society.

This alternative will require a commitment to national action—compassionate, massive, and sustained, backed by the resources of the most powerful and the richest nation on this earth.

Violence cannot build a better society. Disruption and disorder nourish repression, not justice. They strike at the freedom of every citizen. The community cannot—it will not—tolerate coercion and mob rule.

Violence and destruction must be ended—in the streets of the ghetto and in the lives of people.

Segregation and poverty have created in the racial ghetto a destructive environment totally unknown to most white Americans.

What white Americans have never fully understood—but what the Negro can never forget—is that white society is deeply implicated in the ghetto. White institutions created it, white institutions maintain it, and white society condones it.

Our recommendations embrace three basic principles: To mount programs on a scale equal to the dimensions of the problems; To aim these programs for high impact in the immediate future in order the close the gap between promise and performance; To undertake new initiatives and experiments that can change the system of failure and frustration that now dominates the ghetto and weakens our society.

These programs will require unprecedented levels of funding and performance...There can be no higher priority for national action and no higher claim on the nation's conscience.

New York wasn't spared completely as rage erupted in Harlem after the assassination of Martin Luther King Jr. in May 1968.

University. It was headed by the legendary *Washington Post* journalist Robert C. Maynard and later named for Michele Clark, whom the program trained and who had become one the rising stars in the broadcast industry before she was killed in a plane crash. The accelerated three-month program was supported in its infancy by all three major networks and by newspapers around the country. In time, the program moved to the University of California and through the leadership of Maynard and his wife, Nancy, the Maynard Institute produced Pulitzer Prize winners, top editors, managers, and publishers. Lindsay and the Kerner Commission were responsible for the beginning of the diversity movement within the American media industry.

Reflection

ROBERT CURVIN, a long-time civil rights advocate, served on the editorial board of *The New York Times* and as director of the Ford Foundation's Urban Poverty Program.

In Mayor John V. Lindsay, the tall, blond, handsome patrician who led New York City from 1966 through 1973, blacks and Hispanics saw a leader who understood their pain and sense of isolation, and used his power and prestige to deliver on some of their deeply felt aspirations for recognition and advancement. In return, they showered him with adoration.

When Martin Luther King Jr. was assassinated in 1968, black communities in cities throughout the nation erupted in violent protest. But New York City's black neighborhoods did not resort to violence. Mayor Lindsay ventured into Harlem, Bedford-Stuyvesant, and other black areas of the city, apparently convincing residents that they did not need to vandalize or damage their neighborhoods to be heard.

Lindsay's forays into the dark ghettos of New York were extremely important, but that is not what won such deep respect from people of color. Using city resources and the substantial largess flowing to urban communities through federal programs, he delivered jobs and resources to the black and Hispanic communities, and opened doors in city government that previously had been closed to them.

His first bold move was the appointment of a black career fireman, Robert Lowery, to become fire commissioner, to head an agency that had a notorious reputation for racial (and gender) exclusion. He appointed several blacks to the bench, including Judges Joseph B. Williams and Bruce Wright. Hector I. Vasquez became the first Puerto Rican member of the New York City Board of Education. The Lindsay administration supported vigorous civil rights enforcement and appointed the energetic and vocal William Booth to head the city's Human Rights Commission. In 1970, Joseph L. Searles, then a young lawyer and protégé of the mayor, became the first black person to have full membership on the New York Stock Exchange. Former Representative Major Owens of Brooklyn, whom Lindsay brought into government, said Lindsay gave blacks the opportunity to develop a base at the community level, which allowed us to challenge the political clubs.

Regrettably, Mayor Lindsay found himself in the middle of several racial imbroglios, which cost him dearly among white voters. When he supported the decentralization of public schools, the Ford Foundation's plan blew up amidst protests by the teachers' union, which, in turn, were countered by vitriolic antiwhite and anti-Semitic attacks against the union by blacks. An exhibit on Harlem at the Metropolitan Museum of Art turned into another clash between blacks and Jews over what was considered an anti-Semitic essay in the exhibit catalogue, actually partly pilfered from a passage in a scholarly writing by Nathan Glazer and Daniel Patrick Moynihan. The origins of the strategies or the hateful writing and literature did not matter. In the minds of working-class ethnics, Mayor Lindsay was the culprit.

When the fiscal crisis hit New York City in 1975, under the leadership of Mayor Abraham D. Beame, numerous critics and journalists blamed Mayor Lindsay, arguing that the generous settlements he had given unions and the social and welfare benefits he allowed to flow to minority populations had stretched the city's budget far beyond capacity. Some added that he gave too much attention to issues of the poor and minorities, while ignoring the needs and interests of white middle-class residents. The criticisms rang true for working-class white ethnics. But countless black and Hispanic New Yorkers remember John V. Lindsay as a close friend in difficult and changing times; a rare political leader who understood the impact and cost of injustice and discrimination, and a courageous man who did all he could to change the way cities and the nation address problems of racial inequality.

Racial Battles

But John Lindsay was unable to put out all the fires that erupted during his two-term tenure. One of his baptisms of fire came during the summer of 1967, when the New York City Board of Education, backed by the Ford Foundation, launched a program in the predominantly black Ocean Hill-Brownsville area of Brooklyn. It was an experiment known as "community control" that was aimed at giving local residents an opportunity to run their own schools, in the hope that officials who looked like the students in their charge would be more successful in motivating them and enabling them to succeed.

While the aim was laudable, and the initiative spread to Harlem and other areas, it created one of the most racially divisive moments in Lindsay's tenure, if not in the city's history. At the time, only 8 percent of the city's teachers and 3 percent of its administrators were black, whereas the student body was over 50 percent black. The newly empowered Ocean Hill-Brownsville board fired 19 teachers in the spring of 1968, setting off demonstrations by the predominantly white teacher's union. Racial and religious tensions that may have been silently simmering exploded. The acrimonious dispute triggered three teachers' strikes and was a turning point, producing a breach in the historical compact between blacks and Jews—partly because many of the city's teachers were Jewish—that lingered long after Lindsay's tenure.

To some New Yorkers, his heartfelt empathy for minorities made Lindsay the city's first "black mayor."

One of the other Lindsay initiatives that aroused intense anger and furthered racial polarization was scatter-site housing—a plan to build low-income apartments scattered among the city's working and middle class communities, including the Forest Hills section of Queens. But ultimately few minorities were housed under this plan, due to massive white resistance.

Lindsay's liberal politics cost him his party's nomination in his second run for mayor in 1969, but it was clear that he had the support of those whom he had championed. Running on the ballot line of the tiny Liberal Party and with the support of the city's blacks, including Brooklyn Representative Shirley Chisholm, Lindsay won with a slightly lower percentage than in his earlier victory.

While Lindsay's actions aimed at empowering minorities and the poor may have alienated people who looked like him, his unwavering commitment to that goal and his steadfast moral authority earned him the gratitude of countless black and Hispanic New Yorkers and a place in the pantheon of great mayors of the 20th century.

June 1968:
The mayor often made unannounced visits to local communities, like this one in Bedford-Stuyvesant, Brooklyn.

"I had never in my life met a white Protestant Republican–I had heard they existed, but I had never seen one. And maybe that is why he was so special–because he didn't act like he was white, he certainly didn't act like a Republican and he did act as though he wanted all people to feel like he did: that we were the tops."

– Charles B. Rangel,
the Harlem congressman

FRED HARRIS was a United States senator from Oklahoma who served with John Lindsay on the Kerner Commission.

As well or better than any other public figure of his generation, John Lindsay understood, was intuitively in tune with, in step with, the great upheavals and popular movements of the 1960s—the civil rights movement, the youth movement, the feminist movement, and the anti-Vietnam War movement.

Someone reported to President Johnson that John Lindsay and I were more or less dominating the work of the Kerner Commission and that the commission's report would not have a good word to say about Johnson's great civil rights and antipoverty initiatives (which, of course, was false). So, when, with another senator, I went to see the president one day in the Oval Office on a minor mission, he said to me with great sarcasm as he shook my hand, "I'm surprised to see you up, Fred." I said, "Sir?" Johnson said, "I heard old John Lindsay had you down and had his foot on your neck." I later learned that Johnson suspected that John was preparing to run against him. I tried unsuccessfully to disabuse the president of that idea.

And, sadly, President Johnson, who accomplished more in the struggle for civil rights and against poverty than any president before him, eventually rejected the findings and recommendations of the Kerner Report without reading it. He believed the false word someone gave him that the report actually condoned and encouraged riots and gave his administration virtually no credit.

JUAN GONZALEZ has been a columnist for the *New York Daily News* since 1987 and is co-host of the radio and television current affairs-program Democracy Now. He has won the George Polk Award for his reporting and is the author of several books, including *Harvest of Empire: a History of Latinos in America.*

East Harlem was like every other inner-city neighborhood in America in 1969, simmering with anger and unrest. That summer, I helped found the Young Lords, an unlikely collection of rebellious Puerto Ricans in their teens and early 20s, some of us ex-gang members and former heroin addicts, others college dropouts. New York's rich and powerful had long regarded the 600,000 working-class Puerto Ricans who settled here during the 1950s as one huge uneducated and unim-

We in the Young Lords were part of the second generation. We'd watched our parents mistreated and abused in the garment factories and restaurant kitchens of this great city, and we had vowed to gain new respect for our community.

Much to our surprise, an idealist patrician Republican politician named John V. Lindsay became one of our biggest allies.

None of us in the leadership of the Lords ever met Lindsay. But we ended up dealing constantly with his young, street-savvy aides: Barry Gottehrer, Sid Davidoff, Teddy Gross, Arnie Segarra, Frank Espada. The in-your-face protest tactics that became a trademark of the Lords, the very tactics that helped us achieve so many important reforms in government policy, would not have had the same success if someone other than Lindsay had been mayor.

Some of us might not even be alive today but for Lindsay's cool-headed response to our most radical actions.

We did not understand that back then, of course. Age teaches you things.

In July of 1969, we started sweeping the garbage-strewn streets of East 111th Street. Those mounds of trash, we knew, said more about City Hall than it did about the residents of El Barrio's overcrowded tenements. The fact is, the Sanitation Department wasn't picking up trash on schedule. Days would go by without trucks appearing.

So we started sweeping the streets and neatly packing up all the trash, and when the sanitation trucks didn't come, we threw all the bags in the middle of Third Avenue and Second Avenue and set them on fire. The press promptly labeled our protest the East Harlem garbage riots.

Lindsay dispatched Arnie Segarra, who already knew some of us personally, to negotiate a peace. "Stop blocking traffic and we'll make sure that Sanitation picks up the trash," Arnie assured us. We stopped, and the city reinstituted regular service.

That September, we teamed up with students from the old Flower and Fifth Avenue Hospital's medical school. We went door-to-door collecting urine samples from tenement children and tested them for lead poisoning. Our results documented alarming lead levels in many kids.

A young reporter with thick black glasses had begun writing articles in *The Village Voice* about the lead-poisoning epidemic in the city. His name was Jack Newfield, and he was eager to publicize our test results. Newfield's lead-paint-removal program.

But Newfield and we in the Lords needed someone in authority who could listen to the people, and Lindsay was that leader.

That December, a few hundred of us occupied East Harlem's First Spanish Methodist Church. The pastor had refused to allow us unused space in the church to run a free breakfast program for local school children (this was before federal school lunch and breakfast programs). Instead he called in the police to arrest us in a confrontation where several Young Lords members were savagely beaten by the police.

We responded by occupying and barricading the church for more than 10 days. Segarra lost his job for daring to publicly support what we were doing. He would later become a confidante and aide to Mayor David Dinkins. Lindsay had just been re-elected in 1969 to a second term. Still, he resisted the call of many powerful people, including top brass of the Police Department, to launch an assault on the church and drag us out.

The mayor instead sent his aides and a few influential Puerto Ricans like Herman Badillo to try to negotiate a settlement with us. He even appointed a Puerto Rican, Amalia Betanzos, as a new top City Hall aide on December 31 – during the very time we were still occupying the church. It wasn't a purely selfless strategy on Lindsay's part. He did have presidential ambitions, and a police raid that risked a possible riot in East Harlem would not help his long-range goal. But the key point is, he chose negotiation over rash action.

We eventually agreed on a resolution to the standoff: we would not resist the police when they came in, and City Hall would guarantee no violence from police. All told, 111 of us were arrested for criminal trespass in early January 1970. The charges were later quietly dismissed. The protest instantly made the Young Lords the best-known radical Latino group in the country.

In July of 1970, we once again occupied a building. This time it was the old Lincoln Hospital, in the South Bronx. City officials had been promising to build a new hospital for more than 25 years – the old one was falling apart and was notorious for its terrible care. More than 100 of us sat in early one morning and barricaded the nurses' residence. Every news outlet in the city covered the protest. We demanded the construction of a new hospital.

Lindsay immediately sent Davidoff and Gross to meet with us. They climbed in one of the first-floor windows and tried to convince the key leaders, Felipe Luciano, who would later become a reporter for both WNBC and Fox, and Pablo Guzman, now a veteran of WCBS-TV News, and myself, to surrender. If we left peacefully, they told us, no one would be arrested. The city would make no public announcement of a deal, but they gave us their word that a new Lincoln Hospital would be built.

Late in the afternoon, as the police were breaking down the barricades at the building's main doors, all of us escaped via a delivery platform in the back that had been miraculously left unguarded. We made no announcement afterward. But the Lindsay administration kept its word to us and the new Lincoln Hospital was built.

There are other amazing examples I could give of how Lindsay and his aides adopted a governing style toward the Puerto Rican community of listening first, rather than reacting rashly. He understood what few politicians do today that when ordinary people get angry at government, there is usually a good basis for their anger. His unflagging compassion for the downtrodden was what made him unique among New York's mayors, at least in my lifetime.

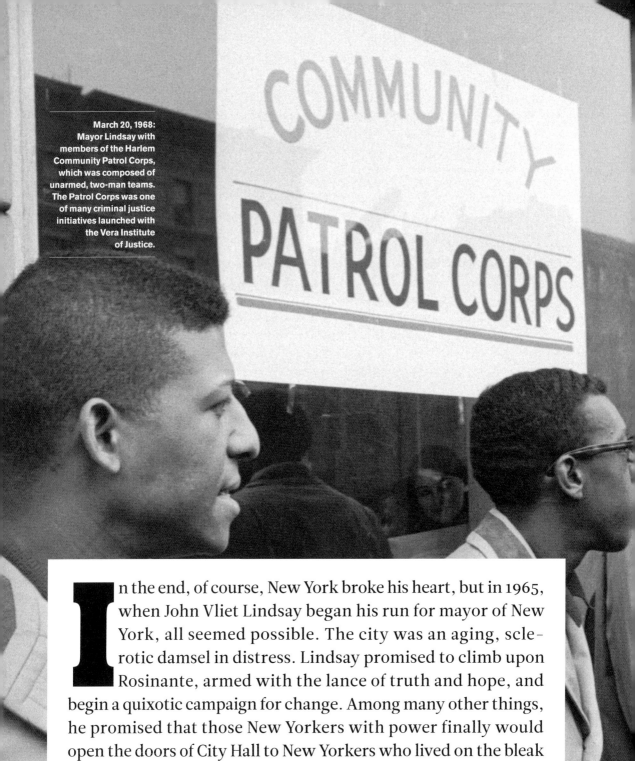

March 20, 1968: Mayor Lindsay with members of the Harlem Community Patrol Corps, which was composed of unarmed, two-man teams. The Patrol Corps was one of many criminal justice initiatives launched with the Vera Institute of Justice.

In the end, of course, New York broke his heart, but in 1965, when John Vliet Lindsay began his run for mayor of New York, all seemed possible. The city was an aging, sclerotic damsel in distress. Lindsay promised to climb upon Rosinante, armed with the lance of truth and hope, and begin a quixotic campaign for change. Among many other things, he promised that those New Yorkers with power finally would open the doors of City Hall to New Yorkers who lived on the bleak margins. There were many huzzas, some tinged with irony.

PETE HAMILL is a veteran journalist and the author of more than 20 books, including 10 novels and several short story anthologies. Born in Brooklyn to Irish immigrant parents in 1935, he became a newspaperman in 1960 at the *New York Post*. He has covered wars, urban riots, political conventions, prizefights, and an occasional World Series. He is a Distinguished Writer in Residence at the Arthur L. Carter Journalism Institute at New York University.

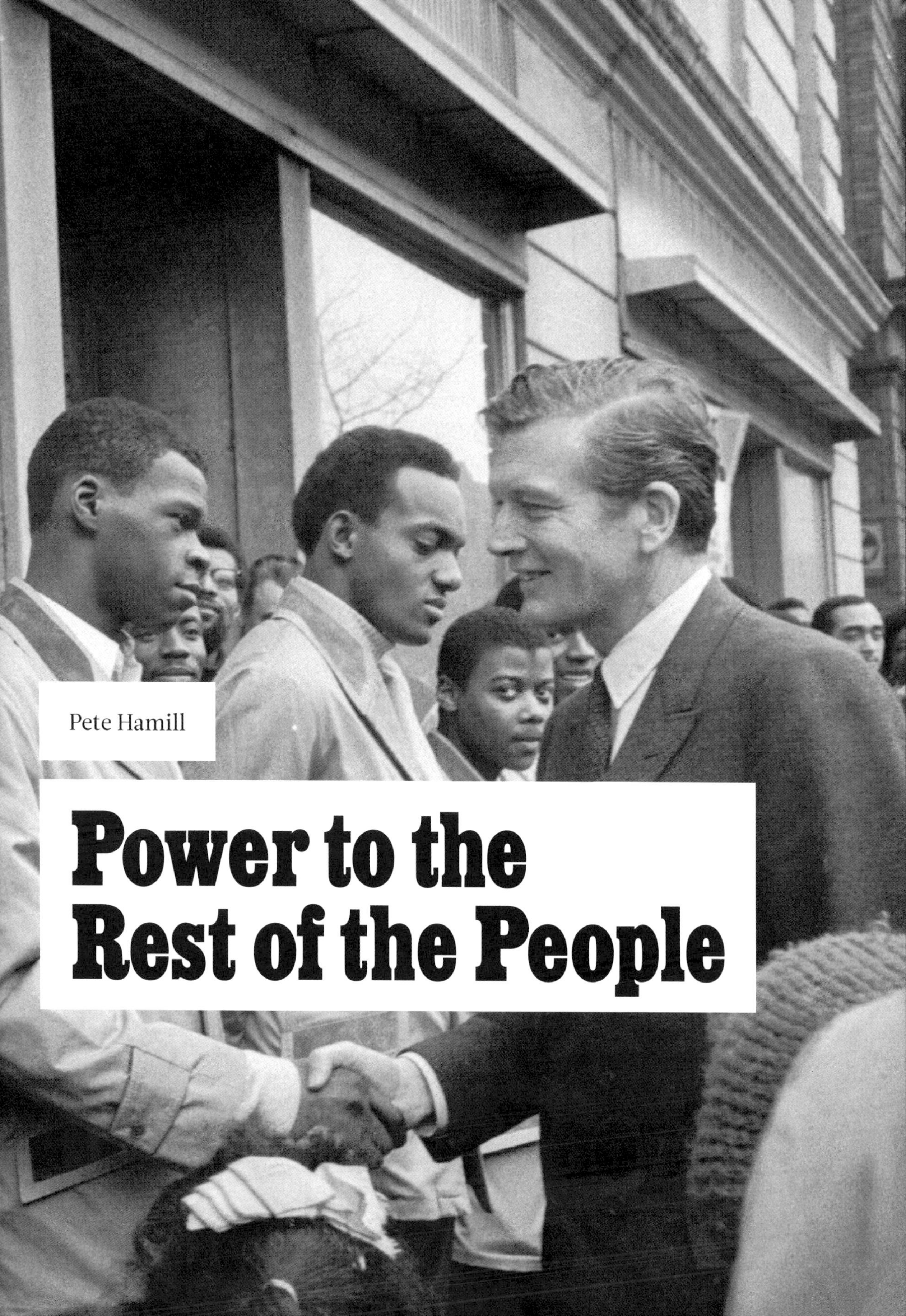

Pete Hamill

Power to the Rest of the People

The implication of the columnist Murray Kempton's line that Lindsay was fresh and the others were tired was obvious: New York was in terrible shape, fractured, exhausted, cynical, in need of fresh faces, fresh ideas, a fresh style that would take all of us to a brighter future. Including the poor.

Yes, the times they were a-changing, as Bob Dylan told us all in those years. And so was New York.

By 1965, the population was certainly changing. The phenomenon sloppily called "white flight" was under way (it was actually "middle class flight" since the diaspora included many middle class blacks). For 20 years, the G.I. Bill was a major engine of change in the city's working class neighborhoods. Young veterans of World War II or Korea used housing benefits to choose life in the suburbs. Or they chose college educations that were never available to their blue collar (often immigrant) parents. They gained admission to the Wall Street houses, the white shoe law firms, the private clubs, the wood-paneled rooms where power flourished.

At the same time, the great highway programs of the Robert Moses era carried many middle class New Yorkers out of the city, usually for the rest of their lives. They took stability with them, and taxes too. Even the civil servants—cops, firemen, teachers—used the highways to live somewhere else, while working in New York City.

But in those same years, while John Lindsay was serving his political apprenticeship, a huge new migration to the city was under way, made up of American citizens: African Americans from the South, and young people from Puerto Rico. Most (not all) were from agricultural backgrounds, like the Irish and Italians of the 19th century. As so often happens, timing was everything. It was their bad luck that they arrived during the same period when the manufacturing jobs were vanishing. Those jobs had made New York lives of dignity possible for millions of earlier newcomers like my father. In the postwar years, some new arrivals found work. Many did not. During the last years of Wagner, the welfare rolls began to escalate. Those numbers would grow even more drastically in the years to come. The Lindsay years.

So would the statistics of violent crime. They were driven by the terrible new combination of heroin and guns, both of which began flooding New York in the late Wagner years. In neighborhoods all over the city, ordinary working people learned to live with fear, with triple locks on the doors, with gates over windows. And fear was not confined to those areas that were collectively called "the ghetto."

No wonder that, in his last year as mayor, Wagner looked like a defeated old commander of cavalry in the age of jet fighters.

Enter John V. Lindsay.

A Vanishing Breed

In 1965, John V. Lindsay was 44, handsome in an Arrow shirt style, tall and lean. He faced the world with a ready smile and a relaxed, graceful demeanor. That is, he was perfect for the now dominant medium of television, which placed image before message.

From the start, Lindsay was a Republican. More than that, he was a *liberal* Republican. In addition, he was a W.A.S.P. That is, he was a member of a very

The antiwar movement divided the city. It also played a vital role in reelecting Lindsay.

"Power to the People" manifested itself in more decentralization of government and more community control and, sometimes, more controversy, as seen in Ocean Hill-Brownsville.

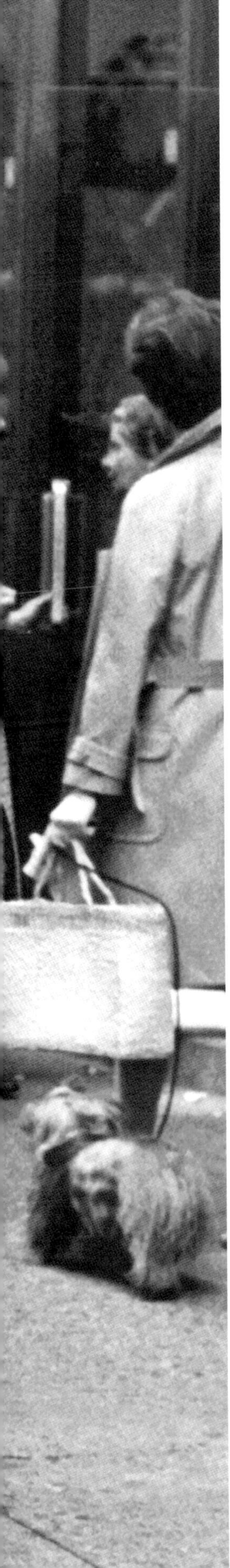

small minority group, without a natural ethnic constituency in the five boroughs of New York. (Like La Guardia, he was an Episcopalian). He did not come from an old wealthy family. His father worked his way up from a job at a bank, showed great talent, became sufficiently "well-off" to move from the West Side to Park Avenue. But when John Lindsay married Mary Anne Harrison in 1949, they moved into an apartment in Stuyvesant Town. This was a new development for middle class families, its red brick facade visually resembling low income projects. Stuyvesant Town was a short walk to the slums of the Lower East Side, once inhabited by the German, Irish, and Jewish poor, and now housing a growing number of the Spanish-speaking new arrivals.

Almost from the beginning of his political career, Lindsay was passionate about the American struggle for full civil rights. That struggle was being fought primarily in the South by courageous young African-American college students who thought any American could choose to sit at a lunch counter, or in the front of the bus. Above all, every American should possess the power that came from voting. The struggle was made vivid to New Yorkers by the growing power of television news, and from 1950s reports by Kempton, and a brave black reporter named Ted Poston in the then-liberal New York Post.

There appears to have been no single epiphany that made Lindsay a passionate liberal on race. But he must have seen that the struggle for genuine power for black Americans was not unique to the South. All he had to do was take a walk. Or read the papers. In his time in the House, he often voted with the Democrats on these issues. In the years ahead, parts of the struggle assumed multi-syllabic labels: democratization, decentralization. For Lindsay, it was surely about fairness. Power to all the people.

In the 1965 election for mayor, Lindsay ran against the city comptroller, 59-year-old Abraham D. Beame, the choice of the Brooklyn Democratic machine and what remained of Tammany Hall. Beame's short stature made Lindsay look even taller. Born in London, raised on the Lower East Side, Beame was educated as an accountant. For the rest of his life, he was a Democrat and an accountant. As budget director in the 1950s, and then as comptroller, he was methodical, careful, unimaginative, and decent. He had pride, but no vanity. He was totally devoid of any messianic impulse and did not believe in utopias. Abe Beame was steady, he was loyal, and he could count. Poor Abe Beame discovered, when the counting was over in the election, about 2 a.m., that John V. Lindsay had won by 100,000 votes.

Cautiously Optimistic

Among many citizens that night, there was hope for a luminous future. Lindsay did not exactly have a mandate; he garnered 43.3 percent of the vote in the three-way race. Still, the Manhattan reformers were almost giddy with the possibility of regeneration. Even the younger regular Democrats I knew were cautious, but optimistic.

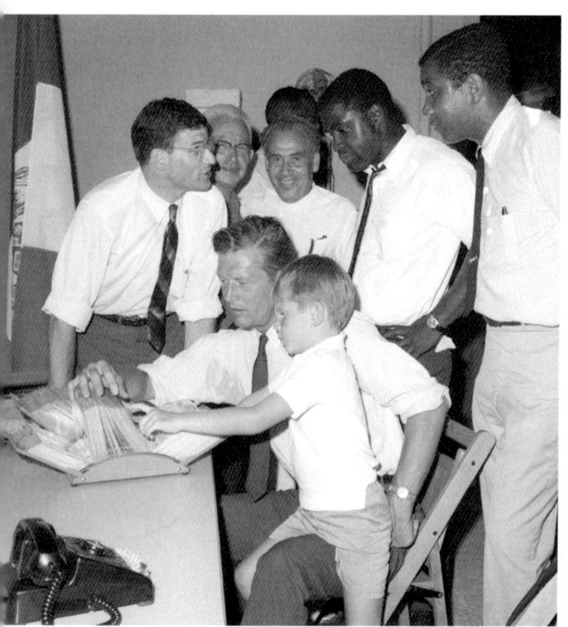

August 1966: Little City Halls, an outgrowth of the 1965 Lindsay campaign storefronts, helped bring direct access to vital city services and a sense of empowerment to local neighborhoods.

But on his first day in office, Lindsay blundered into a calamity: the city-wide strike by the Transport Workers Union that stopped bus and subway service all over the city. The 12-day strike incited fury among millions of New Yorkers who used the subways and buses every day. It might be possible to walk to work from Greenwich Village, or midtown Manhattan. Try doing it from Bay Ridge or Far Rockaway or the north Bronx. The so-called "outer boroughs" were not separate cities; they were part of one immense city that was lashed together by the more than 700 miles of subway lines. Now they could not get to work. They could not shop in the big Manhattan stores. The term "limousine liberals" began to be heard. The columnist Dick Schaap picked up a casual remark from Lindsay and began using the phrase "Fun City." In New York, irony is used as a weapon and as a form of armor. In all the dark days and nights that lay ahead, the ironic notion of Fun City remained alive. Almost four centuries earlier, the Illustrious Don from La Mancha was immune to irony. That belonged to Sancho Panza. Lindsay seemed to be a young man with no interior Sancho Panza.

In the end, Lindsay's first major crisis was a dreadful failure. The TWU boss Mike Quill died of heart failure a few days after the settlement was reached, but he had won a victory more dominant than even he could have imagined. To pay for salaries, job security, pensions far more generous than even the rank and file could have expected, the 15-cent fare would rise quickly to 20 cents. Lindsay would soon ask for (and receive) a city income tax and a commuter tax. All costs were rising, but the transit strike was the first jagged rise in the charts. Years later, my friend Paul O'Dwyer, another Irish immigrant, a staunch liberal reformer, said to me: "Wagner always knew that you had to give Mike Quill a place to fall. A half a loaf. So that he could sell it to the membership. The Lindsay people didn't know how to do that." O'Dwyer laughed. "And, of course, Mike was an old Red. He saw Lindsay as a symbol of the class struggle."

Race and Class

The template had been cut. Lindsay and his young staff certainly learned from the mistakes of those early days, but most of his future crises were also driven by class—and its twin brother race.

Lindsay moved ahead, determined to push hard to bring blacks and Latinos into the mainstream (social and political) of New York life. He wanted to give parents of public school children a greater say in the educational system. There were about one million such children, many of them from the marginalized, and the parents soon began serving on community school boards. He created

Every day was a "Day of Outrage" in the late 1960s, as repressed groups found their voice. Here, a demonstration is held outside Weinstein Hall at New York University.

June 28, 1970: The Christopher Street Liberation Day parade. The gay rights movement was born with the 1969 Stonewall police raid in Greenwich Village.

AMALIA V. BETANZOS who was Lindsay's relocation commissioner and youth service commissioner, went on to become president of Wildcat Service Corp, which ran the John V. Lindsay Academy

Mayor Lindsay gave New York's Hispanic communities hope that their version of the American dream could come true. That their children could triumph and become the leaders of tomorrow. That they had important opinions and city government wanted to listen to them and take action based on their needs.

RONNIE ELDRIDGE, a West Side Democratic district leader, and former special assistant to Lindsay, became a City Councilwoman

He had a soul that wasn't as patrician as his appearance I think. And I don't know where he learned it from but his family was pretty much the same way I think. They just had a sense of understanding.

People knew that City Hall was a place of power that would listen to them. The Welfare Rights people camped in City Hall Park. The first Gay Rights march took place the year after Stonewall. The Cambodian crisis brought students from all over the country to City Hall... Permits were always issued. No one was stopped. No one was hurt, either. He was the perfect mayor for those turbulent times.

JEFFREY KATZENBERG was 15 years old when he began working for John Lindsay's mayoral campaign as an advance man in the summer of 1965, he became a prominent film executive and is now CEO of DreamWorks Animation.

The fact is that Lindsay was out and about the streets of New York 24/7 and really it was very much a signature of him and his administration, which was to open the doors of government to respond to the disadvantaged in a way that no one had done before, and it is why when we got to 1968 and cities across the country erupted, this one didn't. And it's not simply that he was there in the streets on those nights personally doing it. That was the culmination of several years of investment in opening up the pressure cooker of frustration that minorities were feeling around this country and obviously in this city."

It wasn't just a kind of sizzle. There was real substance underneath it.

I think there were aspects of him that were very humbling and gracious, and at the same time I think there were aspects of him that were very cold cut, and a very practical tough fighter. You can't be in that seat and not be expedient. It comes with the territory. And you know, expediency is not always so pretty.

DAVID N. DINKINS was a newly minted Democratic district leader in Harlem in 1969 when he rejected the Democratic mayoral candidate and endorsed John Lindsay, Dinkins was mayor of New York from 1990 through 1993.

John and his wife Mary were just likeable people and not every wealthy person, not every person born with a silver spoon in his mouth so to speak is concerned about the least among us. And that was John. He cared.

Women demand equal rights during a demonstration in 1968. In 1970, Lindsay played a key role in the passage of New York State's liberalized abortion law.

December 8, 1967: Mayoral aide Sid Davidoff keeps watch during an anti-draft demonstration. The patrolmen's union and some elected officials accused mayoral aides of political interference with the police and demanded their resignation.

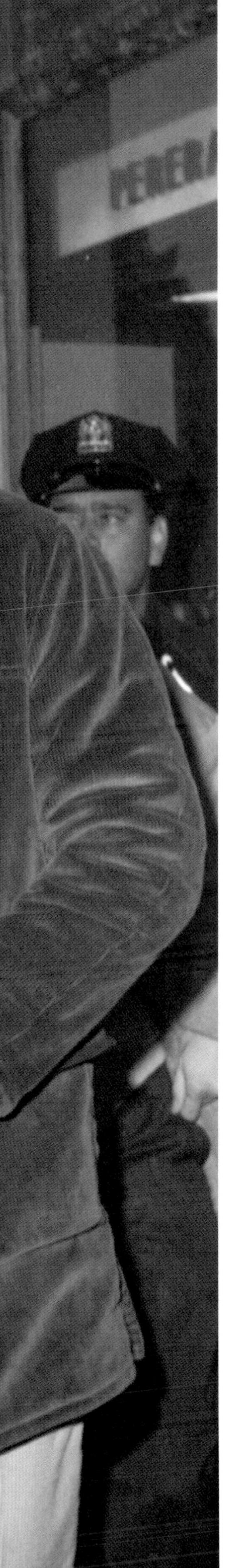

"Little City Halls" in storefronts scattered around the boroughs, to process complains, urgent needs, and warnings. He eased the rules for applying for welfare. He established local community boards, with a powerful say over planned local developments, changes in infrastructure, the establishment of rowdy businesses. He restructured some government agencies to save money and increase efficiency.

By 1968, which began so ominously with the Tet Offensive in Vietnam (Lindsay opposed the war from his time in the House), revolt was in the air, among university students, old Village radicals, artists and musicians and writers, along with growing numbers of middle class baby boomers. And there was a counter-resistance too. Lindsay struggled with it on the local level. Fury was also being decentralized. Race and power were part of the anger.

There seemed to be too many crises. The long teachers strike triggered by the consequences of community control in Ocean Hill-Brownsville, the sanitation strike that led to bonfires in the streets, the early stages of a dispute over low-income housing in Forest Hills, slowdowns by policemen, and threats of a strike by firefighters. The bitter teachers strike and Forest Hills helped to fracture the old bonds that united so many liberal Jews and African Americans; the vocal anti-Semitism present in these disputes was becoming more common among a minority of black citizens. Too many younger African Americans were raising the clenched fists of black separatism, cheering the Black Panthers, applauding the Black Power rhetoric of H. Rap Brown and Stokely Carmichael, sneering at notions of integration (for which many white liberals had been beaten, arrested, and killed). It was as if in distant Mississippi in 1964, Andrew Goodman, Michael Schwerner, and James Chaney had died for nothing. Nobody knew it at the time, but the neo-conservative movement was being born.

Lindsay's liberalizing changes—particularly over welfare—were also enraging the city's remaining white working class. As one ironworker said to me in that period: "I don't pay taxes so some guy can sit on the stoop."

And yet that era of ugly impulses, glib half-baked ideologies (often spouted by Marxists who had never read Marx), and anarchic violence was also the time of some of Lindsay's finest hours. The Watts riots of 1965 and the Newark and Detroit riots of 1967 triggered no huge echoes in New York. Those riots were not strictly race riots; they were riots against property, not attacks by blacks on whites. In New York, Lindsay had gone out of his way to cure some of the ills of black New York. One technique: visibility. He walked the streets of Harlem on summer nights. He was gracious with ordinary black citizens while also befriending blacks with true power, politically and in trade unions. As vice-chairman of the Kerner Commission investigating the 1967 riots, he was a strong advocate for telling the blunt truth about the consequences of white racism. As mayor, he put money into summer job programs. His Little City Halls were not simply another way of building a network of predictable middle class sources. Those urban consulates were also charged with opening contact among non-conventional groups, including militants, gang leaders, sports groups. They were a big city version of an early warning system.

"It was the symbol of 'you count' that was shown to the rest of the world. There were hundreds of those symbols that this city knew that he did without the camera on him, in community meetings, in walking down the street. But it was–the culmination was in that moment in time when he put his body on the line and went to the people who most were affected by what had happened that night, the dreams that they had, the dreams that Martin Luther King gave them, that he understood it and had to be with them, that was–it showed that he really did care."

–**Sid Davidoff** *was assistant buildings commissioner in the first Lindsay administration and one of the key aides in Lindsay's outreach efforts to the city's black communities.*

The great test came on April 4, 1968, when Martin Luther King was assassinated in Memphis. That night, ghettos all over the United States exploded into violence. Lindsay was at the Alvin Theater (opening night of *The Education of H.Y.M.A.N K.A.P.L.A.N*) when he heard the news. The mayor immediately went to the lobby and called his police commissioner. Reports from Harlem were ominous. Angry crowds were filling the main streets. There was not yet any violence, but anything might spark the fire this time.

Lindsay went first by limousine to Gracie Mansion, where a crisis center was being formed. Then, against the wishes of some advisers, he headed for Harlem. His media adviser, David Garth, drove him and a black detective named Ernest Latty in the Lindsay family station wagon. They stopped at Second Avenue and 125th Street. Lindsay and Latty got out of the car and walked west toward to the crowd. "I put my hand on the shoulder of each man we passed," he said in his memoir of the first term, "and expressed shared sorrow." He made no prepared speech, nothing to match the speech that Robert F. Kennedy was making that night in Indianapolis. He simply said, "This is a terrible thing." Hearing complaints that a police barrier was enraging some residents, he ordered it taken down. The crowds thickened. On all sides, Lindsay could hear the sounds of grief. Sobs. Moans. Two groups of men—men he knew—started arguing about the best route for Lindsay to take. "It was later reported that I had been wedged in between hostile groups and had been driven off the street," he wrote in his memoir. "In fact, the opposite was true. I was in the best of hands."

Eventually, he was steered to a car driven by Percy Sutton, the Manhattan borough president, and returned to Gracie Mansion. There the mayor received reports from around the city, and saw television coverage of burning cities across the country. He went back again to Harlem, walked again through the crowds. Harlem was holding. So was the larger city.

To be sure, there was minor looting, broken store windows, 12 arrests (including two in Brooklyn). Two people had died: one stabbed in a crowd, the other trapped in a burning building. The total damage was about $3,000,000. Across the country, during four days of rioting, there were 43 deaths, 23,987 arrests, almost 2,000 homes and shops destroyed. Total property damages came to almost $40,000,000. Almost 73,000 Army and National Guard troops were called into action, with the worst scenes taking place in Baltimore, Washington, D.C., and Chicago. Tanks rolled through American streets.

Not in New York.

Confronting Dragons

After that April night, many things got worse. There was a hardhat riot. There were riots in prisons. Snipers were killing policemen. The policy of "open admissions" was instituted at the City University, and the once rigorous educational standards of the free university began to crumble. Crime kept rising, along with a wider variety of drug use by the young. Heroin wasn't enough;

mood-alteration was now the goal. Every weekend, it seemed that a white kid playing at poverty on the Lower East Side walked off a rooftop, high on acid, thinking he could fly. Vietnam got worse, as did the opposition to the war. The welfare rolls almost doubled, peaking after Lindsay ended his second term in 1973 at 1.2 million human beings. That meant that New York contained within its boundaries a second city that was totally impoverished.

As a reporter, I interviewed some teenagers who had never known anybody on their blocks who actually held a job. What was called "relief" by its New Deal creators during the Great Depression and World War II—the word implying temporary government help for the poor—had become permanent for many people. The second generation welfare family became a fixture in many neighborhoods.

Lindsay looked more tired, more susceptible to bleakness, even after he won re-election in 1969 as the Liberal Party candidate. He had learned the hard way that saying something didn't make it happen. The snow storm happened earlier in 1969 and he was reviled by citizens in Queens. For some reason, he began to think about running for president, and switched parties, becoming a Democrat. Most likely, he knew there was no room for the likes of John Lindsay in the new Republican Party. The presidential bid didn't work. Lindsay had become a symbol: for urban chaos. In 1972, he finished fifth in the Democratic presidential primary in Florida and, after finishing sixth in Wisconsin, gave it up. The following year, he announced that he would not run for a third term in City Hall and when it was over, and Abe Beame at last had become mayor, Lindsay virtually disappeared. We saw him occasionally, and even when smiling there was a wounded look in his eyes. He must have known that he was seen as a symbol of liberal futility. He had started his first term as Quixote and he endured the second term as Sisyphus: rolling the boulder up the mountain with full knowledge that it would almost certainly roll back down.

But for me, he will always be that man who went to the churning streets of Harlem one terrible night in the spring of 1968. Sometimes, dragons really are dragons, and John Lindsay that night confronted the dragons of a possible urban apocalypse. Guns did not fire. There are men and women alive today who might have died that night except for Lindsay's uncommon valor. Many sneered at his notions of extending power to all of the people. I often wish that he had lived to see a black American sworn in as president of the United States of America. Quixote or Sisyphus, he helped make that happen too.

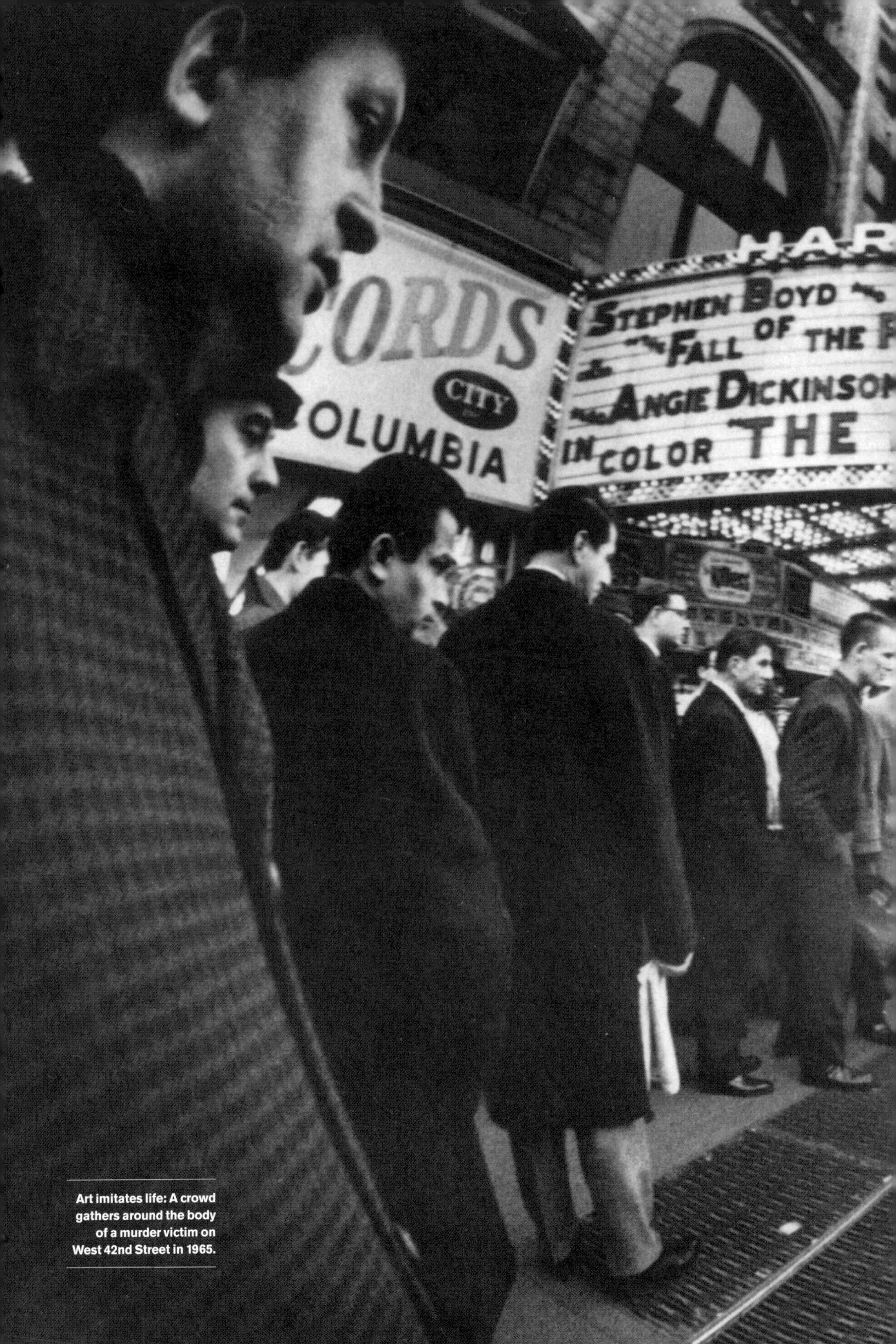

Art imitates life: A crowd gathers around the body of a murder victim on West 42nd Street in 1965.

Nicholas Pileggi

Crime and Punishment

For John V. Lindsay it was very simple. New Yorkers should be able to wander around their city without being robbed by muggers or harassed by cops. Before Lindsay's election in 1965, it was routine for police officers in radio cars to pull over minority youngsters whom they saw walking along Park Avenue, or any other predominantly "white" street, and ask whether they lived around there.

NICHOLAS PILEGGI worked at the Associated Press in New York City before joining *New York* magazine at its inception in 1968. Pileggi's 1987 book, *Wiseguy*, became the movie *Goodfellas*, the script of which he wrote with its director, Martin Scorsese. In 1990 he wrote the book *Casino*, which was turned into a movie that he also wrote with Scorsese.

"One of the most important things for the Lindsay administration is to prevent riots, to prevent rioting in the streets. That's why in terms of law enforcement, and in terms of welfare rights, the idea... from the Lindsay administration was if you get more people on welfare, if you can kind of help them, then that will keep the streets quiet, and that's what they wanted to do."

–Vincent Cannato, *author of* The Ungovernable City, *in an interview with Michael Epstein for the film* The Lindsay Years, *produced by Thirteen for WNET.org*

"No," was the usual answer, but even if the youngster turned out to be Ambassador Ralph Bunche's son walking home along Sutton Place from prep school, the police admonition was invariably the same: "Just get the hell out of here. If we see you around here again, you'll be sorry."

This was 40 years before "profiling" became a verb, but the longstanding discriminatory practice ended with Lindsay's election (at least official tolerance of it did) and it was just the beginning of the changes he brought to the Police Department and law enforcement in New York. Even before his election, while he was still a campaigning congressman, Lindsay challenged the entrenched brass at Police Headquarters and the politically powerful Patrolmen's Benevolent Association (P.B.A.), the police officers' union, in a speech to a bar association, calling for the establishment of an independent Civilian Complaint Review Board. That speech demonstrated from the very beginning his confrontational commitment to opening government and its processes to minority groups.

In the speech, Lindsay said that the New York City Police Department had become a remote, intransigent, and unaccountable city agency. Civilian complaints about police brutality and corruption were either dismissed out of hand or heard behind closed doors, where only the most egregious "bad apple" examples were suspended or dismissed. Most of the complaints filed would slowly wend their way through the Police Headquarters bureaucracy until they simply disappeared.

New York City, 1964: "Wanted" posters routinely adorned subway token booths.

Modernizing the Police Department

Lindsay not only campaigned for a Civilian Complaint Review Board, but he also made it clear that he planned to modernize a department that he felt had become calcified. The P.B.A. fought him at every turn. Hundreds of noisy off-duty police officers filled City Hall Park and cheered when Police Commissioner Vincent Broderick warned that Lindsay's plan for a Civilian Complaint Review Board would "tie the hands" of law enforcement. Uniformed police officers started walking the beat wearing "Buckley-for-Mayor" buttons, a form of electioneering that is against the department's rules and regulations, but no one at headquarters seemed to notice.

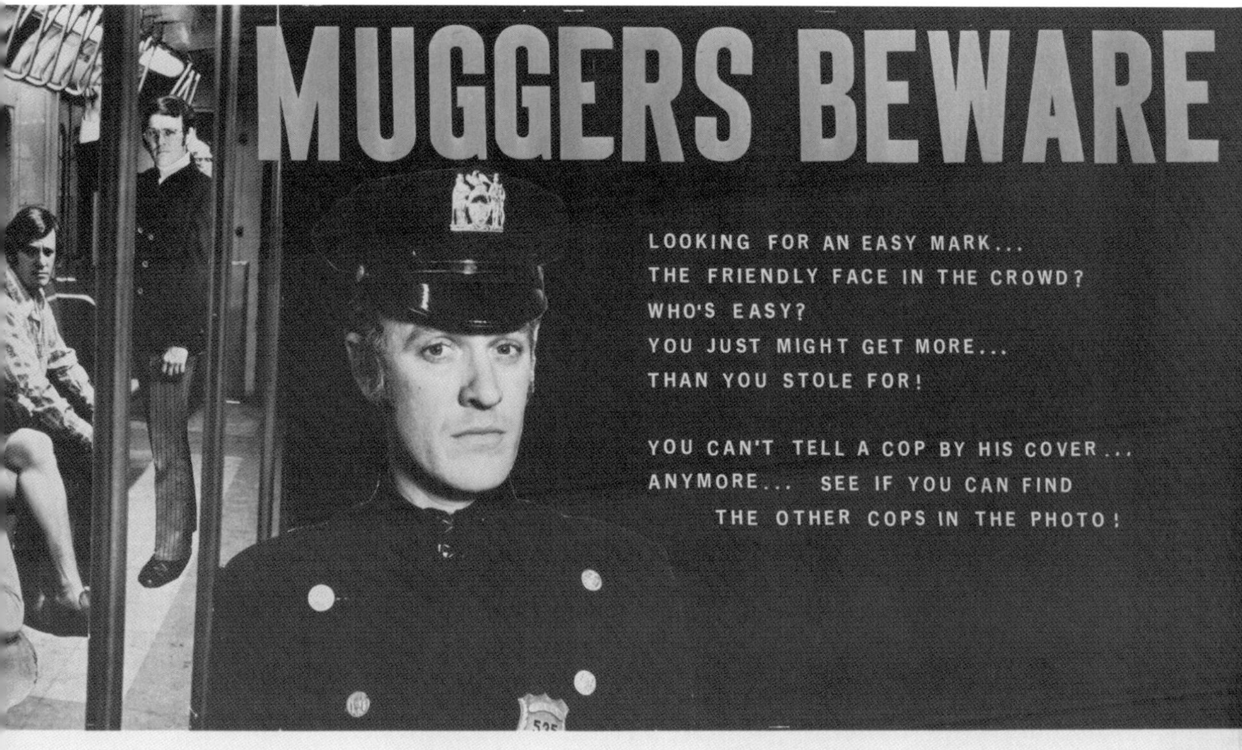

MUGGERS BEWARE
LOOKING FOR AN EASY MARK...
THE FRIENDLY FACE IN THE CROWD?
WHO'S EASY?
YOU JUST MIGHT GET MORE...
THAN YOU STOLE FOR!
YOU CAN'T TELL A COP BY HIS COVER...
ANYMORE... SEE IF YOU CAN FIND
THE OTHER COPS IN THE PHOTO!
by
ERNESTINE McCLENDON AGENCY
56 WEST 45th St.
N.Y.C. TN 7-2287

By 1971, Lindsay's efforts to quell crime included public campaigns warning criminals that their next victim might, in fact, be an undercover cop.

Once Lindsay was elected, he appointed Philadelphia's Howard R. Leary as police commissioner. Leary got the job because he was totally committed to implementing Lindsay's C.C.R.B. but also because he was from out of town and not a part of the department's old-boy political network. It might have been smart politics for Lindsay to soften his stand on the C.C.R.B. and modify some of his other positions, but he refused. Lindsay was just as adamant about changing the Police Department after his election as he was during the campaign.

Unable to deter the new mayor from his plan to create a Civilian Complaint Review Board, the P.B.A. initiated a citywide referendum to ban the creation of such a board. The P.B.A.'s print and TV campaign featured images of cops handcuffed, claiming that they could not do their jobs and appealing to middle-class voters with claims that a crime wave would sweep the city if the mayor's C.C.R.B. was allowed to stand.

Lindsay did have the New York Civil Liberties Union's support. It used the slogan: "Don't Let New York Become a Police State," but its high-brow campaigning was no match for the P.B.A.'s street-smart political savvy and its paid TV ads about rampant street crime. The core of the P.B.A. position was that Lindsay was coddling blacks and criminals by preventing cops from acting aggressively. As a result, the proposed Civilian Complaint Review Board was voted down by an almost three-to-one majority in the referendum. For Lindsay, it was a huge political defeat during his first year in office, but even

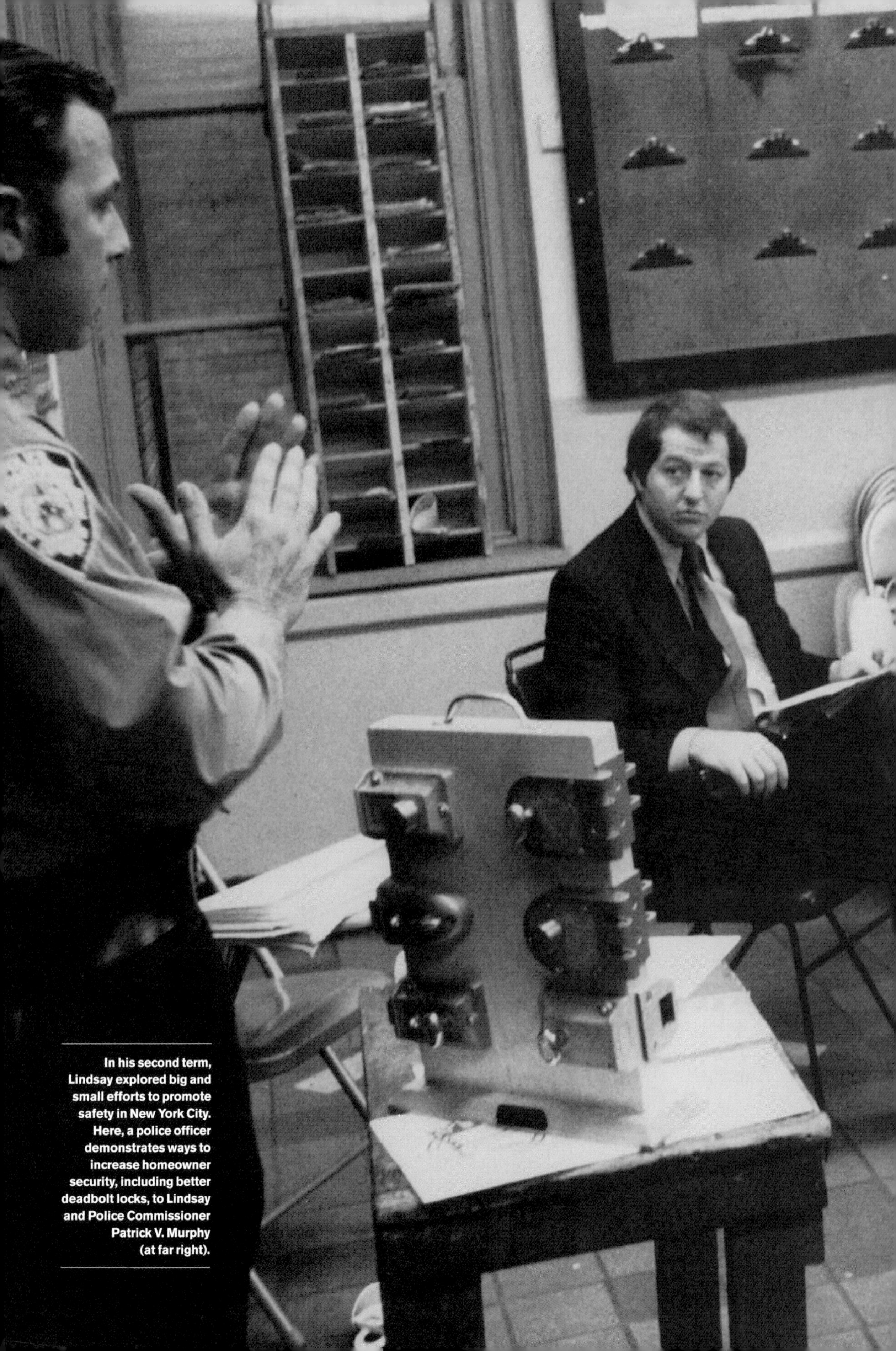

In his second term, Lindsay explored big and small efforts to promote safety in New York City. Here, a police officer demonstrates ways to increase homeowner security, including better deadbolt locks, to Lindsay and Police Commissioner Patrick V. Murphy (at far right).

"The police really disliked Lindsay. The police were another set of power brokers that Lindsay was out to break. It was the so-called Irish mafia that ran the police department, and the Lindsay administration wanted to break that up. They put in place the top two cops, well the top three cops are an Irish Catholic from Philadelphia, a Jewish American and an African American on top, and he basically pushes out other top leaders of the police department, and they're not happy about this. Lindsay, in some ways with this, paints the police as the enemy and that's the flip side of the moralizing. The flip side of the crusading John Lindsay is that crusaders or moralizers have to have an enemy against which they fight, and in this case the enemy was the police in a time when crime is severely rising. I mean, crime rates had gone up over 100 percent in the 1950s, they're going to go up another 100 percent. Fighting a war against the police is probably not the best strategy."

–**Vincent Cannato,** *author of* The Ungovernable City, *in an interview with Michael Epstein for the film* The Lindsay Years, *produced by Thirteen for WNET.org* more devastating, as far as he was concerned, was that the P.B.A.'s campaign to defeat the C.C.R.B. had deeply divided the city along racial lines.

Mayor Lindsay and members of his Urban Action Task Force tour East Harlem in the summer of 1967. They were the shock troops in responding to citizens' complaints.

A Policy of Restraint

Undeterred by the loss, Lindsay began making the kinds of changes within the department that could not be thwarted by a referendum. He began promoting blacks for the first time into the senior ranks of the uniformed force, with Lloyd Sealy as the first black assistant chief inspector, Ed Waith as deputy chief inspector, and Artie Hill as an inspector. Lindsay instructed his City Hall aides, including Barry Gottehrer and Sid Davidoff, to monitor police behavior at protest demonstrations. When Gottehrer and Davidoff showed up at a potentially volatile Vietnam protest in December 1967, the P.B.A. and City Council President Frank O'Connor attacked the mayoral aides for "interfering" with the police and called for the aides' resignations.

The idea that Lindsay would not let the police do their job was heightened at a Neighborhood Youth Corps rally in front of City Hall. The rally got out of hand when some black youths seeking summer jobs jumped on a Cadillac belonging to City Councilman Joe Modugno of Queens. The police gave chase the youths, but failed to make arrests. City Hall aides at the scene decided that since there was no serious damage done to Modugno's car, arresting and cuffing some black youths in the middle of a boisterous rally would have been a mistake. In fact, arresting the kids there could have helped escalate the rally into just the kind of disturbance Lindsay was hoping to prevent. While the policy of restraint would contribute to the deep racial divide, the Kerner Commission, which Lindsay was vice chairman of, later validated his insistence on police restraint in the face of provocation. Its report confirmed in meticulous detail that in one case, some of the worst rioting and looting in another city took place after police officers, who found themselves in a tenuous and tense situation, unwittingly escalated the situation by mistaking a 14-year-old with a sandwich for a man with a gun.

Despite the P.B.A.'s anti-Lindsay position, there were those within the department—from top brass to the uniformed officers on the beat—who agreed with many of Lindsay's ideas about modernizing it, and shortly after the election the new team at headquarters began implementing some of Lindsay's plans.

Restraint coupled with deploying overwhelming numbers of officers were two of the keys to Lindsay's success in keeping the city relatively cool. In East New York during the summer of 1966, a turf war between black and Italian-American youths threatened to explode until Lindsay and Leary ordered a massive infusion of over 1,000 uniformed cops to the area. No one in the neighborhood had ever seen so many cops before. They were deployed to stand just a few yards from each other. As a result, the rabble-rousers,

Molotov cocktail-tossers, and potential looters the police had been warned about never materialized. In the end, not one head cracked and although one person died, he was shot by a sniper, not by the police.

Of course, it helped that Lindsay had about a 32,000-member police force, so that he was able to saturate such areas, but there was more to the plan than just overwhelming numbers. The uniformed officers were purposely deployed during daylight hours, so they would become acclimated to the area before dark, a departure from the traditional practice of sending cops into a potential riot in a strange neighborhood at night. That only heightened the fears on both sides.

The individual police officers were urged to restrain themselves from the use of force. Uncertainty was taken out of the equation. It was intended that a police officer should never feel the pressure or fear that might cause him to fire his gun. In addition to the safety of large numbers, there were also large numbers of sergeants, lieutenants, and captains standing just feet away to answer any questions about how to act. As a result, many of the cops assigned to potentially dangerous situations later said that they never felt threatened enough to act in self-defense.

Lindsay also created the Urban Action Task Forces, under Gottehrer, to work within the city's most troubled neighborhoods. The task forces reached out to all kinds of community leaders in powder-keg neighborhoods with the idea of defusing potentially volatile situations before they occurred. Gottehrer, an ex-newspaper reporter, did not limit his contacts to traditional community leaders, like city social workers, political district leaders, and local clergy. Aware that Lindsay saw the police as a peacekeeping force to maintain order, not provoke it, Gottehrer realized that the city also had to reach out to the kinds of people the police would be more inclined to arrest than cajole. Gottehrer would meet with anyone who could insure neighborhood peace. He began recruiting street-gang leaders and ex-cons from troubled neighborhoods around the city. He reached out to the kinds of local troublemakers who did not spend a lot of time around political clubhouses and churches. Gottehrer even recruited the organized crime mobster Joseph (Crazy Joe) Gallo to defuse a potential battle between black and Italian-American youngsters in Brooklyn.

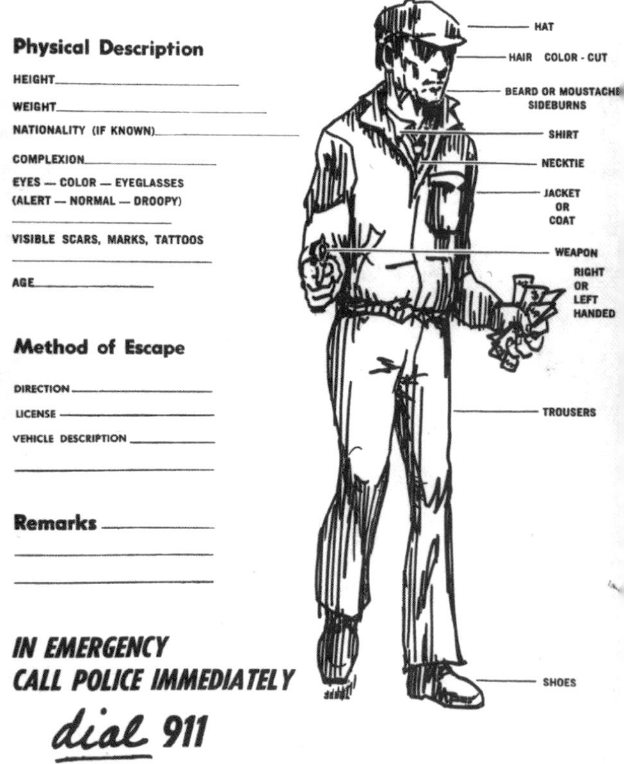

CRIMINAL DESCRIPTION SHEET

Physical Description

HEIGHT

WEIGHT

NATIONALITY (IF KNOWN)

COMPLEXION

EYES — COLOR — EYEGLASSES (ALERT — NORMAL — DROOPY)

VISIBLE SCARS, MARKS, TATTOOS

AGE

Method of Escape

DIRECTION

LICENSE

VEHICLE DESCRIPTION

Remarks

IN EMERGENCY CALL POLICE IMMEDIATELY

dial 911

POLICE DEPARTMENT CITY OF NEW YORK

PIB #71

A description sheet helped New Yorkers report criminal activity in their neighborhoods.

By 1968, cities across the country were going up in flames. Governors and mayors were desperate. News photos of Lindsay and his aides walking through angry tenement streets where an army of cops could not have

April 1968: A botched response to taunting student protesters at Columbia University turned into a police riot.

saved them were in marked contrast to what was happening in other cities. Detroit. Watts. Block after block of arson and ruin. Looting was so bad during riots in Chicago after King's assassination that its mayor, Richard J. Daley, ordered his police to "shoot to kill" any arsonist or bomb-thrower and to "shoot to maim or cripple" looters. When Lindsay was asked whether he planned to take similar action if widespread looting came to the city, he answered: "We are not going to shoot children in New York City."

Lindsay's policy of police restraint might have run counter to the national political mood at the time, especially with candidates like Richard M. Nixon running on law-and-order platforms, but there was no arguing with the results.

Statistics and Strategic Planning

But changing policies about suppressing riots was just one of the transformations Lindsay had in mind for his department. Many of his decisions about improving the police were not seen as politically beneficial, but he did not seem to care. For instance, when Lindsay ordered Commissioner Leary to start keeping accurate crime statistics, it was a move, his political aides said, that would produce a marked jump in the city's crime statistics and could be used against him by his political enemies.

Lindsay accepted that risk. The city needed crime statistics accurate enough to be able to deploy officers where and when they were needed. Until Lindsay, the city's crime rate was among the lowest in the country. But the rate was low only because most felonies were reported as misdemeanors, if they were reported at all, and murders were not reported unless they were solved. Civilian complaints were invariably "filed" with "Detective Can" in the trash. The city's crime statistics were such a joke that the F.B.I. refused to accept them as part of the bureau's annual compilation of crime in the country.

One year after Lindsay ordered the Police Department to start keeping accurate records, the city's crime rate jumped 70 percent. While his political enemies and the tabloids had a rousing time discussing "Lindsay's Crime Wave" and his "coddling" of thugs, he kept pushing the department forward. For instance, he started the first 911 police emergency number, with a computerized dispatch center. This not only meant that more people than ever would be able to report crimes and emergencies, but it also made the cops on the beat much more accountable.

Until 1964, all calls from the public went to one of the 76 local precinct houses. This cumbersome system assumed that citizens in need of immediate assistance knew not only the precinct in which they happened to find themselves, but also that precinct's phone number. Lindsay also issued the first walkie-talkies for every officer on patrol. He tripled the number of police radio frequencies.

Sometimes it seemed that every innovation became an intense political battle. Lindsay's idea for one-man radio patrol cars was condemned by the P.B.A., which said it feared that the practice was unsafe and would cut into the department's manpower. Lindsay said that with the new communication equipment, the one-man radio cars would not decrease manpower but increase coverage and efficiency.

Lindsay's creation of a fourth platoon also required his winning a political battle in Albany against the P.B.A. He had to amend a 1911 law that limited the department to three tours of duty a day—8 A.M to 4 P.M., 4 P.M to midnight, and midnight to 8 A.M. Four police commissioners who preceded Leary had unsuccessfully tried to amend the rigid shift structure. The city's newly accurate crime statistics showed that a fourth shift would allow cops to be assigned from 6 P.M. to 2 A.M., the hours when most crimes were being committed and officers were most active responding to citizen emergency calls.

The three-platoon system, under which officers rotated shifts, which meant that an equal number of officers covered each shift whether they were needed or not, led to all kinds of inefficient habits, including "cooping"—cops sleeping in radio cars, hotels, churches, and the back rooms of all-night diners and grocery stores during the midnight to 8 A.M. shift. One night, a perhaps apocryphal account had it, a mounted cop who patrolled the West Side piers stashed his horse in an idle railroad boxcar during the midnight tour. When he woke up the next day, he found himself and his horse hundreds of miles away, in Buffalo. The department quietly sent a horse van to retrieve him.

The P.B.A. fought Lindsay, too, when he freed thousands of cops from clerical desk duties by hiring civilians for routine paperwork and hired civilian traffic-control agents to give out parking tickets, freeing additional cops for more-important duties.

Police presence was hotly contested during the Columbia University strike in the spring of 1968. Mayor Lindsay sent three aides to negotiate with Columbia, its striking students, and other factions.

The Lindsay administration also built on the early experiments begun under Mayor Wagner to integrate Herb Sturz's Vera Institute of Justice into the Police Department's strategic-planning arm. As the city's chief magistrate, Lindsay persuaded turf-conscious judges, court administrators, and prosecutors to join together in a Criminal Justice Coordinating Council. Jay Kriegel, who would serve as Lindsay's chief of staff and special counsel, enlisted Sturz in diverse projects to treat Bowery alcoholics instead of recycling them in and out of detention pens (a job that beat cops despised and that cost the department overtime for processing thousands of useless arrests).

DAVID BURNHAM was an award-winning *New York Times* reporter from 1968 to 1986 and covered police corruption. His editor was the legendary Arthur Gelb. He is the author of three books, is the co-founder of the Transactional Records Access Clearinghouse, which tracks staffing, spending, and enforcement activities of the federal government, and is an associate professor at the S.I. Newhouse School of Public Communications.

Within the ranks of the New York Police Department during the late 1960s and early 1970s, a "substantial majority" of the 30,000 patrol officers eventually were determined to be accepting bribes routinely. At the same time, many detectives assigned to the department's elite squad, created to combat the most serious narcotics dealers, were taking five-figure payoffs to close their eyes to massive drug violations. While this flood of corruption was swamping the city, Police Commissioner Howard Leary decided to shrink the internal affairs division that was established to stanch it.

Later, Governor Nelson A. Rockefeller would appoint a special prosecutor to take over the prosecution of police-misconduct matters after he decided that the city's five district attorneys had failed to properly handle the problem. And a top Patrolmen's Benevolent Association official privately asserted that the millions in dollars of illegal payoffs each year were considered part of the city's "pay package."

(above) In 1971, the Knapp Commission concluded: "This was the first time–in this or perhaps any other city–that the official ultimately responsible for a police department's conduct had authorized public investigation of allegations of police corruption." From left, Cyrus Vance, later Secratary of State; Joseph Monserrat, later president of the Board of Education; John E. Sprizzo, later a federal judge; Franklin A. Thomas, later President of the Ford Foundation; and the commission chairman Whitman Knapp, who also went on to become a federal judge.

Sitting on top of this toxic stew was John Lindsay. Two of his close associates, a young special assistant for police matters (Jay Kriegel) and the investigation commissioner (Arnold G. Fraiman) were eventually found to have failed to act on credible reports from Frank Serpico, a plainclothes officer, and Detective David Durk, that virtually all the officers in the department's anti-gambling squad received regular payoffs.

I covered that police corruption story for *The New York Times*. Forty years later, considering only the hugely perverse impact of the city's upside-down "war on drugs," the costs of corruption to New Yorkers are almost impossible to overstate. One reason we know so much about these sordid events was Lindsay's 1970 decision to create an independent commission to investigate some of them, and especially his choice of Whitman Knapp, a prominent New York lawyer and later a federal judge, to be its chairman. Knapp proved himself an unusually tough, canny, and highly principled street fighter who, in the end, concluded that Lindsay, as chief executive, "cannot escape responsibility for widespread corruption" in the department.

Lindsay's decision to create a commission was not a good-government reaction of a reform-minded politician. Rather, it was a defensive public relations move taken shortly after his press secretary learned that *The Times* was about to publish a major investigative article on police corruption. The front-page article, on April 25, 1970, said that narcotics dealers, gamblers, and businesses in New York City were making illicit payments of millions of dollars a year to the police and that high officials in the Police Department and the administration looked the other way.

The Knapp Commission's impact was vast. In 1992, another investigation, this one by Judge Milton Mollen, a former presiding justice of the Appellate Division of the State Supreme Court, found that while some corruption endured, "unlike the situation a generation ago, this commission can confidently report that the vast majority of New York City police officers are honest and hard-working and serve this city with skill and dedication each day."

The administration invited Vera to launch the city's first ambulatory methadone-maintenance program to reduce the criminal repercussions of addiction (but stopped short of a politically toxic experiment in heroin maintenance as a last resort). In a political coup of sorts, Lindsay also appointed Robert M. Morgenthau, dumped by the Nixon administration as the chief federal prosecutor in New York, as a deputy mayor whose portfolio included criminal justice and narcotics control, the first such deputy mayor that the city ever had.

Fighting Police Corruption

The impact of modern management on the Police Department was profound. But for all the changes, large and small, the seriousness with which Lindsay eventually took on the overwhelming problem of systemic police corruption would probably most distinguish his relationship with the department. As tough as it was to accept, the institutional "Guys and Dolls" corruption that had been quietly allowed to exist concerning illegal gambling had begun to spread into the far-less-palatable world of narcotics.

Frank Serpico testifies in 1971 before the Knapp Commission, accompanied by his attorney (and former U.S. Attorney General) Ramsey Clark. If City Hall was slow to respond to his reports of corruption, that was because the mayor couldn't afford to alienate the police further when he depended on their restraint in dealing with civil unrest. "I guess that's up to history to judge," Serpico said later. "One would like to think when you go to a government agency or someone in charge they would take immediate action. Without David Burnham, nothing would have happened."

Federal undercover agents, posing as drug dealers, were suddenly and routinely being robbed by New York City detectives unaware that their victims were federal agents and that the rooms they burst into were as wired with cameras as a television studio. *The New York Times* gave prominent headlines to revelations from two cops, Frank Serpico and David Durk, about systemic corruption, including an organized system of collecting bribes from most or all the local merchants in a precinct, which were shared by virtually every cop in the precinct. Perhaps this was one institution that City Hall, already under siege for its influence over police policy, was wary of confronting. But in 1970, after *The Times* revelations and when 79 pounds of pure heroin, much of it seized in the famous French Connection case, vanished from the Police Department property clerk's office, Lindsay created a Commission to Investigate Alleged Police Corruption. Commonly known as the Knapp Commission, after its chairman, Whitman Knapp, a New York lawyer, the five-member panel held a series of public hearings beginning in October 1971 and issued a final report in December 1972 that recommended sweeping institutional changes. Implementation of the commission's recommendations, like holding commanders accountable for their subordinates' actions, deploying undercover informants, and improving screening of officers, changed the department forever. The level of departmental pride and professionalism that survives to this day has to be traced back to the city's 103rd mayor.

James Sanders

Adventure Playground

Lindsay established the Mayor's Office of Film, Theatre and Broadcasting in 1966, the first such office in the nation. Here, Lindsay (second from right), his wife Mary (far left), his son John Jr. (center), and his daughter Anne (far right) visit Audrey Hepburn on the set of *Wait Until Dark* in 1967.

In recent years, it has been scarcely possible to walk down the streets of New York (especially in good weather) without sooner or later coming across a film crew at work: fleets of specialized vehicles and dozens of dedicated craftspeople—directors, cinematographers, camera operators, production designers, property masters, gaffers, grips, and, of course, celebrated or world-famous actors and performers—busily transforming the everyday landscape of the city into the setting for some larger-than-life cinematic vision of urban living.

JAMES SANDERS, AIA, is an architect and writer whose multi-disciplinary work has won him a Guggenheim Fellowship and the Emmy, Peabody, and DuPont-Columbia awards among other honors. With Ric Burns, he co-wrote the award-winning eight-part PBS series, *New York: A Documentary Film,* and is the author of *Celluloid Skyline: New York and the Movies,* which was hailed by the late Jane Jacobs as a "marvelous—miraculous—book." His architecture and urban design firm, James Sanders+Associates, has completed numerous projects for government, corporate, and private clients in New York, Los Angeles, and elsewhere.

Similarly, it is scarcely possible to walk into a movie theater or look at a television screen today and not soon find New York City serving as the setting for—and often enough the subject of—romantic comedies, thrillers, police dramas, science-fiction fantasies, or any of a dozen other film genres regularly shot on location in the city. Over the past decade, no fewer than 200 feature films, and hundreds more episodes for television, have been filmed each year in the five boroughs of New York, a total that no other American city—not even Los Angeles—can match. Thanks to this pervasive filmic presence, audiences across the country, and indeed all around the world, have come to know New York as well as—or better than—their own hometowns.

A frequent visitor on film shoots, Lindsay enjoyed hamming it up with actors Peter Falk and Jack Lemmon during the filming of *Luv* on the Williamsburg Bridge in 1966.

The city's onscreen prominence is so taken for granted today that it is hard to imagine that as late as 1965—the last year of Robert F. Wagner's mayoralty—New York hardly appeared in films at all. That year, only two features were shot substantially in the city: *The Pawnbroker*, an early landmark in the career of veteran New York director Sidney Lumet, and *A Thousand Clowns*, directed by Fred Coe, which used extensive location work to "open up" a Broadway stage hit of a few years earlier by the playwright Herb Gardner.

This big change, of course, was due to Wagner's successor as mayor, John V. Lindsay—who, soon after taking office in 1966, made New York the first city in history to *encourage* location filmmaking: establishing a simple, one-stop permit process through a newly created agency (now called the Mayor's Office of Film, Theatre and Broadcasting), creating a special unit of the Police Department to assist filmmakers, and ordering all city agencies and departments to cooperate with producers and directors.

The founding of the Mayor's Film Office—the first agency of its kind in the world—remains to this day one of the Lindsay administration's signal achievements, an innovation in governance that has since been replicated by agencies or commissions in almost every state and big city and in scores of countries and provinces around the world. In New York alone, it helped to usher in what has become virtually an entire new industry, generating over $5 billion a year in economic activity and bringing work to more than 100,000 New Yorkers: renowned directors and stars, working actors and craftsmen and women, and tens of thousands of people employed by supporting businesses—from equipment-rental houses to scenery shops to major studio complexes that now rival those of Southern California. Along the way, it has also helped to ensure that New York retains its status as one of the most familiar and compelling urban landscapes in the world.

Yet in retrospect, the creation of the Mayor's Film Office, important as it was, can be seen as simply one piece of a much larger and more pervasive shift that was introduced during Mayor Lindsay's two terms in City Hall. It is a change in sensibility so pervasive—from the city as a place of function, in essence, to a place of pleasure—that today it surrounds us, almost invisibly, having quietly revolutionized the way we think about the meaning and purpose of New York and other American cities.

To understand and appreciate this subtle yet tectonic shift there is no better guide, ironically, than those last two films of the pre-Lindsay era, *The Pawnbroker* and *A Thousand Clowns*, which serve almost perfectly to frame the dramatic change in perception that was about to come.

The Pawnbroker centers on a middle-aged Holocaust survivor named Sol Nazerman (Rod Steiger), the proprietor of a decrepit pawnshop on East 116th Street, who fills out his days in his shabby store amidst a universe of unwanted objects—clocks, jewelry, appliances, musical instruments—and trudges to work and back each day through the grim streets of East Harlem.

Though the horrific past of its main character inevitably gives *The Pawnbroker* its special import and trajectory, it is easy to look beyond the particulars of its story to see the film in broader terms, as a period portrait of the kind of ordinary working life that prevailed across much of Manhattan in the first half of the 20th century—the city that remained very much in place through Mayor Wagner's three terms in office. It is, in fact, a portrait of the classic industrial city: a place of endless labor, devoted primarily to the making, moving, and selling (in this case, *re*selling) of physical goods. (The pawnshop, in its way, represents a small corner of the vast wholesale and retail industries that did so much to build and sustain the city's economic engine in the hundred years or so from the 1850s to the 1960s.)

For Nazerman, as for so many of the unsung millions of men and women who toiled in the city's factories, warehouses, and stores, the city is above all a place for *work*: a cheerless, essentially functional environment in which to spend five or six days each week, to be valued as a place of gainful employment, perhaps, but certainly not to be treasured as a source of delight or even regarded, in some sense, as a setting or "landscape" at all. Indeed, Nazerman barely notices the city as he walks to and from his shop each day, except to take note of an occasional strange sight or distant horror, triggering a flashback of his nightmarish past. Otherwise, the gray, gritty city simply passes by—not a "place" at all, really, but merely a serviceable location for economic activity.

Sol Nazerman (Rod Steiger) opens his East Harlem pawnshop on the set of *The Pawnbroker*, filmed in New York in 1964.

A Thousand Clowns offers a completely different view of the city—and not only (or even mostly) because its main character, a comedy writer named Murray Burns (Jason Robards), is part of the city's new "post-industrial" economy rather than the

Jason Robards filming a scene for *A Thousand Clowns* along the East River waterfront in 1965.

Leo Bloom (Gene Wilder) and Max Bialystock (Zero Mostel) at the Lincoln Center fountain in *The Producers*, 1968.

older, goods-oriented commercial world of Sol Nazerman. In fact, during most of the film, Murray is out of work entirely, having chosen sometime earlier to quit his job on a children's TV show. Instead, he spends much of his time touring the city with his live-in nephew (Barry Gordon) and, later, a new girlfriend (Barbara Harris)—meandering the city on foot and by bicycle, binoculars in hand, seeking out picturesque corners of the urban landscape, enjoying a range of unusual or eccentric attractions (often on or near the water's edge) outside the mainstream of busy, white-collar Manhattan. His relationship with the city is based not on its role as a center for commercial activity at all, but on something else entirely: as a kind of spectacular, full-sized stage set, through which he is free to wander joyfully, like an overgrown child, finding delight in its endless surprises and discoveries, its hidden corners and unexpected vistas. For Murray, the great urban construct that is mid-century New York serves, at some real level, as a giant playground.

If Sol Nazerman's New York was, in effect, the city of Mayor Wagner—a gray, functional environment, dedicated largely to commercial pursuits—then *A Thousand Clowns* perfectly presaged the new vision of the city that John Lindsay and his colleagues sought, consciously or not, to put forward: a new, officially sanctioned spirit in which the city was actually to be *enjoyed as a place*.

The notion itself was hardly new. For decades, individual writers, artists, filmmakers, and others had drawn attention to distinctions and pleasures of New York as an urban environment, one that—though devoted largely to commercial purpose—could offer a romantic, exciting, and even delirious sense of place. But rarely, if ever, had there been any *official* approval or appreciation of the city's existing physical environment, as such. Indeed, by the late 1950s and early 1960s—as urban renewal and highway programs leveled and rebuilt one neighborhood after another—exactly the opposite was true. "Everyone, it would seem, is for the rebuilding of our cities," the editor and critic William H. Whyte observed in 1958, "with a unity of approach that is remarkable."

> *But this is not the same thing as* liking *cities.... [M]ost of the rebuilding under way and in prospect is being designed by people who don't like cities. They do not merely dislike the noise and the dirt and the congestion. They dislike the city's variety and concentration, its tension, its hustle and bustle.*

By contrast, Lindsay and his colleagues generally *liked* cities, in the particular sense described by Whyte and portrayed in *A Thousand Clowns*. But that was only part of it. In a striking variety of ways, Lindsay and his team would also seek to promote the other notion suggested by the film: that the urban landscape of New York could be considered a kind of giant outdoor "stage"—one that could be enhanced, moreover, as a theatrical designer or art director might transform a stage or film set: with "scenic" improvements that would allow it to serve as a setting, or frame, for the widest imaginable range of public and private pleasures.

The most obvious example of this was the administration's effort to encourage film production, which set off a sudden explosion of creative energy, as dozens of filmmakers fanned out across the city's landscape, eager to exploit it as (literally) a giant stage, and determined to adapt it to their own purposes. (In 1967, just a year after the Mayor's Film Office was founded, 42 feature films were produced in New York.) Audiences tended to imagine that location-shot films represented some kind of documentary-like "truth" about their setting, but nothing could have been further from the case: cinematographers, production designers, and set decorators almost always modified or transformed real locations—sometimes quite ambitiously—to meet the needs of story and script. This was most evident in period films, which employed ingenious production-design and set-dressing techniques to allow contemporary New York streets to be turned back to the 1920s (for *The Night They Raided Minsky's*, 1968) or the 1940s (for *The Godfather*, 1973). But it also held for films set in the present day, which adapted the city's urban landscape no less imaginatively to their own ends—turning Lincoln Center's central fountain, for example, into a thrilling set piece in *The Producers* (1968), its waters exploding into the sky to underscore the joyous moment when a repressed accountant, played by Gene Wilder, agrees to join forces with the larger-than-life impresario played by Zero Mostel. Or transforming the contemporary high-rise landscape of New York—by eerily emptying it of people—into a haunting and somehow timeless setting for a retelling of St. Matthew's Gospel in *Godspell* (1973).

Lindsay's radical new approach to location shooting—encouraging moviemakers to transform (or creatively reimagine) every corner of the city's urban landscape—was plainly the most literal embodiment of the impulse to turn New York into a kind of giant outdoor stage. But that same impulse underpinned a far more ambitious effort by the Lindsay administration: to extend the approach to the actual fabric of the city, which was not only to be regarded as a source of delight, but manipulated and enhanced as if it, too, were a kind of scenic environment.

The obvious place to start was the city's parks—one of the few places, even in the days of the traditional, relentlessly commercial city, to be specifically dedicated to the unworldly values of pleasure, respite, and even joy. Yet in practice, New York City's parks, for decades under the firm and heavy hand of Robert Moses—who had headed the Parks Department as commissioner from 1934 to 1960, then ran it through faithful surrogates in later years—had been curiously dull and joyless places. Obsessed with orderliness and propriety, Moses had tirelessly sought to disallow any type of behavior outside the strictest possible norms (an authoritarian instinct embodied almost comically by the wooden sign posted at every park and playground entrance in the city, featuring a giant printed "NO" followed by a long list of proscribed activities). Though he had been known in his youth (nearly 40 years earlier) for the imaginative and even whimsical approach he brought to the design of Jones Beach and other state parks, the structures and equipment that the older Moses installed in the city's parks and playgrounds in the 1950s and after were almost uniformly grim, banal, and uninspired, seemingly designed more for ease of maintenance and discouraging vandalism than with providing any sense of delight or whimsy.

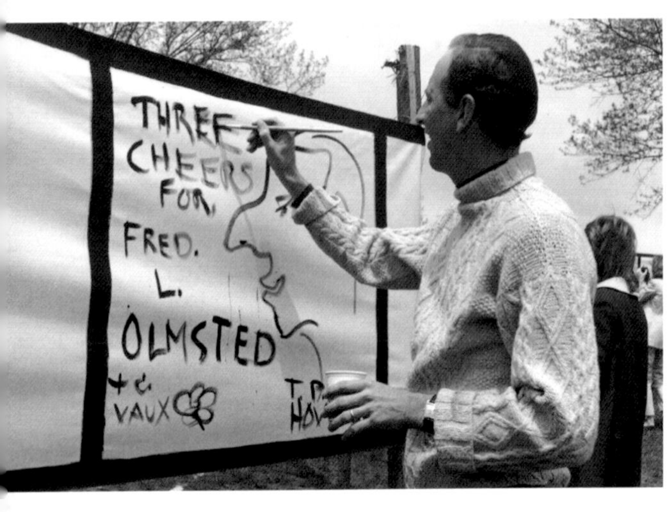

May 15, 1966: Parks Commissioner Thomas Hoving participates in a "Paint-In" at Cedar Hill in Central Park.

But all that would change overnight, when, even before Lindsay officially took office, he appointed Thomas P.F. Hoving, an iconoclastic 34-year-old curator at the Metropolitan Museum of Art, as the city's new Parks Commissioner. Declaring that "the old rinky-dink, hand-me-down stereotype of the park is out, OUT!" Hoving proclaimed the advent of the "park as public theater"—and within months had initiated a series of stunning initiatives to fulfill his promise. To the astonishment of cab drivers (and the traffic commissioner, Henry Barnes, who predicted traffic jams stretching from Maine to Florida), Hoving ordered Central Park's drives closed to auto traffic on Sunday mornings to encourage bicyclists to savor its 19th century landscape (much as Murray Burns had done in *A Thousand Clowns*). He borrowed an art-world idea from the curator Alan Kaprow and introduced what were soon dubbed "happenings": loosely structured—or entirely *un*structured—public events and gatherings in the city's parks, from a 500-person game of "capture-the-flag" on Central Park Mall to a Gay Nineties-themed cocktail party at the Naumburg Bandshell, that drew 35,000 participants. There were "kite happenings," a "folk song happening," and a nighttime "scientific happening" to observe a meteor shower.

"A park is like a stage," Hoving declared, in no uncertain terms. "If you leave it sitting, nothing good is going to happen." Having re-envisioned the city's parks as an almost theatrical environment, Hoving now sought to enhance the "scenic" elements, through a series of innovative, small-scale interventions designed specifically to help bring life to pre-existing spaces. At Bethesda Fountain in Central Park, he created an open-air "Fountain Café," which disposed of the need for major permanent structures to achieve its effects, using instead lightweight canvas canopies and outdoor café seating—elements that were suggestively scenery-like in their portable, casual, temporary nature. In place of the standardized, almost grudging playground designs of the Moses era, meanwhile, Hoving commissioned an "Adventure Playground" near West 67th Street in Central Park, which, drawing on the ideas of "participatory play" popular in England and Scandinavia, offered a stylish, exuberant design by the architect Richard Dattner, plainly intended not only to engage the imagination of children, but also to engender pleasure and delight in adults.

A "happening" in Central Park around 1967.

As the years went on, Lindsay's colleagues—some in government itself, others in arts groups that worked closely with the city—sought to extend the same spirit still further, reaching beyond the leafy confines of the parks and into the streets of the city itself. If less explicit than Hoving in comparing the city to a stage, these groups were motivated by deeply similar goals and means: to celebrate the existing urban environment—and enhance its appeal as a pedestrian setting—through small-scale, imaginative, often temporary or portable elements or installations. In this case, however, these scenic elements would take the form of public art—not traditional statues of civic worthies, but unconventional, often lighthearted works that would at once animate the urban landscape and encourage it to be seen and enjoyed afresh. In 1967, the city's Office of Cultural Affairs mounted a temporary open-air exhibit called "Sculpture in the Environment," whose 26 artworks, placed in pedestrian spaces around the city, were like nothing ever quite seen before: striking, often playful set pieces with no purpose other than to enhance the public's enjoyment of the larger urban landscape (at least until the run of the show was over, when, like any theatrical experience, they receded into collective memory).

From "Such an Amusing City..."

DICK SCHAAP

The New York Herald Tribune, January 7, 1966

At a January 2, 1966, press conference at City Hall, Mayor Lindsay was asked what message he wanted to send New Yorkers beleaguered by the transit workers' strike. He replied: "Thanks for cooperation and for toughness, for good spirit and good cheer. This is a fun and exciting city even when it's a struck city." His remarks inspired this column by Dick Schaap in *The New York Herald Tribune* and immortalized the phrase Fun City:

Not long after the transit strike began the other day, Mayor John V. Lindsay went on radio and television to announce that New York is a fun city. He certainly has a wonderful sense of humor. A little while later, Lindsay cheerfully walked four miles from his hotel room to City Hall, a gesture which proved that the fun city had a fun mayor.

The funniest thing was that New Yorkers were actually finding humor in the absence of buses and subways. One citizen was very concerned that the pickpockets and muggers, the true New Yorkers he called them, would get out of shape. He offered to give them a room where they could practice on each other for the duration of the crisis. A local radio station, WNEW, added a special crisis record for its disc jockey shows.

The station, bowing to nostalgia, played a tape of a roaring subway train, as a public service for those people who miss the sound. Other people took subway tokens they had purchased in advance and stored them away with their Confederate dollars.

And somebody kept telling people who live in Brooklyn how they could get to Times Square by public transportation with a minimum of walking. They could take the Long Island Rail Road to the Jamaica Station in Queens, then take the Long Island Rail Road to Penn Station in Manhattan, then take the Hudson Tubes to New Jersey, then take the bus from New Jersey to the Port Authority Bus Terminal, which is so convenient, right next to Times Square. Then, if they had enough time and money left, they could turn around and go home.

New Yorkers' sense of humor spread out of town. In Philadelphia, nearly everyone was talking about the contest in which first prize was one week in New York and second prize was two weeks in New York. Even in Los Angeles, which had been told by the McCone Commission that it had one of the most inadequate transit systems in the country, people had to smile a little.

Probably the best joke of all was Mayor Lindsay's suggestion that employers should not dock the pay of their employees who chose to help the city by staying away from their offices during the transit strike. The employers laughed very hard at this one.

And Bill Buckley, who had run for mayor last year on the Conservative party ticket, must have found New York a fun city, too. He had suggested during the campaign that the city build bicycle paths above the streets to relieve traffic congestion. Everybody had made great fun of Buckley's suggestion. At the time, Lindsay almost broke up laughing. I think he suggested covered wagons as an alternative.

"Can you imagine people bicycling to work in the middle of the winter?" Lindsay said in the fall. The covered wagon will be ordered next.

Robert F. Wagner, who had been mayor of New York for 12 years before Lindsay took over, chose to spend the first week of 1966 in Acapulco, another one of those fun cities. He thought it was kind of funny that the city had never had a transit strike when he was mayor.

Even policemen were groping for jokes. "It could be worse," said a policeman on duty at City Hall early in the week. "It could be snowing. It could be the Christmas shopping season. And Consolidated Edison could have another blackout." Some fun.

The theatrical parallel grew more obvious a few years later, when Doris C. Freedman, a public arts advocate who had organized the open-air sculpture exhibit for the city's cultural affairs office, established a group called City Walls to sponsor murals on the blank walls of New York buildings. Among their most notable projects was a five-story-tall painting by the artist Richard Haas on a building on SoHo's Prince Street, using *trompe l'oeil* techniques to recreate, on an exposed brick side wall, the ornate cast-iron architecture of the building's facade—an unmistakable piece of urban sceneography, rendered at the grandest scale.

Dreary and impersonal standardized equipment was replaced with imaginative exploratory experiences in what was naturally dubbed an "Adventure Playground." This one, designed by Richard Dattner at Central Park West and West 68th Street, opened in 1966.

The ironies could not have been more stark. Just a few years earlier and a few hundred yards away, Robert Moses, with the blessing of Mayor Wagner, had sought to destroy hundreds of similar cast-iron buildings to clear a path for his Lower Manhattan Expressway, with no thought whatsoever for the area's historic architecture; now, under a new mayor, that same architecture was not only being saved (in part by new zoning provisions designed to encourage its reuse) but also being lovingly and imaginatively reinterpreted. The desire to actively enjoy the existing landscape of the city—to find delight in its idiosyncrasies, its mixture of new and old, its picturesque vistas and tucked-away corners—was no longer the private, somewhat suspect pleasure of a few eccentric individuals like Murray Burns but had come to be societally approved and officially supported.

Toward the end of Lindsay's second term in office came his administration's most ambitious attempt to remake the fabric of the city as a kind of a open-air setting or stage for city-dwellers: the Madison Avenue Mall. Conceived by a city agency called the Office of Midtown Planning and Development—one of a handful of young planning teams created by Lindsay to promote advanced urban design ideas—the project called for the stretch of Madison Avenue between 42nd and 57th Streets to be closed permanently to cars (buses would still be allowed down a center lane) and re-landscaped as a pedestrian-only promenade. The plan had been inspired by street closings for the first Earth Day, in April 1970, which had drawn tens of thousands of joyous pedestrians down the middle of Fifth Avenue: a kind of theatrical Hoving "happening" that had somehow burst the bounds of Central Park and occupied the heart of the city—and now, at last, was about to receive a permanent, dedicated outdoor "stage," 12 blocks long.

112–114 Prince Street, Manhattan, before (left) and after the *trompe l'oeil* mural by Richard Haas.

Rendering of the proposed Madison Avenue Mall, 1971. The project was defeated by the Board of Estimate in 1973 after an intense public campaign.

Yet in the end, the Madison Avenue Mall was killed: defeated at the Board of Estimate in July 1973, five months before the end of Lindsay's second term, by the joint efforts of the city's taxicab industry and department-store interests, fearful of a loss of business from well-heeled cab-riding customers.

In retrospect, the death of the mall project seemed to be a harbinger, as the brave new approach to the city that Lindsay had almost entirely pioneered was soon overwhelmed by the tidal wave of troubles crashing over the city.

To be sure, there had been criticism from the start—from skeptical observers who (not without reason) regarded the Lindsay team as elitist, Manhattan-centric, and essentially oblivious to the needs of the working people who made up most of the city's population. Many older, traditionally minded New Yorkers, meanwhile, were suspicious of the anti-authoritarian undercurrents—and sometimes almost reckless tone—in the words and actions of the young mayor and his even-younger colleagues. Prominent among these critics, not surprisingly, was Robert Moses himself. "It has yet to be shown," he declared,

> *that [an] essentially honest, youthful municipal administration based on impulse rather than experience—with…extravagant promises, invitations to disorder in the name of satisfying youth, uncontrollable events and happenings—can maintain New York's supremacy and livability. We must soon decide whether we want a fun town [or] one guaranteeing outward order and decency.*

If it was easy to dismiss Moses's attack as the bitter critique of an old lion turned out of power in the city, it gradually became apparent that there was more than a grain of truth in what he said. Hoving's fervent desire to fill the parks with people almost any way he could, for example, began to succeed all too well—as the fragile landscapes of Central Park and other spaces were overrun and trampled by thousands of visitors who, responding to the commissioner's liberatory declarations, felt no need to curb their behavior in any way. Within a few years, the city's parks began to fray and then fall badly into

Reflections

HAL PRINCE, the theatrical producer and director, has won more Tony Awards than any other individual. Here are excerpts from his recollections of his friend, John Lindsay:

John Lindsay and I met in the early 1950s. I knew his family—his brothers and sisters-in law—and we played tennis on Long Island fairly regularly. The friendship continued for the rest of his life, and the recollections which return most vividly are:

An early-morning phone call from St. James Church to my wife and me, asking us to throw on some clothes and meet him and Mary for a walk down Madison Avenue, at which time he told us he was going to run for mayor, asked me whether I'd help, introduced himself to too many New Yorkers who failed to recognize him as their Congressman, and ended up at the Roosevelt Hotel, looking at empty office space.

His campaign reminds me very much of the national campaign that infused the Barack Obama presidency: many, many young people supporting their young candidate, who was iconic, charismatic, articulate, and idealistic—perhaps too idealistic, so that he was introduced to the rough-and-tumble of politics in the very first weeks of his term.

John Lindsay had the Roosevelt touch, the Kennedy touch, and now the Obama touch. Though a patrician, he had the ability to speak with the people—uncondescendingly, compassionately, and they accepted him as one of their own.

BARBARALEE DIAMONSTEIN-SPIELVOGEL was appointed the city's first Director of Cultural Affairs in 1966.

The Lindsay Team quickly set out to transform the city's parks and open spaces from the staid, controlled rules of the Moses era, to exciting, welcoming places. On a snowy January day in 1967, we opened the first outdoor sculpture exhibition in Bryant Park featuring the enormous black forms created by Hunter College Professor Tony Smith, who was then largely unknown. This exhibition helped give him the visibility that has made him one of our most sought-after creators of large commissioned outdoor pieces.

That summer, the Metropolitan Opera performed for the very first time in Central Park, thrilling an enormous audience under the stars on the Great Lawn with a dazzling *La Bohème.*And our Festival of Films about New York was a great hit, attracting leading critics, actors, and film aficionados, while showcasing the magical iconic celluloid images that have made New York City the most instantly recognized urban brand in the world.

Soon these cultural happenings were everywhere across the five boroughs—poetry readings and ethnic festivals, art shows and food tastings, some planned meticulously, some spontaneous. As New Yorkers flocked to these events, people took back their parks from being an exclusive preserve, asserting a new attachment and ownership that had never existed before.

Lindsay greets Harold Prince (right) at Gallagher's in the theater district.

disrepair—not only from their heavy use and abuse, but also because maintenance and operations budgets were being dramatically slashed as the city began its plunge into fiscal disarray.

But parks were the least of it. As Moses had sarcastically (but more or less correctly) observed, the Lindsay administration's unusual gift for bringing a spirit of joy and "fun" to New York was not matched by an equivalent ability to bring order and safety to a city increasingly besieged by economic and social problems. The soaring incidence of crime and disorder, in particular, made a brutal mockery of the administration's hopeful attempts to inspire a sense of pleasure or delight in the city's landscape. How could one find delight in an urban space that had been vandalized or defaced, or, worse still, in which one feared being mugged or even killed?

Once the city's economic and social fortunes began their sudden, vertiginous descent—coming to a climax in the 1975 fiscal crisis, after Lindsay's mayoralty had given way to that of his successor, Abraham D. Beame—it was probably inevitable that the Lindsay-era approach to the city would be mostly discredited. To be sure, some innovations not only survived, but expanded: Central Park's drives were closed to traffic, for example, not only on Sunday mornings but also weekday evenings and all weekend long—an amenity now taken for granted and regarded almost as an inalienable right. Pedestrian malls, similar to the proposal for Madison Avenue, were eventually completed on Nassau Street in lower Manhattan and on Fulton Street in Brooklyn. And the Mayor's Film Office prospered, encouraging ever more features to be shot on location in the city—though as the years went on, the image of the city that those films presented grew ever grimmer, from darkly expressionistic tones of *Rosemary's Baby* (1968), *Midnight Cowboy* (1969), and *The French Connection* (1971), to the outright city-hating posturing of *Death Wish* (1974), to the nightmarish vision of *Taxi Driver* (1976).

In the 1971 film "The French Connection," a television reporter asks: "Do you agree with a recent survey finding that shows Mayor Lindsay was the sexiest man in the world?"

But for the most part, there was little or no return (at the official level) to the Lindsay administration's initiatives even after the city's fortunes began to improve in the 1980s, under the mayoralty of Edward I. Koch. With the crime rate still high, and New York in many ways still a grim and unfriendly place, it was hard to ignite the kind of optimistic spirit that might see the city's landscape as a source of delight, or a kind of scenic environment.

In a subtle but significant way, however, something new *had* been introduced, a different way of thinking about the city—and as the decades passed, the new attitude began to take hold among much of the population.

Not all, by any means. Many parts of New York, especially outside Manhattan, were being dramatically remade in the same decades by waves of immigrants from around the world—newcomers who, if anything, appeared to share the same attitude toward the city as Sol Nazerman's generation: that the city was primarily a place for hard work, and, with luck, a modest measure of economic advancement. But even as that change was underway, other parts of the city (beginning with "historic districts" in Manhattan and Brooklyn but soon spilling over to other areas) were being transformed by affluent New Yorkers, often with young families, who in previous decades might have fled the city but who now chose to stay—not only because of its traditional draw

Mayor Lindsay gave Duffy Square a symbolic housecleaning as he helped launch "Operation Big Sweep" in 1968, a drive to clean up Times Square. In 1973, Lindsay established the TKTS discount theater ticket booth in Duffy Square, which is still in operation.

as a commercial center but specifically because they *enjoyed it as a place*, valuing its quirkiness and character in place of the perceived homogeneity and dullness of the suburbs. Though the trend could be (and roundly was) criticized as "gentrification," it continued to gain strength throughout the 1980s and '90s, even as a distinct but related change to the fabric of the city was underway. By the mid-1980s, urban observers like Phillip Lopate were taking note of the ranks of young people filling the sidewalk cafés that had sprung up along Columbus Avenue and elsewhere, bringing an almost European, "see-and-be-seen" atmosphere that, Lopate recognized, was essentially theatrical in spirit, turning the sidewalk itself into a kind of extended stage.

In the decade and a half since the mid-1990s, with the crime rate finally under control and the city once again perceived as an essentially benign environment, much of New York has been remade by this flood of newcomers: ambitious young men and women from around the country and the world, attracted—as young people have always been—by the unique economic opportunities the city offered, but perhaps even more by the new sensibility, which looks at the city as the most desirable place possible not only to work, but also to live and, yes, play. (The impact of these newcomers has been amplified by a major demographic shift, in which college-educated Americans choose today to spend 10 or 15 years finding their life partners—rather than the 15 months they once might have spent—and so remain for a decade or more in the city's romantic "market.") To complete the circle almost perfectly, it is a trend that has been dramatically propelled by the portrayal of New York onscreen, thanks the explosion in local film and television production encouraged by the Mayor's Film Office: the countless romantic comedy features, and cable television series like "Sex and the City," whose extensive and effective use of New York locations has extended as never before the Lindsay-era impulse to regard the city's urban landscape as, in some real sense, a giant outdoor stage. Like gentrification, it is a phenomenon easy enough to criticize or mock, but, like it or not, it has given rise to an essential new reality of modern urban life: that cities like New York owe their continued prosperity (and, to some degree, their survival) not only to their traditional role as a functional location for commerce, but instead—as Lindsay and his colleagues had first dared to officially suggest, four decades ago—as a place to be enjoyed, a landscape to be explored, a vast "adventure playground."

The snowstorm that almost buried the mayor: Lindsay in Queens, February 1969.

The political legacy of John V. Lindsay has been thought to be one of failure. Indeed, as his second administration came to an end in 1974, New York City was sinking into a morass of job loss, housing abandonment, neighborhood destruction, white flight, fiscal crisis, and interracial antagonism. Citing Lindsay's purported lack of empathy for the white middle class, Michael Barone, a gifted observer of American politics, concluded that "Lindsay was the most destructive American local public official of the last half-century."

JOHN MOLLENKOPF is distinguished professor of political science and sociology at the Graduate Center of the City University and Director of its Center for Urban Research. He co-authored *Inheriting the City: The Children of Immigrants Come of Age* (Harvard University Press, 2008). His other books include *A Phoenix in the Ashes* (Princeton University Press, 1993), a study of New York City politics, and *Contentious City* (Russell Sage Foundation, 2004), which examines the city's response to 9/11. Before joining the Graduate Center, he worked for the New York City Department of City Planning.

John Mollenkopf

The Politics of Change

New York City certainly took decades to recover from the fiscal crisis of the mid 1970s, to which it is fair to say that the Lindsay administration contributed, especially in fiscal terms. Unfortunately, as a result, his administration's considerable efforts at municipal reform also ended up suffering collateral damage. Every subsequent mayor, with the possible exception of David N. Dinkins, publicly rejected Lindsay's strategy of trying to address the city's social problems, particularly racial inequality, by expanding public employment—even when they were practicing this tactic themselves. And despite the fact that an alliance of white liberals, blacks, and Hispanics would seem to be the natural governing coalition in this very liberal city, these groups have only united to elect a mayor—Dinkins—once since 1969.

Yet many potentially valuable Lindsay-era practices did become part of everyday governance in New York City. The Lindsay administration's idea that decentralization could make city policies more responsive to neighborhood interests was institutionalized in Community School Boards, created in 1969, and Community Districts, expanded in the late 1960s and formalized by the 1975 City Charter. The Lindsay administration's use of policy analysis and output measurement as tools to help city agencies reallocate their resources in ways that improved their results also lives on. Even the Giuliani administration's widely-praised Compstat innovation in the Police Department should be read as a daughter or granddaughter of the fourth platoon deployed by Police Commissioner Howard Leary in 1968. The Lindsay administration's practice of making contracts with community-based organizations to deliver public services (dubbed third-party government by Lester Salamon of Johns Hopkins University) has flourished. New York City remains a laboratory for urban policy experiments.

Beyond the question of how posterity judges the Lindsay administration's specific actions lies a deeper issue, however. That is whether the long-term effort to diminish the influence of party politics on the conduct of government and open up the system to new voices that was launched by Lindsay has had the unintended consequence of eroding New York City's capacity for balancing its conflicting priorities in a democratic way. In this reading, the use of third-party government and municipal labor union support as an alternate political base to the Democratic Party, begun in the Lindsay era but continued by subsequent administrations, undermined a mechanism that, for all its many faults, held spending demands in check and restrained racial and ethnic conflicts with balanced tickets and carefully choreographed ethnic successions. This new method of organizing electoral majorities came with new spending demands, which, in effect, became new forms of political patronage. In contrast to the old patronage, this view holds, those who received the new patronage were not required or even encouraged to engage in independent grass-roots politics. Instead, they became dependent clients. The net result was that the city's governing class could not say no, even in times of recession. In Martin Shefter's classic analysis, extrademocratic means were required to rebalance New York City's political system in the resulting fiscal crisis.

The political scientist Theodore Lowi concluded that the growing power of the unionized bureaucracies during the Wagner and Lindsay years made

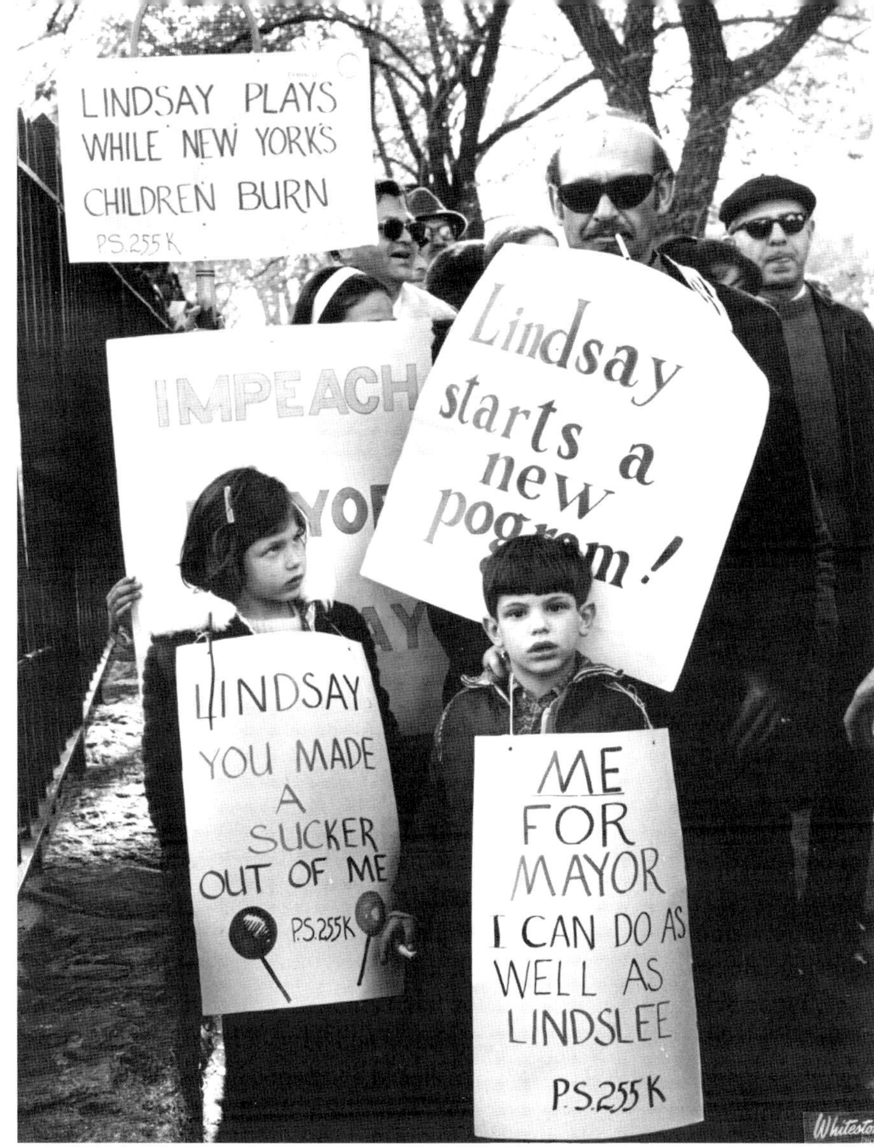

Lindsay promised change. Many New Yorkers, including these students and parents from P.S. 255, concluded that it had not been for the better.

New York "well-run but ungoverned." Their growing electoral power, he thought, eliminated "the popular base of political action." A leading scholar of black politics, Charles V. Hamilton, a political scientist at Columbia University, took this a step further. Certainly, it was necessary to weaken the Democratic Party's hold on public office and the higher civil service in order to bring new groups into the delivery of public services. But the way it was done—through co-optation rather than the creation of an independent power base—led to many compromises with the ideals that motivated this change. By accepting empowerment in the form of jobs managing antipoverty programs, Hamilton argued, black activists became practitioners of "soft money" grantsmanship and converted their constituents from active voters into passive beneficiaries. This transition deflected black activism from the struggle over the "real stakes" of politics and consigned blacks to "demand making, benefit seeking, and invariably subordinate positions." If this outcome, however unintended, is an accurate reading of the long history of the Lindsay era, it is a matter of far greater concern than whether the Lindsay administration had a tin ear for the city's white middle class or ran up too big a budget deficit.

The Successes

Perhaps the most enduring positive legacy of the Lindsay administration is that it helped the long-suffering and often-excluded black and Puerto Rican communities break through some of the old patterns of disadvantage maintained by the white Democratic political establishment. Lindsay's good relationships with black leaders and his willingness to wade into Harlem in the wake of Martin Luther King Jr.'s assassination helped to spare the city from convulsive riots. We should not minimize the symbolic importance of the city's highest elected official endorsing minority-community aspirations and embracing these communities in ways that no predecessor had.

By giving them a start in the antipoverty programs, Lindsay's administration also clearly advanced a new generation of black and Puerto Rican political leaders, who continued to serve New York City with distinction. More generally, the Lindsay administration inspired a generation of young people from many different backgrounds to enter into public service careers. While ambitious young people use every mayoralty as a springboard, the Lindsay alumni association is in a class by itself.

Lindsay also took critical steps to expand the city's revenue base. In his first term, he succeeded in convincing the state legislature and Governor Nelson A. Rockefeller to authorize both a municipal income tax and a commuter tax. In conjunction with growing federal aid, these sources enabled him to triple the size of the city's budget. As long as the city's economy was expanding, which it did quite strongly through 1969, he had the resources to enlarge the size and reach of local government. His new agencies and political institutions included superagencies, neighborhood city halls, and community development corporations (notably the Bedford-Stuyvesant Restoration Corporation). He inspired a new debate among policy elites about the need for structural reform and administrative decentralization, two measures that contributed significantly to what is now called "the new public administration." He created an Urban Design Group to prod the city to be more thoughtful about its public spaces, and he brought in the Rand Corporation to help agencies make operational improvements.

Much of this administrative legacy was institutionalized into the structure of local government through the 1975 Charter Reform, one of the most thorough since the 1930s. It formalized the 59 Community Boards (originally

June 24, 1968: Spectators peer in the window of a new "Little City Hall" on upper Broadway in Manhattan.

contemplated in the 1961 Charter) and required that their borders and those of municipal agencies' districts—like police precincts and sanitation districts—be the same. It set up the Uniform Land Use Review Procedure, which gave community board land-use subcommittees two months to consider proposals before a decision by the City Planning Commission and final review by the City Council. While community boards may not have much impact on major administration initiatives, they often shave the rough edges off smaller proposals.

Finally, the Lindsay administration invented new ways to use neighborhood government to connect neighborhood leaders with City Hall in ways that were not dependent on party politics or elected officials. Other American cities replicated the strategy of using neighborhood-based programs to bring poorly represented minority groups into city government, and indeed, this has become an important part of how New York City delivers social services. In the process, growing numbers of blacks and Puerto Ricans found jobs as managers, professionals, and administrative personnel in the public and nonprofit social services, helping to expand the city's middle class.

September 13, 1968: A member of Youth in Action (left) confronts teachers in front of a school in Brownsville, Brooklyn, during the first of three teacher's strikes that fall.

The Case for Failure

The Lindsay administration faced a broad array of challenges, including strikes by transit and sanitation workers, teachers, and other municipal workers. City workers formed a significant part of the white middle class in New York, and Lindsay's initial unwillingness or inability to conclude prudent contracts with them was taken as a sign of his lack of empathy for them. The slow reaction to the famous "Lindsay snowstorm" in February 1969 was another, leaving white Queens homeowners with snow-clogged streets long after those in Manhattan had been cleared.

While Lindsay was determined to head off black unrest, many of the steps he took to that end created backlashes that led to significant political defeats. His police commissioner established a Civilian Complaint Review Board, only to lose a patrolmen's union-sponsored referendum vote against it in November 1966. He vigorously supported the construction of a high-rise low-income housing project in Forest Hills and the establishment of community control over three school districts, including one in the adjacent communities of Ocean Hill and Brownsville in Brooklyn.

Running for re-election in 1969 on the Liberal Party line against two conservative Italian-American candidates, Mario Procaccino, a Democrat, and John

Marchi, a Republican, Lindsay won with plurality support from liberal white professional areas of Manhattan, the city's black and Puerto Rican neighborhoods, and some Jewish communities in the boroughs outside Manhattan. In the short term, his 1965 and 1969 electoral victories provided a model for liberal biracial coalitions that would challenge white ethnic mayors across American cities. In the long term, however, they bore witness to a growing and persistent racial polarization in New York City mayoral elections. The 1969 victory further positioned Lindsay as the candidate of poor minority groups and well-to-do white liberals against the white middle class Catholics and Jews living outside Manhattan. Perhaps no political leader could have reconciled or bridged the gaps between the worried and threatened white middle class and the growing and no-longer-patient black and Hispanic populations during the turbulent period of the late 1960s and early 1970s, but Lindsay certainly did not.

If growing public revenues enabled him to expand government in his first term, the back-to-back recessions of the early 1970s placed severe fiscal strain on his second term. Having enlisted minority activists with expanding antipoverty programs and placated municipal workers with substantial wage increases, Lindsay was not in a position, nor was he inclined, to impose the necessary fiscal restraint as economic conditions worsened.

The sharp economic downturn, the fast-paced demographic changes taking place in the city, and the decline of federal support led directly to the fiscal crisis of 1975–76. Just as the Nixon administration represented a national reaction against the urban unrest and antiwar protests of the 1960s, the election of Edward I. Koch in 1977, as the one-term mayoralty of Abraham D. Beame sunk under the weight of the fiscal crisis, represented the local defeat of the Lindsay era's policies and political alignments. Although Koch had a background in Greenwich Village reform Democratic politics and succeeded Lindsay in the House of Representatives, he was a strong advocate for the Forest Hills

Outside a school in Ocean Hill-Brownsville in 1968, where the dispute over decentralization and community control disrupted classes for weeks and polarized the city.

From "The Revolt of the White Lower Middle Class"

PETE HAMILL

New York magazine, April 14, 1969

They call my people the White Lower Middle Class these days. It is an ugly, ice-cold phrase, the result, I suppose, of the missionary zeal of those sociologists who still think you can place human beings on charts. It most certainly does not sound like a description of people on the edge of open, sustained, and possibly violent revolt. And yet, that is the case. All over New York City tonight, in places like Inwood, South Brooklyn, Corona, East Flatbush, and Bay Ridge, men are standing around saloons talking darkly about their grievances, and even more darkly about possible remedies. Their grievances are real and deep; their remedies could blow this city apart.

The White Lower Middle Class? Say that magic phrase at a cocktail party on the Upper East Side of Manhattan and monstrous images arise from the American demonology.... Sometimes these brutes are referred to as "the ethnics" or "the blue-collar types." But the bureaucratic, sociological phrase is White Lower Middle Class.

Nobody calls it the Working Class anymore. But basically, the people I'm speaking about are the working class. And they can no longer make it in New York.

It is very difficult to explain to these people that more than 600,000 of those on welfare are women and children; that one reason the black family is in trouble is because outfits like the Iron Workers Union have practically excluded blacks through most of their history; that a hell of a lot more of their tax dollars go to Vietnam or the planning for future wars than to Harlem or Bed-Stuy; that the effort of the past four or five years was an effort forced by bloody events, and that they are paying taxes to relieve some forms of poverty because of more than 100 years of neglect on top of 300 years of slavery. The working-class white man has no more patience for explanations.

In any conversation with working-class whites, you are struck by how the information explosion has hit them. Television has made an enormous impact on them, and because of the nature of that medium—its preference for the politics of theater, its seeming inability to ever explain what is happening behind the photographed image—much of their understanding of what happens is superficial. Most of them have only a passing acquaintance with blacks, and very few have any black friends.

The working-class white man sees injustice and politicking everywhere in this town now, with himself in the role of victim. He does not like John Lindsay, because he feels Lindsay is only concerned about the needs of blacks; he sees Lindsay walking the streets of the ghettos or opening a privately-financed housing project in East Harlem or delivering lectures about tolerance and brotherhood, and he wonders what it all means to him.

"The average working stiff is not asking for very much," says Congressman Hugh Carey, the Brooklyn Democrat whose district includes large numbers of working-class whites. "He wants a decent apartment, he wants a few beers on the weekend, he wants his kids to have decent clothes, he wants to go to a ballgame once in a while, and he would like to put a little money away so that his kids can have the education that he never could afford. That's not asking a hell of a lot. But he's not getting that. He thinks society has failed him and, in a way, if he is white, he is often more alienated than the black man. At least the black man has his own organizations, and can submerge himself in the struggle for justice and equality, or elevate himself, whatever the case might be. The black man has hope, because no matter what some of the militants say, his life is slowly getting better in a number of ways. The white man who makes $7,000 a year, who is 40, knows that he is never going to earn much more than that for the rest of his life, and he sees things getting worse, more hopeless. John Lindsay has made a number of bad moves as mayor of this town, but the alienation of the white lower middle class might have been the worst."

The so-called "hard hat riot" erupted in Lower Manhattan on May 8, 1970 as construction workers clashed with antiwar demonstrators who were honoring the slain student protestors at Kent State University.

homeowners and campaigned against the municipal unions and the poverty programs in a crowded Democratic primary. His victory, and his administration, were in many ways construed as a repudiation of the Lindsay years.

Eroding Democratic Decision-making

Returning to the deeper question posed by Lowi and Hamilton, did the Lindsay era set in motion practices and dynamics that ultimately weakened the city's capacity for making hard decisions and subordinated black and minority political leadership to the new patronage of chasing government grants and municipal wage increases?

The Lindsay years certainly incubated new ways of providing neighborhood social services that initially circumvented, and were designed to circumvent, the local party system. After the federal War on Poverty was created in 1964, Mayor Wagner established a local antipoverty agency run largely by city officials and private welfare-agency leaders that channeled money through existing local organizations and old-line private welfare agencies. Lindsay changed much of that picture. He established a new superagency, the Human Resources Administration, within which a Community Development Agency would administer federal funds, and a Council Against Poverty would distribute funds to 25 poor neighborhoods through newly created community corporations in each of them. This new council had more representatives from poor neighborhoods than it had old-line social welfare agency executives and public officials.

The council, chaired by H. Carl McCall, and the agency, directed by Major Owens, gained a degree of autonomy. While these two leaders shed militant staff and were not always open to demands from neighborhood activists, they committed substantial federal and city resources to the new community corporations and carried out many new activities, including aiding the Ocean Hill-Brownsville community school district. Stephen David, a political scientist, concluded that "by staffing these community-action groups with people from the community and by permitting them to engage in political activities, the mayor increased the possibilities that these organizations would become centers of support for him against the candidate of the regular Democratic organization."

Starting in 1970, the Community Development Agency awarded contracts that granted community corporations fairly unfettered control. These organizations spent $70 million in the first year and $35 million annually thereafter to involve new participants in the political process and train a new stratum of leadership. But their newfound independence did not last long, as local elected officials sought to assert control. When Owens left Brownsville to become the agency's director, Samuel Wright, a Democratic regular, packed his members onto the community corporation board and used outright intimidation to take it over. Low turnout in the 1972 community corporation board elections enabled local political forces to gain the upper hand.

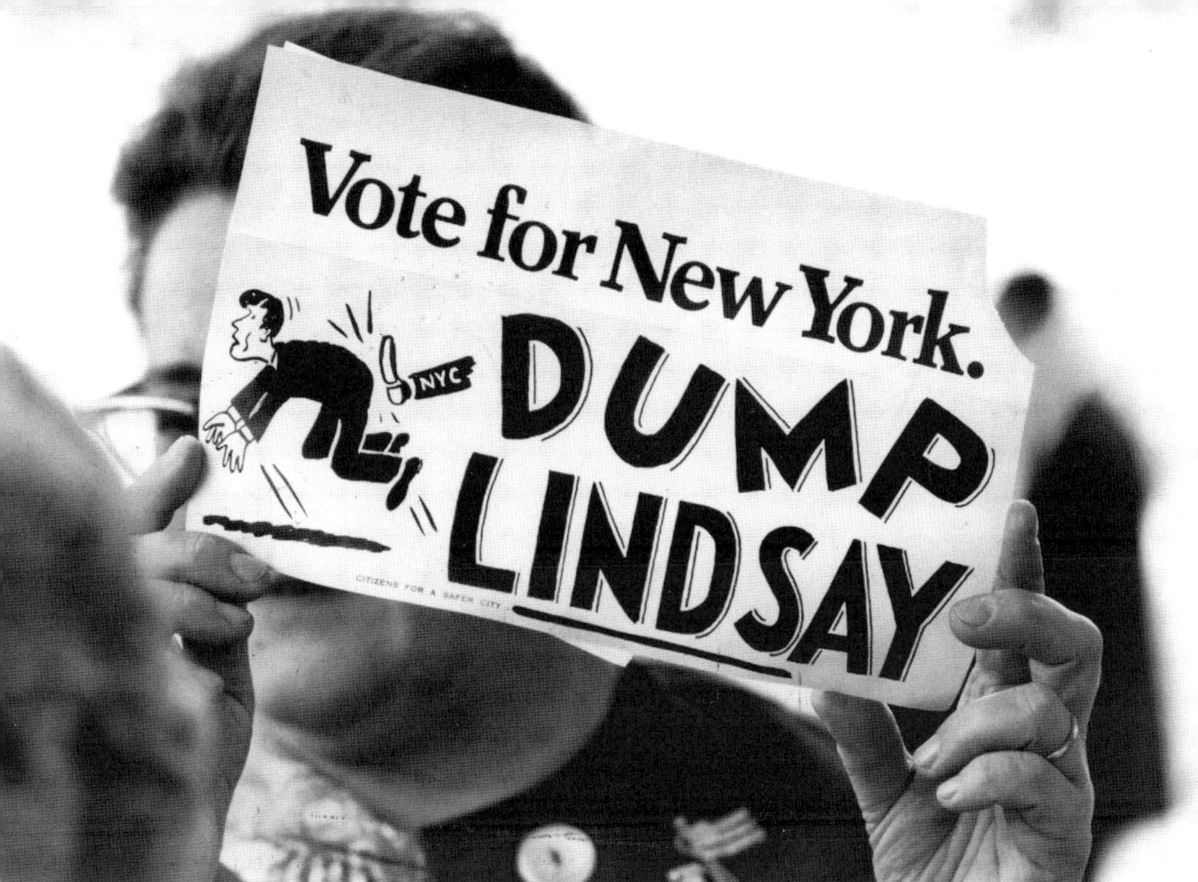

In the summer of 1969, anti-Lindsay sentiment was strong, even from members of his own party. Defeated in the Republican primary, Lindsay ran for reelection as an Independent/ Liberal Party candidate.

The flow of funds changed little through the early 1970s, without evaluation, fiscal monitoring, or even adequate bookkeeping. The boards of funded groups often overlapped with those of the community corporations. The rise of what Ed Koch later called "poverty pimps" or "poverticians" was well under way when the Beame administration took over in 1974. Major Owens would say later that since Beame could not destroy the agency, "he looked the other way while the favored political protégées ran community corporations as if they were their own private plantations."

Today, public funds do not flow only to community organizations that support the mayor or other local elected officials. Yet the relationship between community-based service providers and local elected officials is often symbiotic, and the practice of providing public services through contracts with community-based organizations accounts for a substantial share of the city budget.

The public workforce and public wages also rebounded in the wake of the retrenchment of the mid-1970s. The unionized municipal and social service labor force is also a critical channel of political influence in the city, with political support flowing in one direction and wage and benefit improvements flowing in the other. Overall, more than a quarter of employed black men and almost half of black women in New York City hold jobs in the public sector or in nonprofit health services, social services, and education.

These developments helped to fragment, rather than displace, New York's weakly organized one-party political system. As the political scientist V. O. Key noted, one-party systems "have a weakness of profound significance" as

New York City Expense Budgets and Debts Issued: Fiscal Years 1965–75

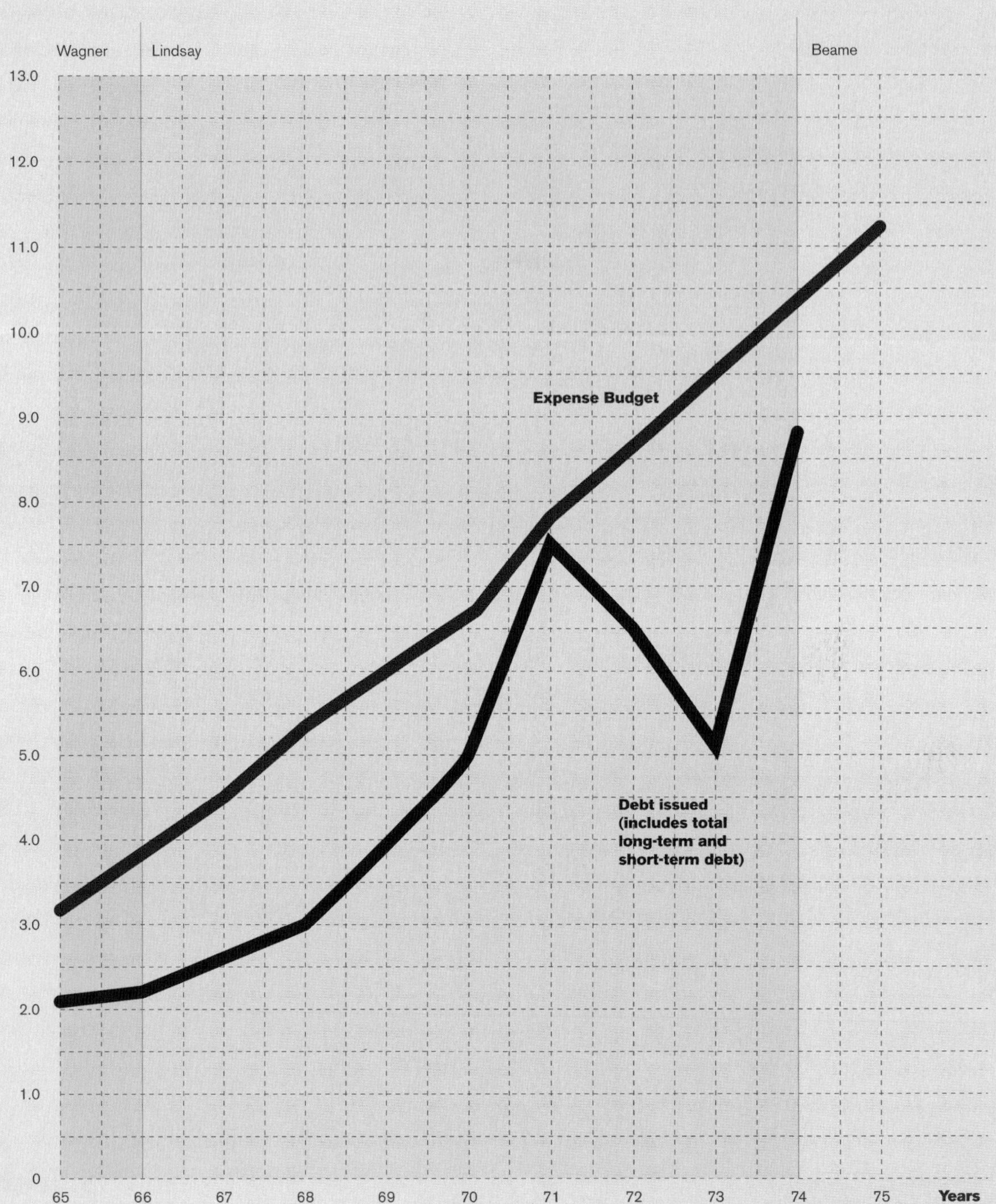

SOURCE
Steven R. Weisman, "How New York City Became a Fiscal Junkie," *The New York Times Magazine*, August 17, 1975, p.191.

Locally Financed Operating Expenditures as a Percentage of the Total Personal Income of New York City Residents 1953–75

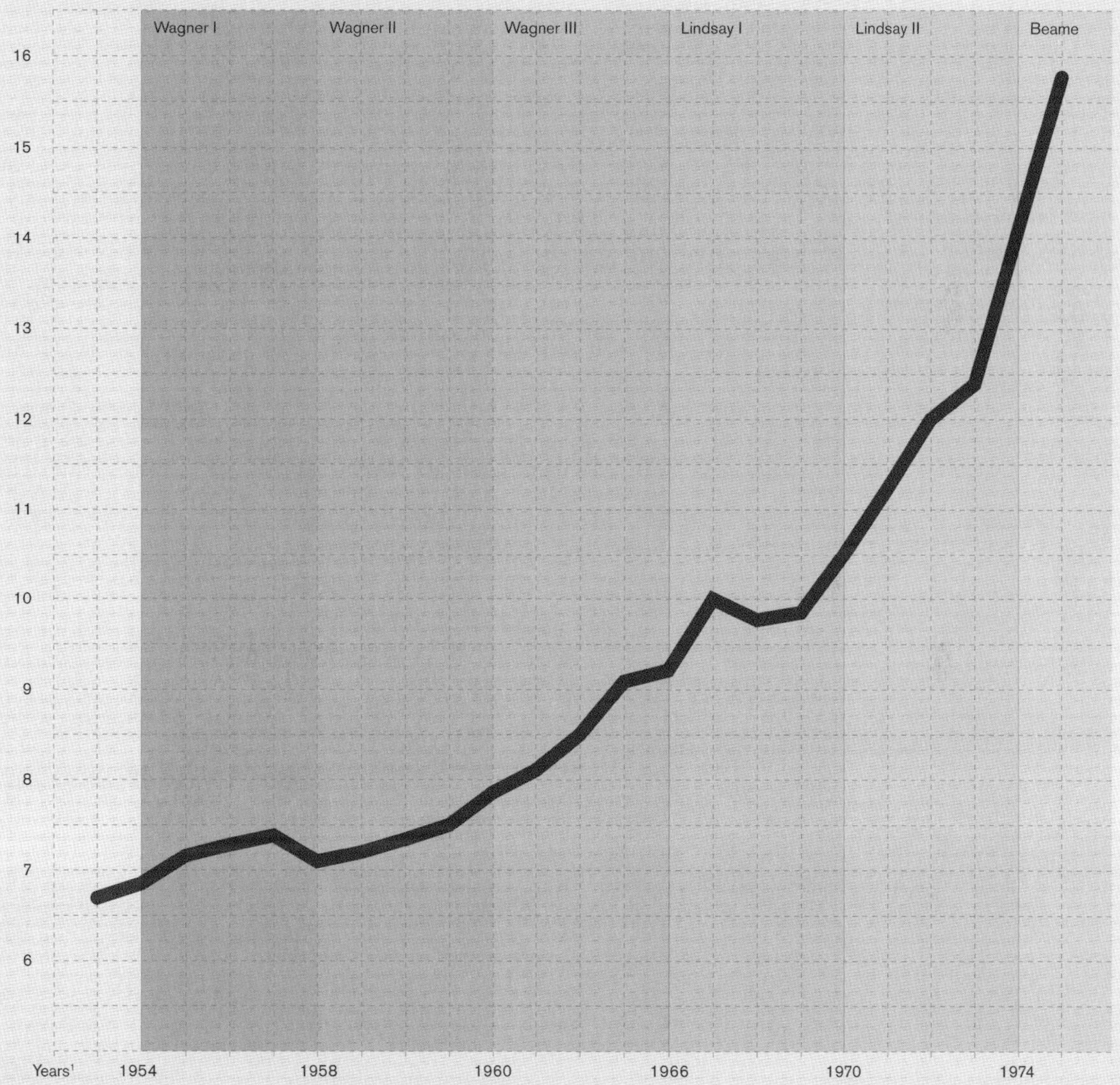

1 Employment data as of December 31 of each fiscal year

SOURCE
Martin Sheffer, *Political Crisis Fiscal Crisis: The Collapse and Revival of New York City.* New York: Columbia University Press, 1992. Reprinted with permission of the publisher.

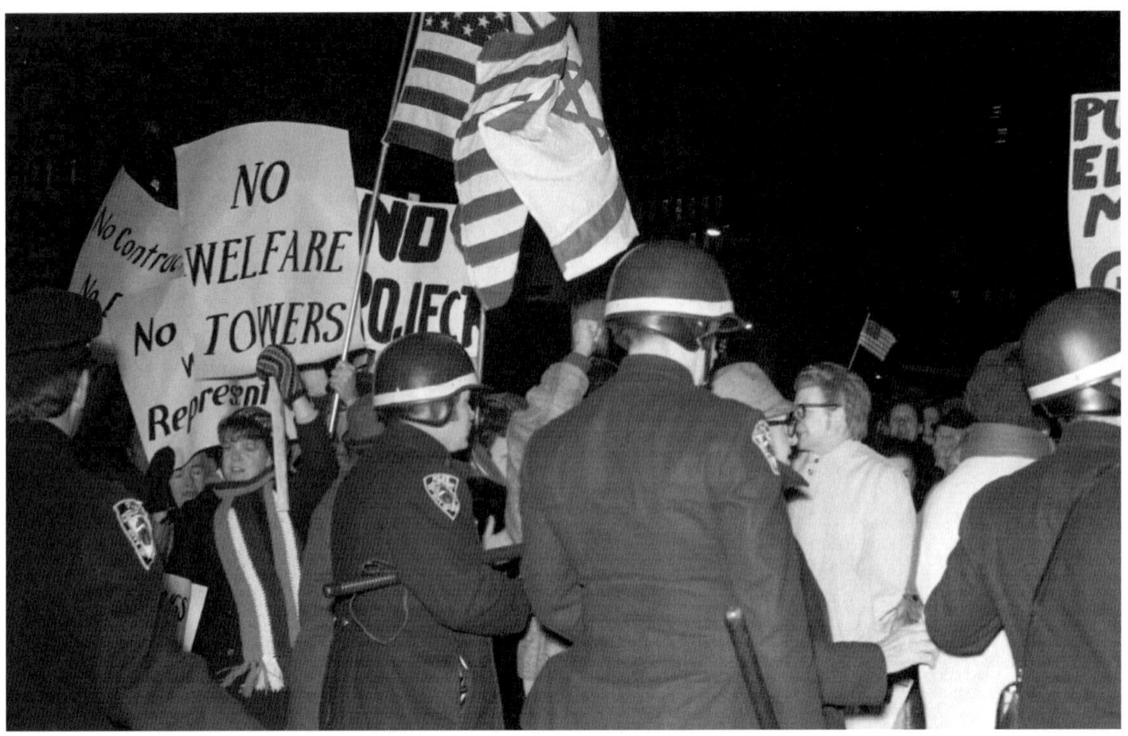

January 1972: **The dispute over a low-income housing project in Forest Hills, Queens, further exacerbated tensions between blacks and Jews. Lindsay called on a Queens lawyer, Mario M. Cuomo, to negotiate a compromise. Cuomo was later elected governor.**

"instruments of popular leadership." Given the heavily Democratic leaning of the local electorate and of public officials, out-groups that want to mobilize for change must do so within the Democratic Party. Meanwhile, in-groups from various ethnic backgrounds and neighborhoods cluster around programs whose budgets they want to expand. This magnifies the racial, cultural, and geographic divisions within the Democratic electorate, resulting, at least at times, in "a veritable melée of splinter factions," as Key predicted. Reform has decayed into a new kind of largely Democratic political factionalism.

These factional allegiances multiply the underlying class, cultural, and ideological differences among white liberal reformers, African Americans, West Indians, Puerto Ricans, Dominicans, and Asian Americans, making it increasingly difficult for them to reconstitute the Lindsay coalition behind a Democratic mayoral nominee. On the other side of the political ledger, the older, better-educated, more-likely-to-be-property-owning white middle class, declining though it may be, has unified behind relatively conservative—indeed sometimes Republican—candidates, including Mayors Edward I. Koch, Rudolph W. Giuliani, and Michael R. Bloomberg. Perhaps the Lindsay era's most profound legacy, unwitting though it may have been, was to pave the way for them.

MARIO CUOMO was the 52nd governor of New York State.

Among the many talented people John Lindsay attracted to government was Mario Cuomo, then a Queens lawyer, whom he recruited as a mediator to resolve two contentious disputes in middle-class Queens over City Hall's commitment to scatter low-income housing projects in sites outside overwhelmingly black and Hispanic neighborhoods. The rejection of a housing project in Corona (replaced by a high school that would require demolition of 69 homes) led to a second proposed site for it, on 108th Street, in Forest Hills and both, Cuomo wrote later, "were born of the same aborted process."

He engineered a compromise in Corona that saved most of the homes. That shifted the pressure to Forest Hills, where predominantly Jewish residents, Cuomo wrote, saw the threat to their community from three 24-story buildings with 842 tenants "as a threat to Jewish survival in the city." Eventually, the project was pared by about half, and the apartments were made available primarily to the elderly.

Forest Hills, Cuomo wrote, "points up the huge gap between abstract sociological propositions and their efficacy—or lack of it—when nailed down to the Procrustean bed of urban reality." Nearly four decades later, Cuomo, who was governor of New York from 1983 to 1994, looked back and delivered this assessment:

Mayor Lindsay was not naïve about seeking to advance integration in the placement of housing for the poor. The underlying purpose was to produce housing for the poor in a way that was integrated, instead of creating another "poor ghetto." That goal was admirable, realistic, and to some extent required by court discussions.

It's true that his own personal history had not given the mayor an intimate knowledge of the cultural implications of the complex mix of ethnicity, race, and color in the highly diverse and constantly bubbling cauldron called Queens, but in the end I think the strongest force at work was not race—black poor people and white middle-class people—or ethnicity that created the most static and occasional explosions; it was class.

At the same time that the Forest Hills Jewish middle class that dominated the 108th Street site was vigorously opposing the potential intermingling with hundreds of black poor families, the black middle-class community of Baisley Park in Queens—not far away—was objecting to a similar "intrusion" by a poor welfare population.

Lindsay's problems were caused by the faulty execution of his policies by his administration's well-intentioned liberals, and the irritating political interventions by clumsy politicians.

He overcame those problems and in the end was responsible for what I believe was the first co-operative low income housing "project" in America. I pass it [the Forest Hills House] regularly in my travels and it has survived and thrived for more that 37 years. Enough said about its success.

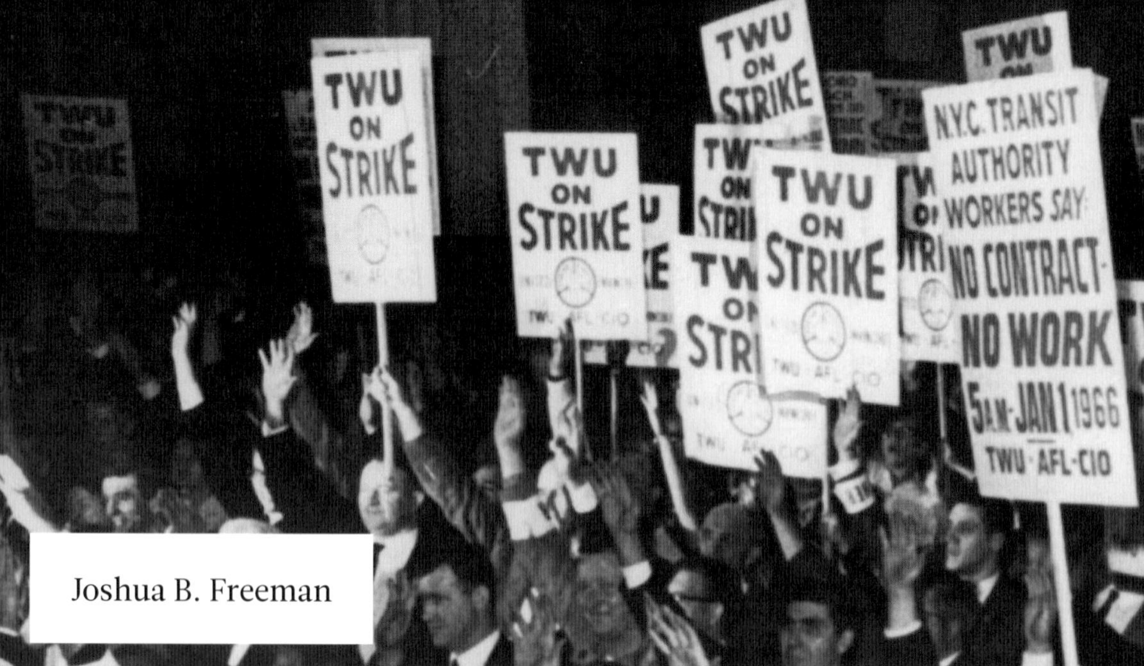

Joshua B. Freeman

Lindsay and Labor

On the evening of December 31, 1965, soon after he took the oath of office to be the 103rd mayor of the City of New York at a private ceremony at City Hall, John V. Lindsay headed back to the Americana Hotel to resume talks with the Transport Workers Union whose contract with the Transit Authority covering the city's bus and subway workers would expire at midnight. By the time Lindsay took the oath a second time at a public ceremony the next day, 35,000 transit workers had walked off their jobs, launching the most crippling strike to hit the city in a half century. For 12 days, New York remained virtually paralyzed, until Lindsay finally reached an agreement with the union ending the walkout.

JOSHUA B. FREEMAN is a history professor at Queens College and the Graduate Center of the City University of New York. His books include *Working-Class New York: Life and Labor since World War II* and *In Transit: The Transport Workers Union in New York City, 1933–1966*. He has written articles and book reviews for *The New York Times*, *The Washington Post*, *Newsday*, and *The Nation* and served as co-editor of the journal *International Labor and Working-Class History*. He is currently writing a history of the United States since World War II for the Penguin History of the United States series.

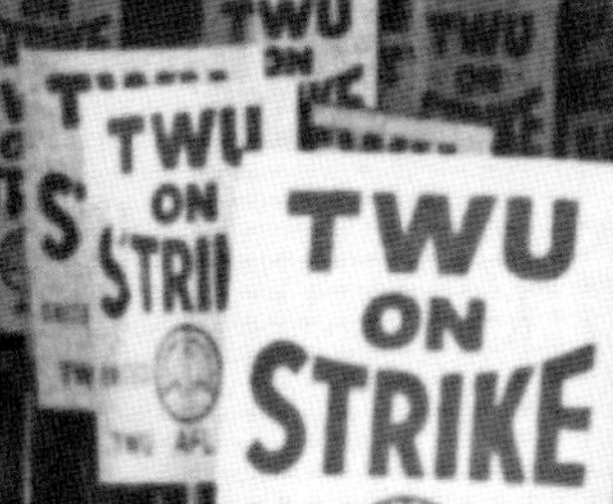

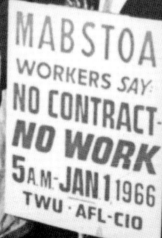

What would become "Strike City" began with the New Year's Day walkout by transit workers. To Michael J. Quill, Lindsay might as well have been the Church of England.

The transit strike proved a portent for the tumultuous labor relations that characterized Lindsay's first term. Walkouts were so frequent and disruptive that *The New York Times* dubbed Gotham "strike city." Labor turmoil contributed to a widely shared sense that New York was out of control. The political and fiscal costs of the labor strife undercut the enthusiasm for municipal reform and liberal social policies that had swept Lindsay into office. So did the mayor's failure to connect with white working-class families. Lindsay eventually established a new set of political and institutional arrangements that stabilized municipal labor relations and brought him some union support. But by then he had lost much of his political capital.

The upsurge of labor militancy in New York constituted an extreme manifestation of a national trend. During Lindsay's mayoralty, strikes nationally reached their highest level since just after of World War II. Private sector workers staged most of the walkouts. During Lindsay's first three years in office, New York experienced strikes by construction, airline, newspaper, cemetery, electrical utility, and package delivery workers, cab drivers, longshoremen, and oil truck drivers (who left thousands of residents without heat). But the greatest challenge to Lindsay came from the city's own employees, who repeatedly walked off their jobs in defiance of the law, leaving the city in seemingly permanent crisis.

No Way Out

Lindsay went to City Hall with much weaker ties to organized labor than most mayors during the previous half century. He won some working-class backing in the mayoralty race as a result of his strong support for civil rights and social welfare legislation. The Liberal Party, largely controlled by the city's garment unions, put him on the top of its ticket, which provided a vehicle for liberal Jewish voters—who would normally shun a Republican candidate—to vote for him. In what turned out to be a close election, Liberal Party votes gave Lindsay his margin of victory. But most unions felt little identification with Lindsay's patrician, good government reformism.

Unions representing New York City workers had mushroomed during Robert F. Wagner's 12 years as mayor. Wagner shrewdly granted them the right to collective bargaining, reaping their political support, while limiting their monetary gains. Lindsay had a visceral distaste for the pattern of backroom arrangements between the mayor and union leaders, expedited by labor relations operators—"power brokers," Lindsay called them—which he believed served private interests at public expense. Egged on by the editorial writers of the city's newspapers, especially *The Times*, which had strongly backed his candidacy, he came into office determined to reduce

the power of union leaders, impose a more formal system of public sector labor relations, and restrain the economic gains (and costs to the city) of the municipal unions. Very quickly he hit a wall of worker solidarity and canny union maneuvering that left him badly damaged.

The transit strike set the pattern for the battles to come. During the Wagner years, the Transport Workers Union president, Michael J. Quill, a flamboyant, Irish-born unionist who relished needling the rich and powerful, repeatedly threatened to call a transit strike, only to reach last-minute settlements with the mayor behind closed doors. His relationship with Wagner and the union's support of the Democratic Party helped the T.W.U. solidify its institutional standing, but transit workers remained poorly paid, on average being able to afford what the federal government deemed an adequate budget for a family of four only when they earned overtime and supplementary allowances in addition to their base pay. As 1965 drew to a close, Quill, with a restive membership and no longer inhibited by his ties to Wagner, sought a hefty new contract to replace the one due to expire as Lindsay took office.

Nothing becomes a union leader more than going to jail for his members, as did these T.W.U. officials. Michael J. Quill, the union president, is not pictured, however; he had had a heart attack while in jail and was hospitalized; he died two days after being discharged.

February 8, 1968: Mayor Lindsay walks along Avenue C and 7th Street on the Lower East Side during the nine-day sanitation strike. Garbage piled up, but Governor Nelson Rockefeller refused to enlist the National Guard.

John DeLury, the canny Uniformed Sanitationmen's Association boss (left), with his lawyer Paul O'Dwyer in the early days of the strike.

Secret Talks Fail

As mayor-elect, Lindsay met secretly with Quill on several occasions, while publicly avoiding hands-on deal-making. But when the transit contract expired, the two sides remained far apart. Lindsay called on transit workers "in the public interest to respect the city in which you live" and not strike. But en masse they walked off their jobs and stayed off their jobs, even after a judge jailed Quill and eight other union officials for defying a state law that banned strikes by public employees. Though the press denounced the strike and backed Lindsay, the wholesale disruption of city life created growing pressure for a settlement. Finally, Lindsay agreed to a contract that gave the T.W.U. virtually everything it had demanded before the strike, with increases that cost twice as much as the agreement the Transit Authority and the union had signed three years earlier.

The transit strike sent a message to municipal workers that militancy paid off. In September 1967, four-fifths of the city's schoolteachers walked off their jobs for two weeks in the first extended school strike in the city's history. It was a startling display by workers who in the past had thought of themselves—and had been thought of by others—as professionals, different in their behavior from blue-collar union members. The United Federation of Teachers demanded not only higher pay but also steps to meet the problems its members confronted in the classroom, including greater teacher authority to remove disruptive students and funding for a union-initiated program of smaller classes and special attention for needy children, politically touchy issues in a school system with an overwhelmingly white teaching corps and a student body that had become one-third black. In the end, the union got most of what it wanted.

The spreading spirit of militancy and a widespread dislike of Lindsay among city workers, particularly blue-collar whites who believed that he had little interest in their lives and problems, made it difficult for municipal labor leaders to restrain their members. When in February 1968 John DeLury, the long-time leader of the Uniformed Sanitationmen's Association, presented a proposed new contract to his members, they booed him off the stage, threw eggs at him, and voted to immediately walk off their jobs. Lindsay tried to make a stand against the sanitation workers in order to stop the increasingly routine resort to illegal walkouts to win better contracts. The city got an injunction against the strike, which led to DeLury's jailing, and Lindsay attempted to get other city workers to pick up the garbage that had begun to pile up, but they refused. He next asked Governor Nelson A. Rockefeller to mobilize the National Guard to clear the growing mountains of trash. Rockefeller turned him down, too. Instead, the governor—a rival of Lindsay's for the leadership of liberal Republicanism—attempted to settle the strike himself, only to have the state legislature reject his effort. The walkout finally ended after nine days, followed by binding arbitration that gave the sanitation men considerably more money than the agreement they had rejected before striking. Police officers and firefighters, determined to maintain their traditional salary differential above the sanitation workers, then launched a series of slowdowns and sickouts before agreeing to new contracts of their own.

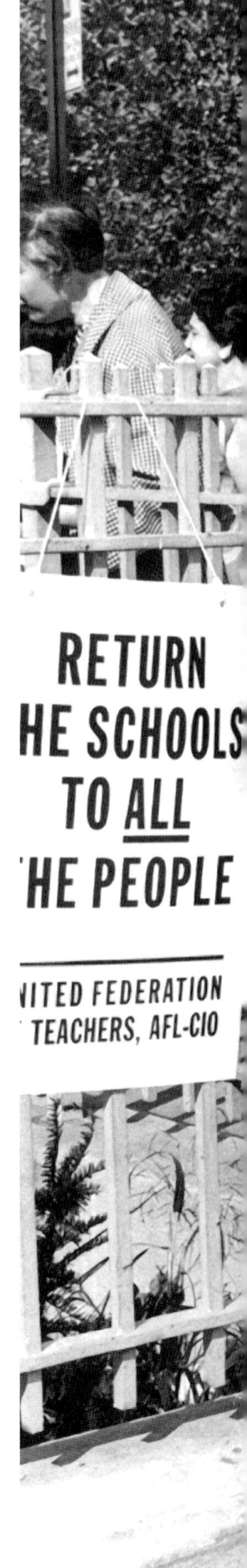

RETURN
HE SCHOOLS
TO ALL
'HE PEOPLE
IITED FEDERATION
TEACHERS, AFL-CIO

Labor Unrest and Other Unrest

The municipal worker strikes came at an unusually turbulent time for New York, as the civil rights movement, anti-Vietnam War protests, student demonstrations, an emerging counterculture, and the Lindsay administration itself undermined the established political and cultural order. Uninterrupted city services became one more thing people could no longer count on, as the previously unthinkable—the subway system shutting down, schools not opening, garbage piling up, police officers calling in sick—became almost routine. The labor strife turned many New Yorkers against the labor movement and greatly frustrated the mayor. But for city workers it proved a heady experience, as time after time they proved their ability to exert power and win concessions by refusing to work.

The display of union power reached its apogee in a conflict that revolved around issues not usually addressed by organized labor. When Lindsay took office, 12 years after the Supreme Court declared in *Brown v. Board of Education* that racial segregation in education constituted illegal discrimination, New York City public schools remained highly segregated as a result of the inherent difficulty of integrating schools in a city of segregated neighborhoods, the indifference and lethargy of the Board of Education, and the resistance of white parents to having their children go to school with blacks. Lindsay, deeply committed to equal rights and to improving the lives of nonwhite New Yorkers, embraced a new thrust in school reform, promoted by some black activists and the Ford Foundation, which effectively abandoned the goal of integration and instead promoted decentralized community

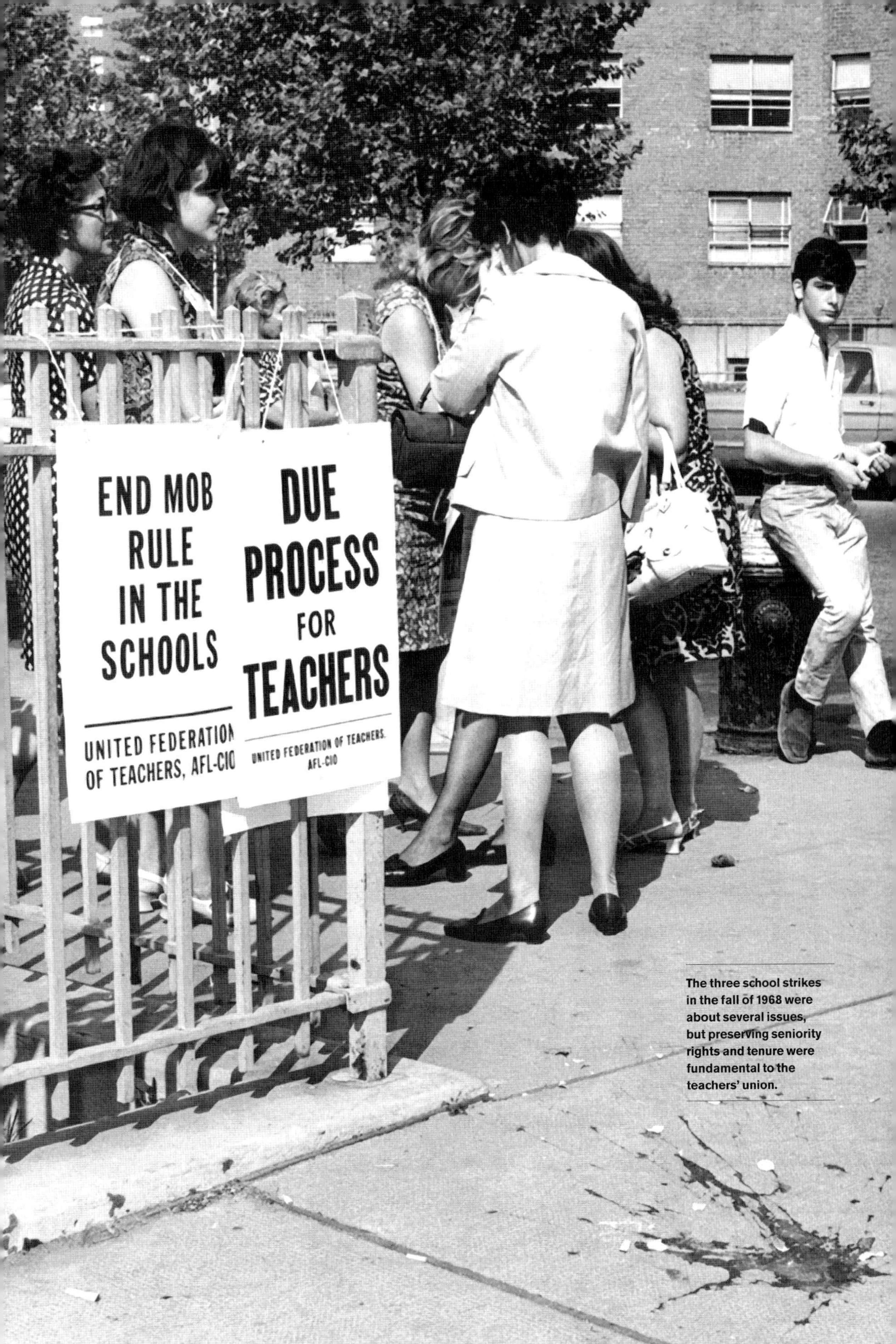
END MOB
RULE
IN THE
SCHOOLS
UNITED FEDERATION
OF TEACHERS, AFL-CIO
DUE
PROCESS
FOR
TEACHERS
UNITED FEDERATION OF TEACHERS,
AFL-CIO

The three school strikes in the fall of 1968 were about several issues, but preserving seniority rights and tenure were fundamental to the teachers' union.

May 23, 1968: Albert Shanker, president of the United Federation of Teachers, exhorting his members at a well-attended rally on Murray Street near City Hall.

control of schools. In 1967, an experiment in decentralization began with the creation of three community school boards, with ill-defined powers. In the spring of 1968, the governing board in Ocean Hill-Brownsville, transferred 19 teachers and administrators out of the district and later tried to fire them without any formal proceedings, and a majority of the teachers in the district went on strike until the school year ended.

In the fall, schools across the city were hit by three successive strikes, as the union demanded that the teachers transferred by the Ocean Hill board be reinstated. The union also insisted that teacher rights be preserved and their safety protected in the face of threats and harassment in the experimental district. The battle divided the city and left parents scrambling to make arrangements for children shut out of school, while the Board of Education, Lindsay, state education officials, the union's president, Albert Shanker, and the Ocean Hill board threatened and denounced one another and seeming agreements to settle the conflict repeatedly dissolved in acrimony. Though they were

formally about due process for teachers, deep distrust and animosity between the largely black Ocean Hill leadership and the heavily white, largely Jewish, teachers' union underlay the strikes.

As the conflict dragged on, week after week, racial tension in the city rose. Lindsay and other political leaders seemed impotent in the face of civic disaster. Finally, in mid November, with growing opposition among black and Puerto Rican activists in other unions to the U.F.T.'s tactics fracturing the once solid labor movement support for the striking teachers, and with Shanker losing some of his support in the state legislature, the U.F.T. ended the battle, having achieved most of its goals. A settlement reinstated the Ocean Hill-Brownsville teachers, put in place a state trustee to oversee the district, and provided further protections for teachers. The following spring, when the state legislature passed a school decentralization plan for the city, in a setback for Lindsay and other community control supporters it denied local school boards the right to hire or fire teachers, placed restrictions on their involuntary transfer and replaced the existing Board of Education, which had supported community control, with a new body, all to the union's satisfaction.

"When you had Lindsay silent, the two main characters then become Rhody McCoy [the Ocean-Hill Brownsville district's administrator] and Al Shanker, it becomes the teacher's union and the Ocean Hill-Brownsville people and all of a sudden Lindsay and the City Hall take a kind of background. And they fade into the background, and that makes the thing that much worse."

–Vincent Cannato, *author of* The Ungovernable City: John Lindsay and His Struggle to Save New York

After the 1968 school strikes, labor strife began to ameliorate. In September 1967, the Lindsay administration established the New York City Office of Collective Bargaining to regulate public employee labor relations and mediate disputes. Based on recommendations of a panel that Wagner had appointed before leaving Gracie Mansion, the new office, supervised by a board with labor and city representatives, set rules for collective bargaining, reduced the large number of municipal bargaining units and stepped in when negotiations reached an impasse. The same year, New York State adopted the Taylor Law, which gave public employees a clear right to collective bargaining but restated the ban on their striking, with new, more effective enforcement procedures. Together, these two steps created a more robust institutional framework for municipal labor relations, and proved successful, over time, in channeling labor disputes into semi-political, semi-bureaucratized resolution procedures. Meanwhile, Lindsay, with an eye toward the 1969 election, reached out to make peace with the municipal unions by agreeing, with little commotion, to a series of generous contracts. The transit workers got a big

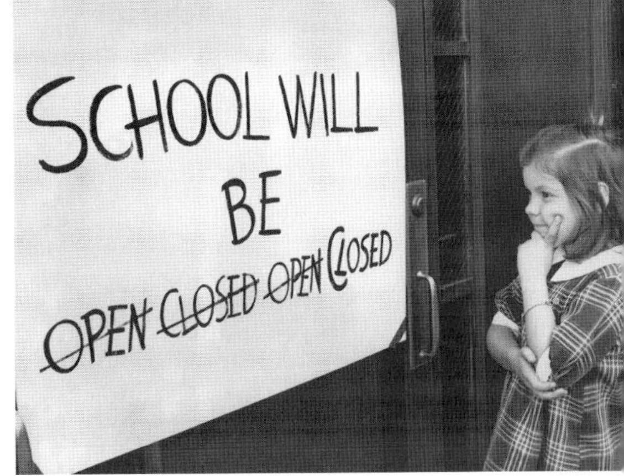

Not an open and shut case: Schools were repeatedly closed over a three month period as unionized teachers clashed with advocates for community control.

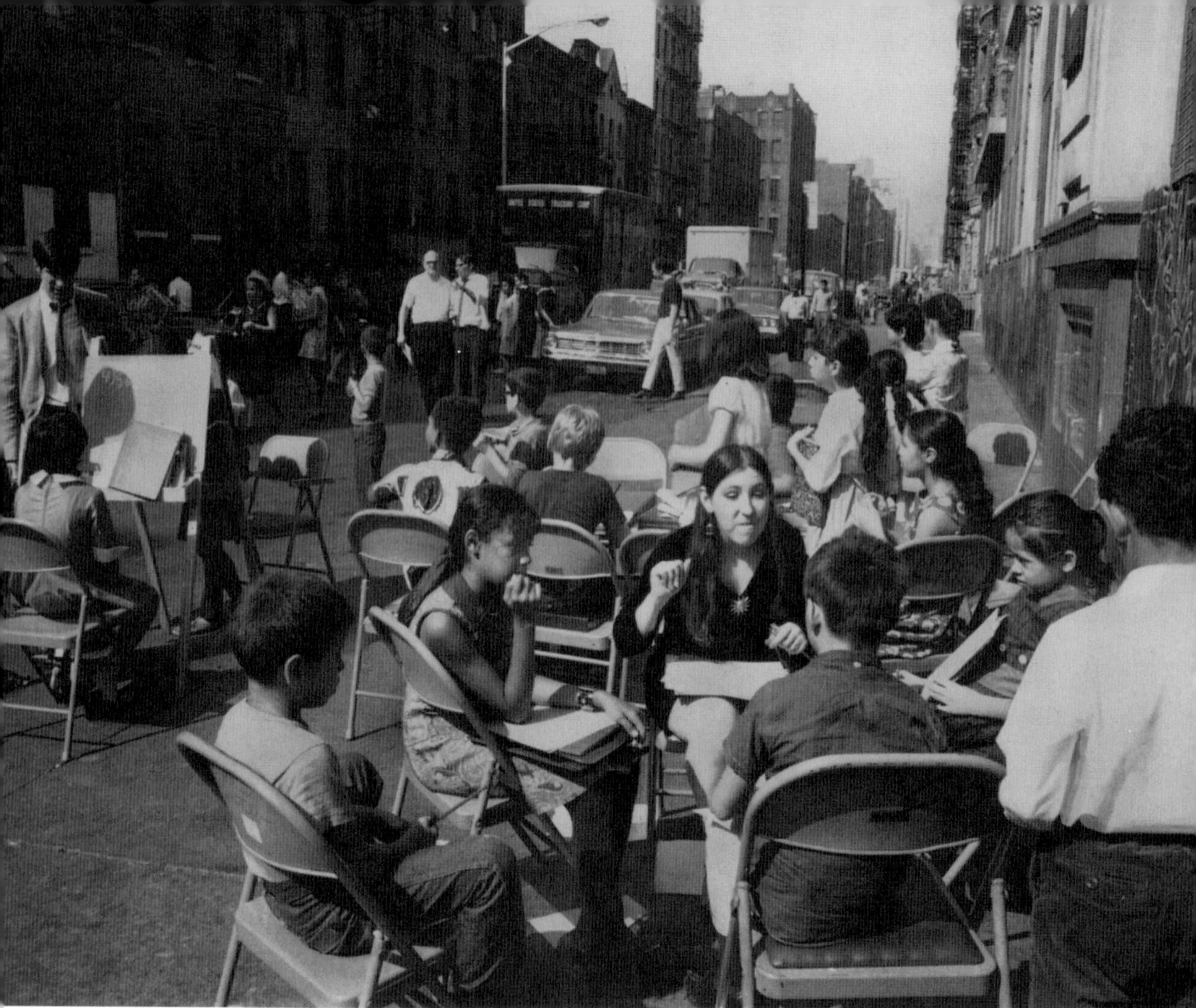

The city as school: Students take an impromptu class outdoors as parents and teachers improvise during the strikes in the fall of 1968.

pay increase, more vacation, and pensions at age 50 after 20 years work. Non-uniformed city workers won a minimum wage of $6,000 (a large raise for many of them) and the right to retire with full pension after 25 years. Teachers saw their salaries jump by 39 percent for newcomers and 22 percent for more experienced teachers.

The Unions Endorse Lindsay

Recognizing the practical advantages of good relations with an incumbent mayor—especially one now willing to open the city coffers to buy labor peace and union backing—key public sector unions, including the Sanitationmen, District Council 37 of the American Federation of State, County, and Municipal Employees (the largest city union), and the T.W.U., endorsed Lindsay for re-election in 1969. The U.F.T. remained neutral, a remarkable turnaround from its bitter denunciations of the mayor just a year earlier. Most private-sector unions stuck with the Democratic Party, but Lindsay again won the nomination of the Liberal Party, engineered by its key boss, Alex Rose, head of the small Hatters union, which proved essential to his re-election, since he lost the Republican primary to John Marchi.

In his second term, Lindsay faced some labor challenges, including a sick-out and slowdown by police officers in 1971 and a short strike by firefighters two years later, but labor issues did not dominate city politics and city life as they had during his first years in office. With the economy turning down, labor militancy in both the private and public sectors diminished. The most disruptive walkout, a two-day strike in 1971 by bridge tenders and sewage treatment workers, which left draw bridges open and raw sewage pouring into city waterways, was directed not at Lindsay but at the state government, for blocking a pension agreement that the city had agreed to, and it ended in failure. In a city that had become acclimated to one labor crisis after another, by the time Lindsay left office he had managed to institute an interlude of relative calm.

By then, though, Lindsay's political career had effectively come to an end. The public sense that he could not impose order in a city made chaotic by, among other things, endless labor disputes, proved politically costly. So did the feeling among many white working-class voters that Lindsay favored non-whites and the poor while holding white families of modest means in contempt. At times, Lindsay had tried to play off non-white New Yorkers against unions, which he saw as agents of white privilege, failing to recognize that the municipal unions were becoming one of the most important channels of upward mobility for African-American New Yorkers, who were moving into their ranks in ever-greater numbers.

When during the mid 1970s, not long after Lindsay left City Hall, New York experienced a severe fiscal crisis that put it on the edge of bankruptcy, many politicians and commentators blamed the former mayor, who had greatly increased the city budget, in part to cover increased labor costs. But Lindsay could not fairly be blamed for the structural problems, including a national

"The status quo was clearly failing. People didn't trust the bureaucracy and integration didn't work and the education was clearly failing. The numbers showed that it wasn't working. Kids were not learning, they were getting taught but not learning.... And parents said, this stinks, we've got to do better and we can't do it so they thought by getting control they could do it."

–Lewis Feldstein *was director of the Office of Neighborhood Government and a mayoral adviser on education during the decentralization crisis*

City Hall was the fulcrum of protest by municipal workers. Here, day care center employees demonstrate in August of 1969.

VICTOR GOTBAUM was executive director of District Council 37 of the American Federation of State, County and Municipal Employees union from 1965–1987

He was a breath of fresh air. He had no baggage and brought a lot of good new people into the administration. His political naiveté was refreshing, It finally defeated him, He called me about running for president. He said, "I want your support." I said, "you haven't built a base." I said, "you're out of your mind." The economy of New York is so dependent on the country and the world, if things are good here you do well and take the credit and if things are bad you take a beating for no fault of your own.

ANTHONY M. SCOTTO was the president of Local 1814 of the International Longshoremen's Association

John Lindsay was a great friend to waterfront workers. He tried to modernize Brooklyn and Staten Island terminals to accommodate containerized shipping. Unfortunately, New York City did not have the resources of the Port Authority, which had predetermined that all this shipping should go to New Jersey ports. When John Lindsay was mayor, Brooklyn and Staten Island piers had over 15,000 employees. They now have probably less than 3,000.

An angry Victor Gotbaum, executive director of District Council 37, the largest union of city employees. As a labor negotiator, Gotbaum said, "I needed a viable Mayor Lindsay." He endorsed Lindsay for reelection in 1969, but refused to support him for president in 1972.

recession and the erosion of the tax base due to suburbanization, which, as much as increased city spending, underlay the crisis.

While receiving much of the blame for the city's later problems, Lindsay rarely received credit for transforming the lives of city workers for the better. When Lindsay took office, many city employees lived in poverty, or close to it. By the time he left office, city workers' earnings had risen sharply and their benefits greatly improved, allowing them to live far more comfortable lives and retire young, with adequate income for their remaining years. Ironically, city employees, who caused Lindsay so many headaches and who so rarely looked on him with favor, ended up being among the greatest beneficiaries of his mayoralty.

It wasn't only about wages: Many unions excluded blacks and Puerto Ricans. Here, African-American men protest the hiring practices of the Longshoremen's Union in September 1970.

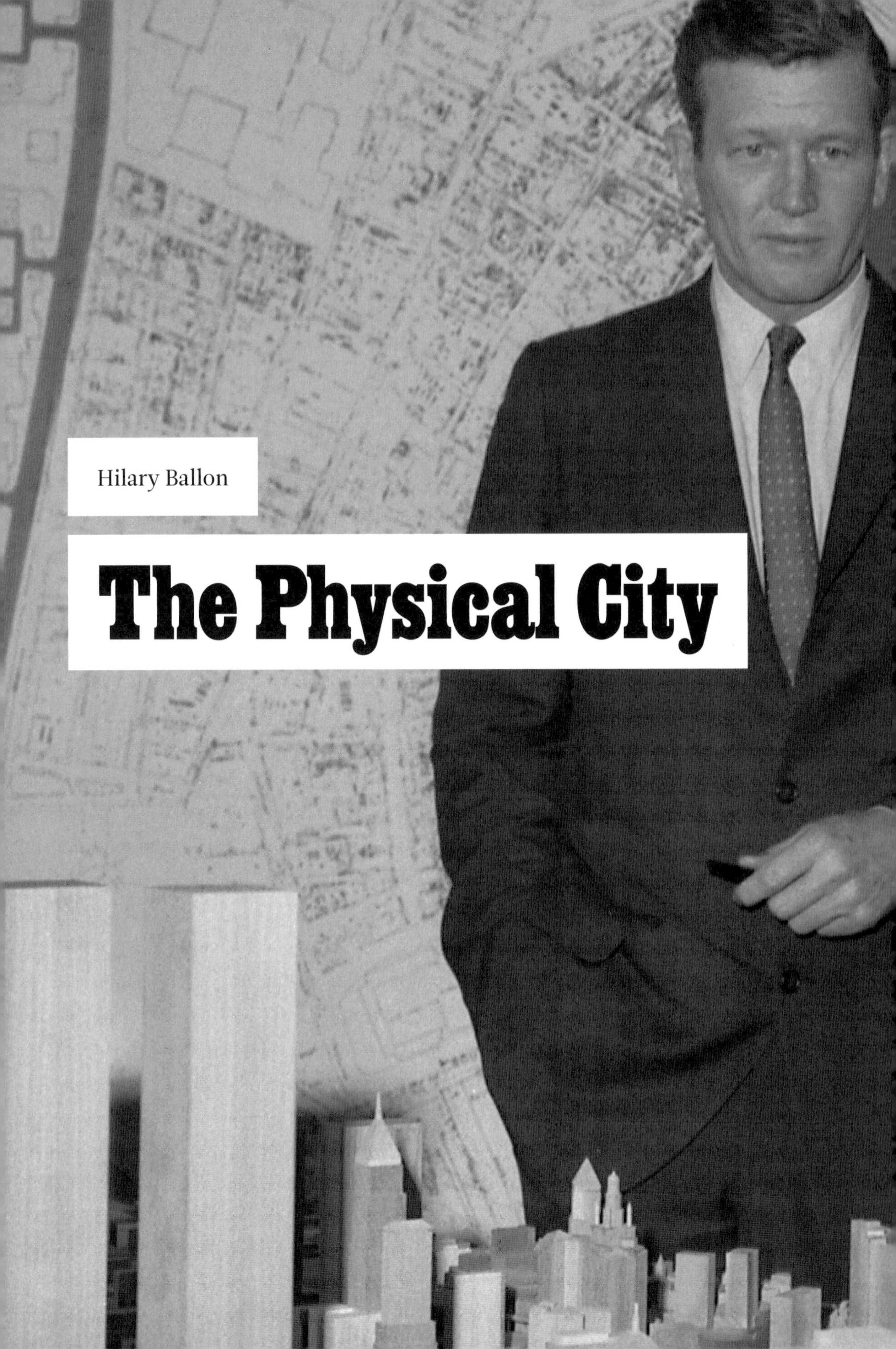

Hilary Ballon

The Physical City

Their kind of town: Lindsay and Governor Nelson A. Rockefeller examine a model of proposed Lower Manhattan development, including the proposed World Trade Center towers at left, in May 1966.

During his run for mayor in July 1965, John V. Lindsay took to the skies for a helicopter tour of New York City, which would not have been remarkable except that two architects, Philip Johnson and Robert L. Zion, guided the tour. The flight, Ada Louise Huxtable remarked in *The New York Times*, was "the first step toward the formulation of a Lindsay campaign platform of urban design." Lindsay saw the city through a design lens, which was an unusual perspective for a big-city mayor, let alone any politician. He believed that poor urban design had

HILARY BALLON is deputy vice chancellor of New York University Abu Dhabi, and professor of urban studies and architecture at the Robert F. Wagner Graduate School of Public Service and university professor at N.Y.U. She curated *Robert Moses and the Modern City*, the 2007 exhibition at the Museum of the City of New York, the Queens Museum of Art, and the Miriam and Ira D. Wallach Art Gallery of Columbia University. Ballon was also a principal author and co-editor with Kenneth T. Jackson of the accompanying book, *Robert Moses and the Modern City: The Transformation of New York*.

"John made public service exciting, challenging, relevant and rewarding because he had a vision of a better New York for all of its citizens. He gave us, on faith, a long rein and strong support. He encouraged us to go all out and took the flak on design issues that had no obvious political payout for him."

–Jaquelin Robertson, *an architect, was the founder of the New York City Urban Design Group and the first Director of the Mayor's Office of Midtown Planning and Development*

damaged the city and that improving the physical environment would improve the quality of life. His achievements in the realm of urban design made his administration one of the most remarkable and creative chapters in American urbanism.

The Lindsay administration was responsible for three major accomplishments involving the urban environment. First, whereas design had previously been regarded as a strictly private concern, Lindsay elevated it to a matter of public policy because of its enduring impact on the city's life. Second, the Lindsay administration advanced a new vision of the good city. The approach used by Robert Moses, though weakened, survived as the Establishment system; it included redevelopment by demolition; the primacy of the automobile; top-down planning without local review; neglect of design; and disdain for old buildings. The democratic urbanism of Lindsay's administration imposed a new set of values: reigning in of the automobile; pedestrianism; lively streets; mixed use; historic preservation; and community participation. Third, the Lindsay administration devised a set of planning tools that succeeded in motivating the private sector to build public amenities. This tool kit remains in use to this day and serves to harmonize private and public interests.

The Urban Design Group

Upon his election, Lindsay appointed a blue-ribbon panel to report on the design of New York City and "how to improve the physical presence of the city for its residents and workers." Akin to President Lyndon B. Johnson's launching of the Great Society programs, he enlisted an expert vanguard and followed the advice he received. William S. Paley, chairman of the Columbia Broadcasting System, headed the task force, which included the architects Philip Johnson, I.M. Pei, Jaquelin Robertson, and Robert Stern, among other informed design voices. Their report, "The Threatened City," issued in February 1967, outlined a pathway to embed design considerations in the planning process.

The crucial recommendation—crucial because the mayor embraced it and because it was superbly executed—was to establish a crackerjack team of urban designers. "This group should be charged with the developing—or commissioning—of concept-designs for rebuilding special-use sections of New York; the conceiving of neighborhoods of residential buildings...; the locating of promising areas of office and commercial building in all the boroughs and the preparing of plans for area development; the preparation of renewal plans for the great avenues of our city, and other such assignments," the report said. The panel envisioned an elite group of designers who would create a prestigious pathway to professional advancement through government service, like that of young lawyers who start their careers as assistant district attorneys. It should be recognized, the Paley report noted, "that in the creation of this special-purpose force...the fourth dimension of design

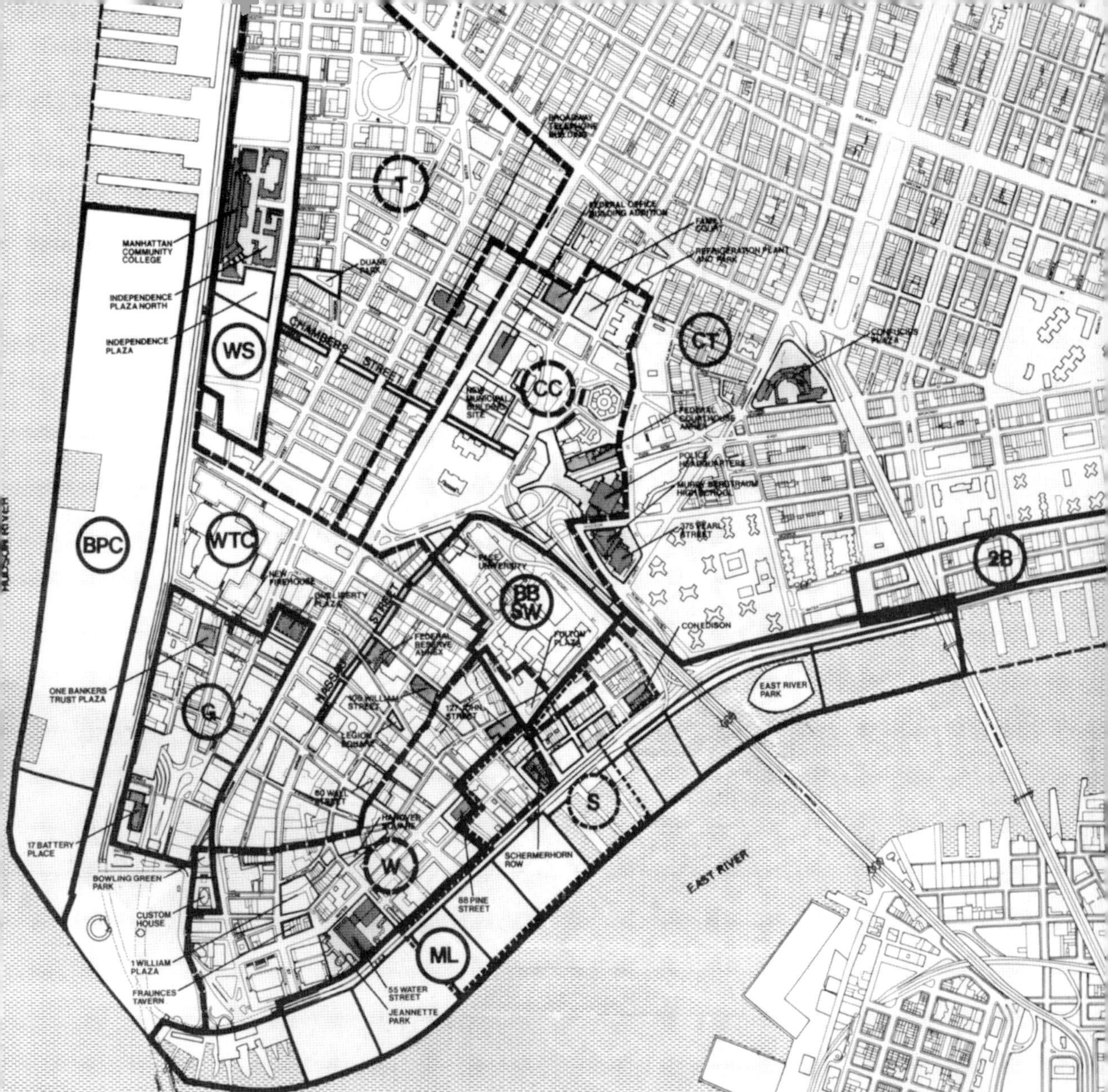

To implement urban design goals, the Office of Lower Manhattan Development envisioned special zoning districts (represented here by coded circles) to facilitate projects like Manhattan Landing, the World Trade Center, and the Special Greenwich Street Development District.

is action." This call to action through design carried the optimism of the mid-1960s and a faith in government service as a means of social change.

In May 1967, appearing at the annual convention of the American Institute of Architects, Lindsay announced the formation of the urban design group, consisting of one of the task force members, Jaquelin Robertson, and Jonathan Barnett, Richard Weinstein, and Myles Weintraub. They were politically energized Ivy League graduates, fresh out of architecture school (three were Yalies, like Lindsay, and the fourth was from Penn), and their combination of talent, youth, and boldness fueled an innovative and ambitious agenda. The Urban Design Group (the plain name stuck) operated within the City Planning Commission, whose chairman, Donald H. Elliott, provided the requisite leadership and mayoral backing as they went about resetting the city's planning approach to development. Perhaps pitching his words to the architect crowd, Lindsay said that the Urban Design Group would seek to "advance the cause of aesthetics in every area the Planning Commission can influence—from street signs to skyscrapers." But aesthetics was not, in fact, the group's focus; designing the city without designing buildings was the objective, as Barnett aptly put it—and doing it through local development offices with community involvement.

Urban design was then a young discipline, floating between architecture and planning. It was introduced as a field of study in the mid 1950s at the Harvard Graduate School of Design and the University of Pennsylvania, and the first graduate-degree program was established in 1960. In an academic context, urban design tended to mean the design of groups of buildings and civic complexes; it was physical, object-oriented, and treated the building group and related open spaces as a unity. The Urban Design Group took a different approach: looking at a structural level above buildings, the team focused on zoning, the intricate set of guidelines that establish the framework within which buildings live. The Urban Design Group grasped the creative capacity of the zoning law to shape the physical environment and achieve a defined set of public benefits. "The whole subject of zoning was a revelation to us," Barnett recalled. "It had always seemed a very dreary subject, of little relevance to any creative endeavor," he said, but "we came to realize that zoning could be made in to one of the basic methods of designing cities."

The Urban Design Group's zoning strategy contrasted with the progressive orthodoxies of the 1960s: comprehensive planning, advocacy planning, and the Jane Jacobs approach. Comprehensive planning took a holistic view of city rebuilding projects. It was an antidote to two failings of the slum-clearance urban-renewal program of the 1950s: the focus on a single project, detached from its context, and a monocular interest in buildings, betting that they alone would generate healthy urban fabric. Comprehensive planning was the basis of Model Cities, the federal program that replaced urban renewal and operated from 1966 to 1974, concurrently with Lindsay's two terms. Model Cities supported rehabilitation, social services, and citizen participation as well as rebuilding. Comprehensive planning reaffirmed the value of an overall master plan, even augmenting its scope by encompassing an expanded range of services.

Advocacy planning, on the other hand, rejected the idea of a correct planning solution and recast the planner as an advocate of an interest group, like a lawyer representing a client. Advocacy planning stemmed from an impulse to empower citizen groups with information to fight government projects. Stung by the criticisms of top-down planning, advocate-planners were enhanced mouthpieces of community groups, a role that devalued expertise as well as design.

The community activists turned on by Jane Jacobs's epochal 1961 book, *The Death and Life of Great American Cities*, were largely interested in halting urban development and did not fundamentally value the enterprise of planning.

The Urban Design Group saw what few architects had seen before: they saw that zoning was a creative tool with which you could do more than restrict

From *The Power Broker: Robert Moses and the Fall of New York*

ROBERT A. CARO

1975

"If you elect a matinee-idol mayor, you're going to get a musical-comedy administration," Robert Moses confided to his aides after his first meeting with the mayor-elect at the mayor's campaign headquarters in Manhattan.

Lindsay had vowed to remove Moses as chairman of the Triborough Bridge and Tunnel Authority and as the city arterial highways czar. Moses, Robert A. Caro wrote in The Power Broker, "had lost enough power so that a tough, canny mayor, skilled in the ways of New York politics, could have given him a hard fight, but his shrewd old eyes had taken their measure of John Lindsay the first time the two men had ever sat down and talked, and he knew that Lindsay wasn't the mayor to do it." Nor was he the mayor to tap Triborough's toll revenues to subsidize mass transit (which Governor Nelson Rockefeller did in 1968, effectively ending Moses's reign). In this edited excerpt, Caro recounts why not:

Lindsay had talked about "the power brokers in our city" but, when pressed by reporters, had never identified them ("Who are the power brokers? They know who they are" was his reply)–possibly because, as he was to demonstrate during his mishandling of the first crisis to confront him, a transit strike, he didn't really know who they were. He was going to find out though–the hard way.

All they were doing, Lindsay's aides could feel, was finally putting into force the proposals reformers such as Citizens Union and City Budget Commission study groups had been advocating for years. What was hard about it? Both authorities, Transit and Triborough, were controlled by the city, weren't they? And John Lindsay was the city now. The ignorance of some of these men concerning the true nature and powers of public authorities would have been ludicrous if it had not been the city's future that that ignorance was jeopardizing. Lindsay was, moreover, full of confidence–overconfidence–and optimism about his ability to run the city; he was going to be another La Guardia, with one exception–La Guardia had never gone on to be president as he was sure *he* was going to; lest anyone miss the comparison with the Greatest Mayor New York Had Ever Had, Lindsay had hardly been inaugurated when he had La Guardia's portrait moved out of another spot in City Hall and into his office, along with La Guardia's desk....

Robert Moses had been taking care of reformers for 40 years....These men with their first taste of power laughed at him; he had not only tasted power but held it longer than many of these men had been alive. Did Lindsay think he had the ability to outsmart Robert Moses? Robert Moses had outsmarted *La Guardia*.

Robert Moses, whom Lindsay tried and failed to break.

height and bulk. The zoning code could be used not just to limit the negative but also to provide incentives intended to achieve defined outcomes, and it could become a tool to achieve specific results, like mixed-use buildings. The Urban Design Group survived until 1973 (in 1969, Alexander Cooper joined the group, Robertson moved to the Office of Midtown Planning, and Weinstein to the Office of Lower Manhattan Development). Seven remarkable years of trend-setting zoning had introduced a new way to shape the city.

Models show how Grand Central Terminal area looked in the 1960s (top) and how it would appear under an Urban Design Group plan to preserve the terminal and transfer air-rights to sites nearby.

Preservation

Mayor Lindsay's urban design policies responded to a painful sense of loss in New York City. By 1965, the city was weary of clearance: clearance for large-scale public-housing projects, for slum-clearance projects that Robert Moses propelled, for Interstate highways, and for commercial redevelopment where real estate wizards saw economic opportunity in underutilized sites. The sense of loss was reinforced by the mediocre new architecture that often went against the neighborhood grain and replaced the fine grain of the old city with superblocks.

Already under Mayor Robert F. Wagner, preservation concerns had infiltrated city planning. The City Planning Commission, under the leadership of its chairman, James Felt, had launched the West Side Renewal Project, which challenged the approach to urban renewal that Robert Moses had ferociously advanced in the 1950s in the West Side Renewal Project. For Moses, urban redevelopment required clearance; it was too expensive to restore dilapidated tenements, and the only cost-effective approach was to demolish them—whereas Felt saw social value and community roots in old neighborhoods. For the first time in New York, the West Side Renewal plan incorporated preservation and renovation of old housing stock in a multifaceted approach to renewal, with demolition used sparingly on a lot-by-lot basis. As a candidate, Lindsay favored this approach and campaigned to save city landmarks, which became possible when Wagner signed a landmarks-preservation bill into law in April 1965. But meanwhile landmarks kept coming down. Pennsylvania Station was demolished between 1963 and 1966; the old Metropolitan Opera House followed in 1967. New York was also fast losing its great mansions and old hotels, as developers gobbled them up to exploit the value of prestige addresses on Fifth and Park Avenues and Riverside Drive. For example, the Savoy-Plaza Hotel, built by McKim,

Artist's rendition of what the South Street Seaport would look like after a proposed historic restoration.

Mead, and White in 1928, stood at Fifth Avenue at 59th Street. It was demolished in 1966 and replaced by the General Motors Building, which incarnated the logic of the 1961 zoning resolution that gave private developers the right to build larger buildings in return for providing amenities like public plazas.

Under Lindsay, the newly created Landmarks Commission had to establish its authority, and it carefully chose its first set of landmarks to win public trust, choosing buildings like the United States Custom House and Grand Central Terminal—whose preservation became all the more charged after the demolition of Pennsylvania Station. The Landmarks Commission designated Grand Central as a landmark in 1967, and in 1969 it blocked the owner's plan to build a 55-story skyscraper designed by Marcel Breuer above it. In return, the city proposed to transfer Grand Central's air rights to another site. The owner sued to block the landmark designation and claimed that the city had violated its property rights. The case was not resolved until 1978, when the United States Supreme Court ruled that no illegal taking of property had occurred. Writing for the majority, Justice William Brennan wrote: "Underlying the opinion is the notion that aesthetic values, particularly historic preservation, are important public interests that justify restrictions on private land." In addition to legal mechanisms, successful landmark designations required support from the private sector to keep the buildings in good condition and private-public conservancies emerged to fulfill this role.

In addition to protecting landmarks, the Lindsay team looked at the ecology of neighborhoods and sought to protect their distinctive characters. The worry

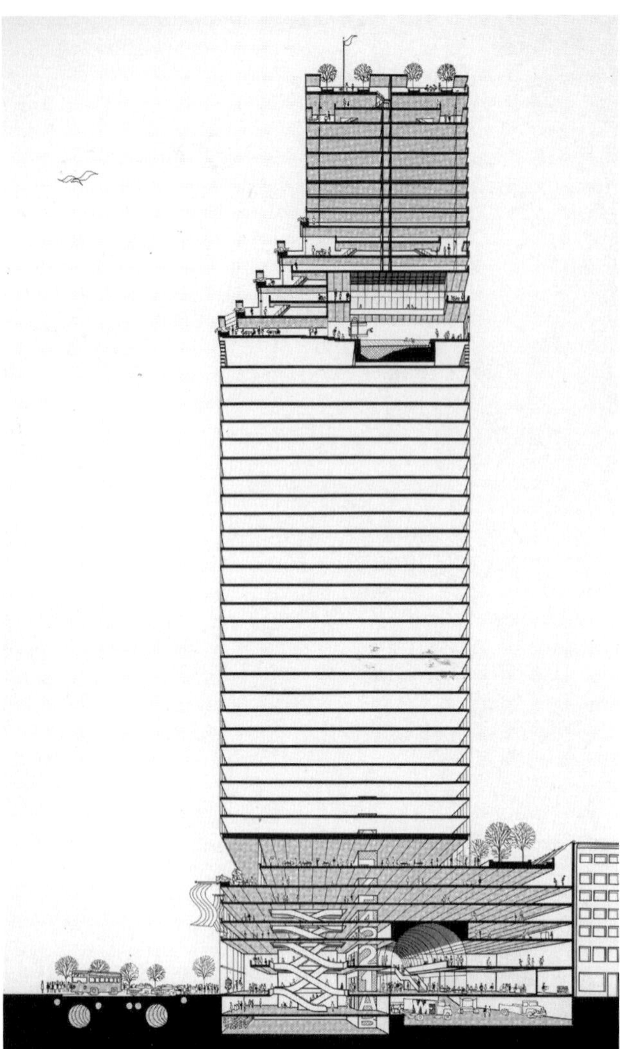

How buildings on the east side of Fifth Avenue would look under special district provisions proposed by the Office of Midtown Planning. Lower floors would be reserved for retail, middle floors for offices, and upper floors for apartments and a swim club.

was that bland office buildings, banks, and airline-ticket offices that could afford to pay high rents would chase out low-rent tenants and endanger the diversity of street life and neighborhoods. The Fulton Fish Market and the adjoining seaport were obsolete and prime targets of redevelopment fever, but under Lindsay, the strategy changed to preservation of the historic building fabric and development of the South Street Seaport Museum District. Boston's Faneuil Hall was a successful example of restoration and adaptive reuse as a downtown shopping center, but Lindsay's team had an even broader vision of a cultural district with old ships, old houses, a seaport museum, and related shopping. Over time, as-of-right zoning impinged on the plan, but the preservation agenda remained intact, and ultimately the real estate market was mobilized to sustain a historic district.

Special Districts

New York's exuberant real estate market, known for buildings with short life spans and skyscraper rivalries, is a metaphor for the city's dynamism; nevertheless, New York has been a pioneer in regulating the built environment. In 1916, it passed the first comprehensive zoning ordinance, which restricted land use and the height and bulk of buildings. The revised zoning ordinance of 1961 took a step in another direction: rather than only limit negative effects, such as bulky buildings that block sunlight from neighboring ones, the 1961 ordinance promoted what the City Planning Commission deemed a public benefit. Based on the premise that open space was needed at street level, the zoning ordinance gave developers an incentive to build street plazas by offering a 20 percent density bonus. Although street plazas proved to be a largely misguided idea, puncturing the street wall with vacant spaces, the Urban Design Group realized that the density bonus provided valuable leverage to achieve various design goals.

Bonus zoning was first applied to the Broadway theater district, whose cultural identity seemed at risk in the 1960s. Broadway had lost 45 legitimate theaters since the 1930s, due to conversions to movie theaters and to demolition. Through the new Office of Midtown Planning, the Urban Design Group acted to halt this trend after the Hotel Astor (Clinton & Russell, 1909), a legendary hotel in the heart of Times Square, on Broadway between 44th and 45th Streets, was demolished in 1966. Encouraged by Lindsay and the city planning commissioner, the Urban Design Group asked the developer to incorporate a theater in his proposed new office building. Despite at first claiming the impossibility of such a solution, the developer was persuaded to build a theater in exchange for being allowed to build a tower 20 percent larger than what the zoning allowed. One Astor Plaza, which was completed in 1972, is a 54-story office tower atop the ground-level Minskoff Theater.

An architectural rendering (top) of One Astor Plaza in Times Square with the Minskoff Theater in foreground. The glass-walled lobbies (bottom) overlook Broadway.

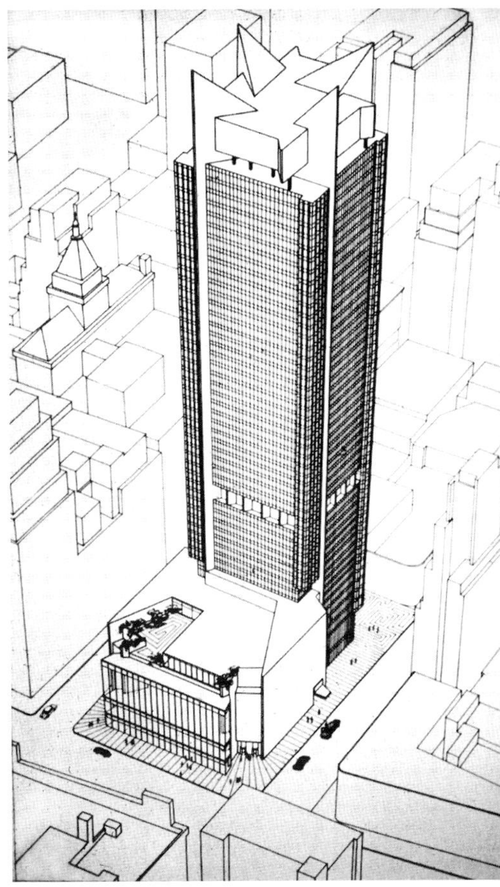

This solution provided the prototype for the Special Theater District and the more widely applied tool of zoning bonuses devised by the Urban Design Group. The Special Theater District encompassed the blocks from 40th to 57th Streets between Sixth and Eighth Avenues. Within that area, a developer could seek a density bonus if a building included a theater, but no standards defined either the bonus or the theater. The process shifted from as-of-right zoning to negotiations between the developer and the City Planning Commission. By offering attractive density bonuses to offset the cost of a public amenity, the Urban Design Group initiated a sort of public-private partnership in which the two parties were required to negotiate a resolution. This arrangement fostered what Barnett called "the negotiation syndrome," with frequent delays, special permits, and case-by-case arrangements, and protracted negotiations made it difficult for the public to understand what was going on.

Negotiation was also Moses's modus operandi with urban renewal developers. Indeed, the Lindsay architects had more in common with Moses than they may have perceived: both were committed to public-private partnerships and understood that in order to influence growth patterns, government had to work with private developers. However, they tipped the scales differently in terms of design, and therein lies the fundamental change in value systems and urban aspirations of the Lindsay years: whereas Moses located design as a purely private sector matter, the Urban Design Group promoted it as a significant arena of public policy.

The Special Theater District worked insofar as it stimulated theater construction. However, the buildings were undistinguished and the theaters were largely invisible structures, submerged in towers and devoid of throbbing marquees and street presence. The Urban Design Group responded to the problem of the disappearing theater district in terms of use, not street character; indeed, Richard Weinstein pronounced the old theaters obsolete and unsuitable for landmarking. Moreover, the special district zoning provided no protection against demolition. In 1982, five adjacent theaters (the Helen Hayes, Morosco,

Astor, Bijou, and Gaiety) were demolished to clear the site for the Marriott Marquis Hotel, on Broadway at 45th Street, designed by John Portman. The hotel included the Marquis Theater on the third floor, but it hardly compensated for the loss of five historic theaters.

The Urban Design Group fashioned several other special districts, the most successful of which was the Fifth Avenue Zoning District. It was developed to protect Fifth Avenue's retail culture as large department stores cashed in on their valuable sites and their buildings came tumbling down. The special district plan required window-shop frontage from 38th to 57th Streets, with office entrances located along side streets. It also promoted a mixture of uses—ground-floor shops, offices above, and residences at the top. Developers satisfying those requirements obtained a 20 percent floor area bonus, but the extra area had to be used for apartments. Olympic Tower (Skidmore, Owings and Merrill, 1975), on Fifth Avenue between 51st and 52nd Streets, the former site of Best & Company, was the first compliant building, mixing retail space, offices, and apartments. The value of mixing uses to populate business districts day and night is now widely accepted, but the Fifth Avenue zoning was the first departure from the single-use zoning enshrined in New York's pioneering original zoning law.

The Lincoln Center Special Zoning District, on the other hand, was hamstrung, and exposed a social blind spot. As Moses intended, Lincoln Center triggered the development of the Upper West Side, but there was no master plan to direct that growth. The Urban Design Group structured the zoning to assure nocturnal street life when theater-goers were in the area; restaurants and shops were permitted, but banks, which closed at night, were restricted. Other aspects of the special district zoning lapsed into design of specific forms: the zoning provided incentives for a building setback at the approximate height of the theaters and a colonnade along Broadway, seeking a unified composition unlike any other Manhattan streetscape. But during the contentious approval process, the Manhattan borough president, Percy Sutton, objected that there were no incentives for low- or middle-income housing. This complaint led to the city's first inclusionary zoning provisions, an important social application of bonus zoning around which there has been continuing experimentation in order to harness market forces to achieve social objectives. If the Urban Design Group was primarily concerned with land use and the physical grain of neighborhoods, the tools they devised were deployable for different ends, and successive generations of city planners have depended on bonus zoning to advance the public interest.

Critics of bonus zoning raise two basic objections. One is that the procedure stimulates increased density and development. This concern connects to a core mission of the planning profession, which was launched, in part, to correct the social and environmental hazards of congestion, but over the course of the 20th century, the profession failed to draw a clear distinction between unwanted congestion, such as overcrowded sidewalks, and desirable density, such as that needed to support mass transit. The environmental awakening of the 21st century has clarified the sustainable dimension of urban density and offers a new perspective on the merits of zoning bonuses. The second objection concerns less the tool than the public benefit that it optimizes. Certainly, what is in the public interest is a debatable proposition. Moses had considered himself a sufficient arbiter of that matter, but reversing his autocratic approach, the Lindsay administration introduced a system of community planning that, if more cumbersome, allowed citizens to arrive by consultation at a more pluralistic understanding of the public interest.

People First

During the Lindsay years, Central Park functioned as an outdoor stage for the political and social movements sweeping the country, second only to the Mall in Washington. Thomas P. F. Hoving, Lindsay's first parks commissioner, served briefly (from January 1966 to April 1967), but in that time changed the mood of the city and the perception of the park, and his policies were largely sustained, although with less fanfare, by his successor, August Heckscher. Moses, the long-serving parks commissioner, had converted Olmsted's pastoral, restful landscape into an exercise arena, by inserting baseball diamonds, tennis courts, playgrounds, an ice skating rink, and a swimming pool in the park. Despite clashing visions, both Moses and Olmsted believed in the elevating effects of the park, its restorative powers, and the requirements of social decorum. Central Park had dress codes and curfews and social norms.

By contrast, Hoving saw the park as a liberating space and organized a variety of "happenings"—rock 'n' roll concerts, mural-painting, stargazing, and sundry be-in's—for frolic and free expression. He also lifted the Moses-era ban on political events and permitted antiwar rallies in the park, the first of which occurred on March 26, 1966. Within three years, the mass events and

Lindsay (center left) and Parks Commissioner August Heckshher (center right) lead a bicycle brigade to Central Park on a car-free Manhattan street—a precursor of today's Times Square.

hippie behavior spurred a backlash, and in the name of landscape preservation, stricter controls were placed on park use.

The value of free play was signaled in the redesign of playgrounds. Moses's exponential expansion of the parks system was facilitated by the standardization of park equipment, from benches to garbage cans to playground equipment. By Lindsay's time, the rationale for standardized equipment had been forgotten, and its impersonality, above all in playgrounds, was bemoaned. As attitudes toward free play changed and its cognitive benefits were better understood, a new type of playground was developed in Central Park. The Adventure Playground, designed by Richard Dattner at Central Park West and 68th Street in 1966, like M. Paul Friedberg's adventure playground a year earlier at the Jacob Riis Houses, offered a variety of exploratory experiences: bumpy slides, tunnels, a tree house, and contoured landscapes of sand, water, and towers.

1970 Joseph Farris cartoon in *The New Yorker*; the caption reads, "I'll bet Lindsay never dreamed *this* would happen!"

The clearest signal that the Moses era had ended, and with it the supremacy of the automobile, came in the summer of 1966, when Hoving initiated a ban on automobiles on the East and West Drives of Central Park. Hoving's proposed test car ban for a few summer weekends led to an interdepartmental spat when the traffic commissioner, Henry A. Barnes, objected; the roads in Central Park, he argued, were under his control, and the displaced traffic would create havoc on city streets. Lindsay stepped in and backed the car ban, and the pilot project almost immediately became standard procedure. The picture of Lindsay leading a bicycle crusade to Central Park captures the ascendant sentiment about the streets: they belonged to the people, not to cars. By contrast, Lindsay's demapping of the Lower Manhattan Expressway, Moses's despised road project that had threatened to destroy what became SoHo, was anticlimactic, coming after a decade of bureaucratic maneuvers, but it signified the end of the Moses-era promotion of the automobile.

In 1969, the City Planning Commission issued a six-volume master plan for New York City. Such a plan was needed to qualify for some federal development grants in order to show how a proposed project related to a comprehensive vision. The City Planning Commission had been founded in 1938 but had never before produced a master plan. To a large extent, that inaction

From the Plan for New York City

1969

The most enduring legacies of the 1969 Plan for New York City were the special zoning configurations that helped resculpt Manhattan's skyline and the imaginative efforts to reshape the social agenda. Many of its proposals represented the last gasp of an expansionist era. Yet the planners were remarkably prescient in defining problems, if less successful in lobbying for solutions.

The "gut issue" of the urban crisis, they said, was to provide more opportunities for the poor. There was a "cruel mismatch" between jobs and education. The welfare system stifled initiative and encouraged dependency. The mayor should be accountable for the school system. The plan sounded what was even then a familiar refrain: develop the waterfront and borough downtowns and New York as the "national" (now "international") city. The authors of the plan concluded:

New York could never be an ideal city. It has too great a dynamism and its problems are immense because they are in part the consequence of it. The slums are a terrible problem, but the blacks and Puerto Ricans came to them because they were looking for a better life, and their new militancy, disturbing as it may be, is a sign of hope and not despair. The fierce competition for land, the crowding, the dislocations of demolition and rebuilding are vexing problems but they are also problems of vitality.

was due to Moses who, planner though he was, disparaged planning and master plans, in particular because their grand scale was not geared to practical action. The publication of the *Plan of New York City* in 1969 thus marks a sea change in the role of the City Planning Commission, which under the leadership of Donald Elliott, its chairman from 1966 to 1973, was an extraordinary laboratory of planning ideas. However, the appeal of top-down master planning had passed; expertise was suspect, and New York City was in the process of decentralizing its services and school system.

Even as the City Planning Commission was producing the master plan, the Urban Design Group was trying to fashion a productive method of local community planning, using the Twin Park vest-pocket housing in East Tremont in the Bronx as a demonstration project. In contrast to the combative approach of advocacy planning, which pits parties against one another, the Urban Design Group formed a local working committee to resolve differences and arrive at a consensual resolution. Twin Park was an exemplar of community involvement and design quality.

Local development offices in Midtown, Lower Manhattan, downtown Brooklyn, and Jamaica, Queens—each of which reported directly to the mayor—planted the seeds for later renewal as the population was replenished. Two new office buildings in Brooklyn for Con Ed and the phone company, arguably, laid the foundation for MetroTech decades later, and Lindsay's insistence that the York College campus be built in Jamaica was intended to encourage later development there.

Motivating the Private Sector

"It is obvious that the large cities are fallen on evil days." Walter McQuade, an architectural critic and member of the City Planning Commission, offered this grim assessment of the urban scene in 1971. From his first day in office, Lindsay grappled with profound social problems—poverty, racism, inequity, violence, and urban decay. The designers on the Lindsay team were mindful that they could not cure those problems. Yet they brought to bear immense creativity in fashioning new tools to motivate the private sector to improve the public domain.

The tools were bonus incentives, air-rights transfers, special zoning districts, landmarking, community participation, and design excellence. These measures were idealistic in inspiration and pragmatic in effect. They did not depend on wholesale adoption in megaprojects; they were tailored to the dynamics of the real estate market and applicable block by block and over time, as developers were attracted to different sites. Finally, these tools were enlisted on behalf of a compelling urban vision, one with lively sidewalks, pedestrian comforts, distinctive neighborhoods, historic districts, great monuments, and cultural pastimes—a city, in short, that enriched human experience.

The Yankees were threatening to leave the Bronx until the city agreed to buy and renovate Yankee Stadium. The $27 million facelift, which began in 1973, eventually cost more than $100 million. The football Giants left for New Jersey, but the Yankees stayed put, going on to win ten American League pennants and seven World Series titles in their new home. Here, Mayor Lindsay supervises start-up on the renovation in October 1973. The rebuilt ballpark reopened in 1976.

"Adding Up the Score"

ADA LOUISE HUXTABLE

The International Herald Tribune, January 20, 1974

Before the assessments of the Lindsay Administration have all been used to wrap yesterday's fish, one part of the score that has been conspicuous by omission should be added to it. The subject is urban design, or as correctly stated in the title of a new book by Jonathan Barnett, *Urban Design as Public Policy* (Architectural Record Books, McGraw-Hill). Mr. Barnett is one of a group of able young people who worked in government to help establish this virtually new field as an integral part of city procedure, and Mr. Lindsay was the mayor who put his weight behind it.

The results, in terms of city development in patterns of great environmental equality, are extraordinary and precedent-setting and, in many cases, visible. They have made New York a pilgrimage point for serious urbanists. It is quite impossible to overstate the vision, skill, importance, and, above all, concrete positive actions that have been involved. Mr. Barnett's is a tell-it-all-like-it-is document that puts this significant chapter in municipal planning history on the record for those who would be informed—including, one hopes, the present administration.

Urban design is a profession that has been developed out of demonstrated need. While planners were allocating resources and specifying land use, no one was aware of how their charts and diagrams would turn out in three dimensions. In the postwar era, renewal schemes that looked fine on paper were considerably less than fine in actuality. The schemes were, in fact, often so bad that the idea of urban environmental quality was born by default out of all those things that were missing—life, interest, convenience, amenity, and pleasure.

And so it became clear that it was not enough to map a logical dispersion of uses, but that someone had to take that scenario and actually project its consequences in an esthetic, sociological, and functional model of the city. In fact, someone had to design the city, not just the buildings. This involves projecting trends and their physical outcome, a process known as conceptualization, or visualization, before the fact. And it also involves dealing with issues as broad as the city's future.

The point is to face problems before they arise, such as the threat of extinction of the theater district, or the effect on circulation and land values of a new subway, or the need to preserve neighborhood character in the face of a building boom, or ways to save services and improve pedestrian features when massive new construction takes place. The effort, generally, is to avoid damage before it is done, and to guide development into the most desirable channels.

In this sense, the urban design process carries much of the responsibility for setting a large part of city policy—what the city will be, or should be, according to specific values and principles. This means that the designer deals with a good deal more than a drawing board; what comes off that board is shaped by economics, law, and politics as well as by design, and increasingly by art and humanism. It is believable and real. And the results are measurable in the shape of the city and the lives people lead.

The Lindsay Administration occupied the historic moment when the profession was beginning to make itself felt. There were a lot of lessons apparent in what had gone wrong in city planning practice in the past, and a lot of realization of what had to be done in the future. But all of the basic questions about how to set up new procedures administratively and how to make them function soundly had to be settled.

The mayor began by accepting the excellent recommendations of his task force on urban design headed by William S. Paley, which called for a permanent urban design force in the city rather than reliance on sporadic reports. In 1967 an Urban Design Group was established within the City Planning Commission, under the director of its chairman, Donald Elliott.

The Urban Design Group immediately became a constructive, trouble-shooting unit. When, for example, it saw a new wave of commercial construction threatening New York's theaters, it devised a zoning plan that would encourage new theaters through bonuses to developers for building them. And when a second wave of Sixth Avenue construction seemed assured, it worked out ways to provide pedestrian conveniences and subway linkage that the first lacked.

But it soon became apparent that more was needed to carry out the proposals. The mayor then established, by executive order and as an extension of his own office, special planning offices for various parts of the boroughs. These have been staffed by a high caliber of architectural professional. The staffs not only deal with problems *in situ*, but have the authority of the mayor's office to coordinate all of the city's departments and agencies to get the job done. In addition, urban designers have been placed in the departments themselves, for further coordination. Subsequently, a civil service category was set up for them, although the special development offices still exist only at the mayor's pleasure.

Those development offices have proved an excellent invention. There are now eleven of them, including those for Staten Island, the Bronx, Queens, Downtown Brooklyn, and lower and Midtown Manhattan. They have not only been extremely effective in dealing with both the political and private sectors; they have also produced outstanding work.

The device traditionally used for shaping the city is zoning, and this has been one of the chief tools of the new process, pushed to creative legal limits by the urban designers. There are at least three innovative zoning uses functioning in New York now and being watched by other cities.

One is incentive zoning, which gives the developer carefully defined bonuses for the inclusion of desirable features that would otherwise not be built. This method tailors the features to specific areas and needs. That procedure led naturally to the creation of the special zoning district, in which character and requirements are defined for a whole area and written directly into the zoning regulations. A third innovation is the extension of air-rights transfers to protect landmarks and historic neighborhoods.

New York's special zoning districts now include, in addition to the theater district, the Greenwich Street area, so well spelled out in form that no discretionary bonuses are needed, Fifth Avenue, upper Madison Avenue, Lincoln Square, Times Square, a Second Avenue transit district, and a series of creative zoning regulations to guide the huge landfill communities going ahead in Lower Manhattan, Battery Park City, and Manhattan Landing.

Downtown Brooklyn improvements are being carried out by the Office of Downtown Brooklyn Planning and Development. Planned unit development zoning to encourage cluster housing over ticky-tacky has been passed for Staten Island. Recently, housing quality in general has been attacked by a zoning study by the Urban Design Group.

It is now possible to see new theaters on the West Side, to use through-block passages in midtown, and to begin to experience some of the intricate and pleasurable pedestrian and open-space amenities in Lower Manhattan. It is a matter of just a little more time before one can enjoy small galleries and small parks and a mix of commercial and residential building where sterile offices have driven out city life.

But the most important, and less immediately tangible, factor is the care, quality, and sophistication of the design attention being lavished on the city now, that is also being so well translated into action through appropriate legal and administrative processes.

It is impossible to name everyone who should be mentioned here, but a few who must be credited are Mr. Elliott, the first and second directors of the Office of Lower Manhattan Development, Richard Buford and Richard Weinstein, as well as of the Office of Midtown Planning and Development, Jacquelin Robertson and William Bardel, and the successive heads of the Urban Design Group, Mr. Barnett and Alexander Cooper.

For the many omissions, we apologize, and refer the reader to Mr. Barnett's fine book. He points out correctly that New York's commitment to urban design has not been matched elsewhere in the country. It is a commitment that deserves to be continued on the highest administration levels.

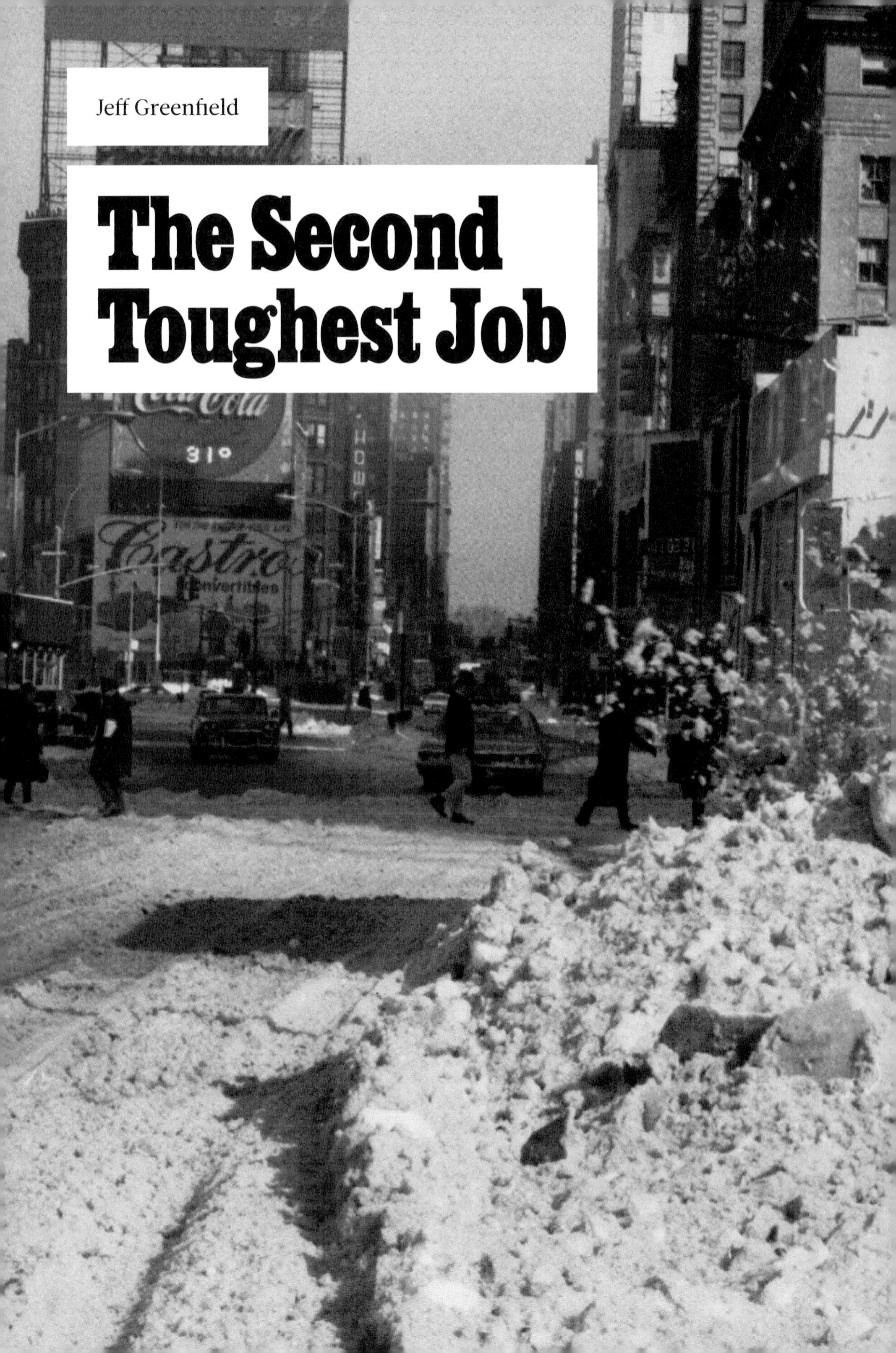

Jeff Greenfield

The Second Toughest Job

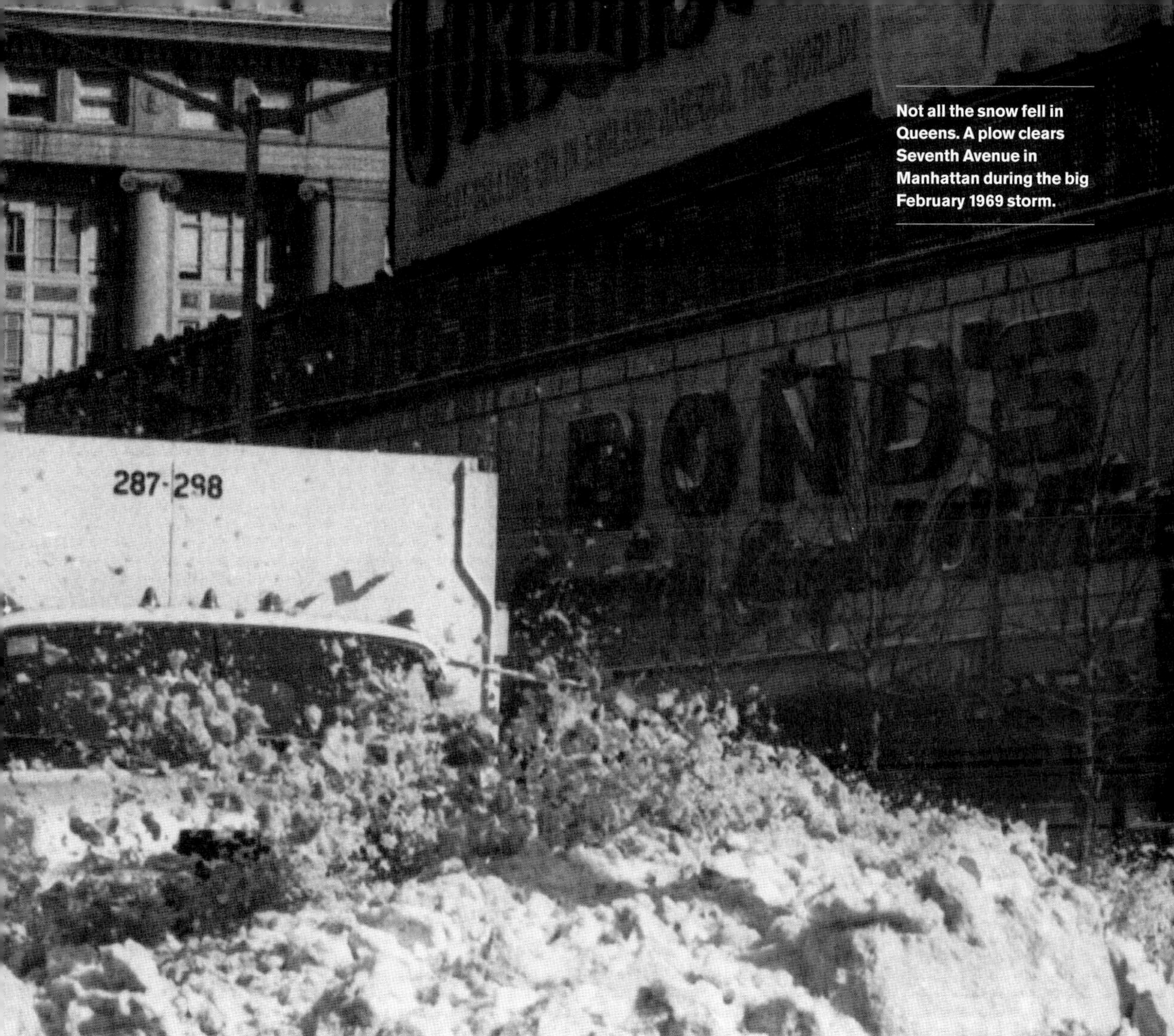

Not all the snow fell in Queens. A plow clears Seventh Avenue in Manhattan during the big February 1969 storm.

There was no way on God's earth that Mayor Lindsay should have won re-election in 1969. He had won office in 1965 at a time when there was a conscious sense that things were going wrong in New York. The months-long series in *The New York Herald Tribune*, "City in Crisis," framed the central theme. This tall, lean, impossibly handsome congressman from the Upper East Side of Manhattan represented a sharp, clean break with the past, a reformer with no ties to the clubhouse politics that had brought the city to its unhappy state.

JEFF GREENFIELD is CBS News senior political correspondent. He previously worked as CNN senior analyst, and ABC News's media and political analyst. He is the author or co-author of a dozen books, including the best-selling political satire, *The People's Choice*. In 1967 and 1968, he worked in the Senate office and presidential campaign of Robert F. Kennedy. From 1968 to 1970, he served as speechwriter for Mayor Lindsay. He is at work now on a book about recent American political history.

September 1, 1969: Everyone's a critic. A heckler (at right) confronts Lindsay at the Clearview Bath and Tennis Club in Queens. In middle is Lindsay bodyguard Patrick R. Vecchio, who was elected in 1978–and still serves–as town supervisor of Smithtown, Long Island.

(When a fractured Democratic primary in 1965 gave the nomination to Comptroller Abraham D. Beame, a product of the Brooklyn machine, Lindsay had his ideal foil.) The columnist Murray Kempton pronounced Lindsay fresh and everyone else tired.

But by the summer of 1969, New York had grown tired of Lindsay. Kempton himself would write that "under Lindsay, the air is fouler, the streets dirtier, the bicycle thieves more vigilant, the labor contracts more abandoned in their disregard for the public good...than any of these elements ever were under the former mayor, Robert F. Wagner."

Even before his first year as mayor was over, Lindsay had drawn the passionate enmity of the rank-and-file of the New York police force with his campaign for a Civilian Complaint Review Board—a campaign that ended in a landslide defeat. As the end of his first term approached, violent crime had risen to levels unseen in the 20th century; the half million on the welfare rolls had swelled to 1.2 million. Yes, he'd engendered good will among liberals and blacks by walking the most dangerous neighborhoods of the city's streets—and making New York one of the few big cities that did not explode into violence on the nights after Martin Luther King Jr.'s murder in April of 1968. But that good will had been overwhelmed by the transit strike, a (brief) firefighters' strike, a police job action, and a teachers' strike that had put the largely Jewish teachers' union and the largely black and Puerto Rican community school boards at war with each other. Even the gods—and a sclerotic bureaucracy—conspired against him; a freak snowstorm in early 1969 that dumped nearly two feet of snow on eastern Queens had paralyzed much of that borough for days, offering a Currier & Ives portrait of a Manhattan-centric mayor indifferent to the plight of the middle-class homeowner. By the time the 1969 campaign moved into high gear, Lindsay had even lost the nomination of the

Republican Party to a conservative Staten Island state senator, John Marchi. That this battered and bruised mayor in fact did win re-election was the result of widely disparate factors: a key strategic move to give the populace a taste of mayoral blood; an ability to link an unpopular war half a world away to the city's woes; an off-hand comment by a legendary crime-fighter; a fortuitous visit by a foreign leader; an opponent whose political skills were that of a baked potato; and...oh, yes, a baseball team.

"I think it was during the Lindsay administration that the job was described as "the second-toughest job in America." Some people outside New York think that's an exaggeration, and humility would probably prevent me from absolutely saying it's correct, but it's not so far from wrong."

–Former Mayor **Rudolph W. Giuliani,** *in an interview with Tom Casciato for the film* The Lindsay Years, *produced by Thirteen for WNET.org*

Re-election Campaign Strategy

The key strategic decision was to acknowledge mistakes; to chip away at the belief that this aristocratic figure believed himself to be somehow "above" the white working-class citizenry, while reminding voters how tough the job of being New York Mayor was. (It was more than a matter of false impression; Lindsay's coterie of elite-educated reformers was often seriously disconnected from the real world of New York City outside Manhattan.) As Fred Hayes, Lindsay's budget director, observed, "the winners we found—the guys who turned out good—were generally those without the education or the experience for the job—because they didn't bring along their preconceived notions." And a young lawyer from Queens named Mario Cuomo, who helped navigate the city through potentially explosive neighborhood issues, observed, "I do think Lindsay couldn't talk to 'us,' didn't understand us. He does not have and could not have that empathy. It's not his fault. It's who he is.'" Thus was born the decision to open the fall campaign with the "I Made Mistakes" TV commercial. Produced by Tony Isidore and Steve Frankfurt of Young and Rubicam, under the direction of Lindsay media maven (and my future employer) David Garth, the ad featured the mayor sitting in shirtsleeves on the porch of Gracie Mansion, looking straight into the camera and saying:

"I guessed wrong on the weather before the city's biggest snowstorm last winter. And that was a mistake. But I put 6,000 more cops on the street. And that was no mistake. The school strike went on too long, and we all made some mistakes. But I brought 225,000 more jobs to this town. And that was no mistake. And I fought for three years to put a fourth police platoon on the streets. And that was no mistake. And I reduced the deadliest gas in the air by 50 percent. And I forced the landlords to roll back unfair rents. And we did not have a Newark or Detroit or Watts here. And those were no mistakes. The things that go wrong in this job are what make this the second-toughest job in America. But the things that go right are what made me still want it."

The first media mayor was a frequent guest on Johnny Carson's "Tonight" show. And New York was often the butt of Carson's jokes.

October 1969: Lindsay's vehement opposition to the war in Vietnam also galvanized supporters of the war.

"I'm Mayor Charles Evers, and I support John Lindsay for many reasons. Number 1, because he's a mayor, as I am, who knows the problems of this country and of these towns. Number 2, because John Lindsay has proven over the years that he's for all the people–the black, the white, the Puerto Ricans, and all of those who need to be cared for. We need a man who's got the guts and courage to stand up and fight for the rights of America...John Lindsay's a doer and a fighter, he's not a talker."

–Charles Evers,
Mayor of Fayetteville, Mississippi, elected in 1969, the first black mayor in the state since Reconstruction

From the Nixon White House Tapes

June 4, 1971

John Lindsay was briefly mentioned as a possible running mate for Richard Nixon in 1968, but ended up seconding the nomination of Spiro Agnew at the Republican convention. Lindsay, a maverick in Congress, alienated the Nixon White House as mayor with his vocal opposition to the war in Vietnam. Lindsay's aide, Sid Davidoff, even earned a slot on Nixon's original "enemies list" compiled in September 1971 by White House special counsel Charles Colson (who described Davidoff as "a first class S.O.B., wheeler-dealer, and suspected bagman").

This telephone conversation between the president and Attorney General John Mitchell was recorded on June 4, 1971, the day after a conference on killings of police officers. New York Police Commissioner Patrick V. Murphy had complained that he hadn't been invited. Here are excerpts:

PRESIDENT NIXON Well, he isn't considered, John, is he, to be a great chief up in New York?

MITCHELL No, no place.

NIXON Good heavens.

MITCHELL No place. He's just a lib politician. That's all he is.

NIXON That's right. And one of a…and one of [New York City Mayor John V.] Lindsay's…Of course isn't it—what do you think of this running battle between Rocky [New York Governor Nelson A. Rockefeller] and Lindsay? Is that just going to go on, or is that just part of the scenario up there?

MITCHELL No, it's going to go on. And as soon as that legislature is out of there, I understand that Nelson [Rockefeller] is interested in taking some definitive steps, such as taking over some of the functions possibly, or——"

NIXON Mm-hmm.

MITCHELL ——possibly putting a commission like the old Seabury investigation in there to see what he's doing wrong. I think he's going to stay with it.

NIXON Mm-hmm.

MITCHELL Because it's going to make him a lot more credible.

NIXON Yeah.

MITCHELL Rockefeller has been refusing to meet Lindsay's state aid request for the reason that Lindsay is not properly administering the city and expending his monies properly.

NIXON Mm-hmm.

MITCHELL So in order to make that credible after he gets this through the legislature, I think he'll take further steps along some lines to prove this to be true.

NIXON That's good, good. As a matter of fact, from all accounts, and of course I guess [Dr. Kenneth W.] Riland is a fellow that colors my comments [chuckles], but I think Lindsay has just been a lousy mayor.

MITCHELL Oh, he's terrible.

NIXON He's a demagogue, and a poor administrator, and a—

MITCHELL What he has done, Mr. President, that has caused him so much trouble, he has gone into this liberal community. There is not a single city employee that is working for him that is worth a damn, all the good ones have up and gone.

NIXON Yeah.

MITCHELL And he has got in all these do-gooders that are trying to run budgets and administer departments, and it just isn't working.

President Richard Nixon (right) and Attorney General John Mitchell were not fans of the mayor.

NIXON The good employees have left? The good, tough–

MITCHELL Yeah, they've all gone. And he had some good ones at the beginning. I helped him get some of them, but they've all packed out here a couple of years ago.

NIXON And what does he have, then, just a set of a bunch of...intellectuals, so-called, or what?

MITCHELL Well, yeah. Take his top man. This [Unclear] is a liberal Democrat who is one of the–

NIXON Oh, boy.

MITCHELL –complete do-gooders, and that's been siphoned on down all through his administrative organization and his advisory commissions and so forth, and they just don't have anybody there that knows anything about municipal government, or how to manage it, or have even a desire to do the right things. In other words, I'll take care of this welfare element and the liberal establishment and to hell with the city's finances and how you administer a city.

MITCHELL And John Lindsay is going to make a commencement address in New Hampshire this weekend.

MITCHELL Yeah.

NIXON That's nice.

MITCHELL He's got three speeches, I understand. He's having quite a bit of difficulty deciding which one he is going to use.

NIXON Yeah. He'll probably kick us on the war.

MITCHELL Undoubtedly that, but he's got one of them that is real hard, and then a middle-of-the-roader and a lighter one, and it may give some indication as to what he's got in mind.

NIXON Yeah. Mm-hmm.

MITCHELL He hasn't got very many places to go, but his people are still toying with it, looking around.

NIXON Mm-hmm.

Bella Abzug, a prominent figure in the anti-war movement, organized rallies on behalf of Lindsay's reelection. In 1970, she was elected to Congress from Manhattan's West Side. Here she speaks at a demonstration on the Capitol steps in May 1971.

Two elements of that ad are worth special attention. First, the only mistakes the mayor acknowledged were a) poor judgment as a meteorologist, and b) shared responsibility for the school strike. Second, it took by the count of one observer fully 33 takes for the mayor to deliver that minute of modified contrition. The second strategic decision was to get the undecided New York voters to focus on matters beyond the city's boundaries. By 1969, the Vietnam War was in its fifth year of full-blown combat, and it was being prosecuted not by a Democratic president, but by Richard M. Nixon, a political figure whom many liberal New Yorkers held in minimal high regard. Lindsay had been an outspoken critic of the war for years; and, as luck would have it, having lost the Republican primary, he had no bridges left to burn with his party. (Nor did the presence of a Republican, Nelson A. Rockefeller, in the governor's office hold any sway: the relationship between Lindsay and Rockefeller was somewhere between icy and toxic). So Lindsay made the Vietnam War, and the billions it was costing, a central theme of the campaign, arguing that resources needed for New York and other cities were being diverted into "massive military weaponry, and a war we should never have fought." Disillusioned liberals might be angry at the garbage in the streets and disruptive strikes and a dangerous city; but they were even more incensed by the quagmire that was Vietnam; and it was Lindsay's great good political fortune that neither of his challengers was inclined to raise that banner.

By contrast, Vietnam became an integral part of Lindsay's re-election message, so much so that the mayor's office plunged full-tilt into the October 15th "Vietnam Moratorium" day. There was a vigil on the steps at City Hall rally that morning (I was one of the speakers) and the flag atop City Hall was lowered to half-staff—a gesture that so infuriated a Queens City Councilman, Matthew Troy, that he climbed onto the roof and raised the flag himself. (There were even plans to lower the flag at Shea Stadium before the World Series game, but the Marine band let it be known that they would not play the national anthem unless the flag was at full staff. It was.)

Crucial Support

Lindsay's campaign also got a boost that had nothing to do with any tactical or strategic brilliance, thus proving once again the wisdom of Joe DiMaggio's observation that "I'd rather be lucky than good." Nothing made New Yorkers more unhappy about the state of their city than the rise in crime; and no figure in the city was more admired as a crime-fighter than Manhattan District Attorney Frank S. Hogan, who had held the job since 1941. Hogan was leaving Gracie Mansion one afternoon when a reporter asked him what he thought of Lindsay's crime record.

"He's the best mayor for law enforcement we've ever had," Hogan said, adding that he couldn't vouch for Lindsay's ability when it came to snow removal. As the columnist Jimmy Breslin wrote of that moment, "Anybody that thought he was the limp-wristed John Lindsay, who won't protect you from the blacks, the crimes, this and that, it shut everybody up."

Mayor Lindsay presents Israeli Prime Minister Golda Meir with a key to the city in September 1969. Her state visit and embrace of the mayor generated goodwill among Jewish voters.

Well, maybe it didn't shut everybody up. For large swaths of middle-class voters in Brooklyn, Queens, and Staten Island, Lindsay was too liberal, too elitist, too ineffectual, too distant, to gain their votes; and, to be blunt, this Manhattan W.A.S.P. was having a particularly tough go with many Catholic voters; his battles with the largely Irish and Italian police, firefighters, and sanitation workers, his identification with racial minorities at a time when black-white ethnic tensions were rising, all made those voters elusive targets at best. Jewish voters, on the other hand, were a target of opportunity. Despite the growth of black-Jewish tensions, symbolized by the fight over school decentralization and community control, Jews—many of those in the more affluent neighborhoods of Manhattan, Queens, and the Bronx—were sympathetic to Lindsay's efforts to preserve racial peace and potentially receptive to a liberal message on the War in Vietnam and on civil rights and liberties. Indeed, Jews had formed the key constituency behind the Reform Democratic movement that began on Manhattan's West Side and Greenwich Village in the late 1950s and flourished through the 1960s. For a wider cross-section of Jews, including those far less inclined toward a reflexive liberalism,

Re-Elect Mayor Lindsay

Campaign ads, 1969

• **JOHN V. LINDSAY**

For one afternoon this fall, a baseball team brought this town together like it's never been brought together before. At 3:17 on a cool afternoon a bunch of kids, named Koosman and Agee and Weis brought about the impossible dream. And all of a sudden New Yorkers forgot about their differences, and it showed me how close this city really can be. For the fact of the matter is that the Bay Ridge homeowner and the Forest Hills schoolteacher and the jobless teenager in Bedford-Stuyvesant are not natural enemies. And there are people trying to divide this city, and we can't let them do that. The man in this office, who occupies this chair, has to reach all of the people in this city and bring them together. And if anyone tries to tell you that it can't be done, remember the Mets. If they can do it, we can do it.

• **JOHN V. LINDSAY**

This is Mayor Lindsay. New Yorkers send three billion dollars every year to the war and another six billion into the war machine. That's more than our entire city budget, and you and I have to tell them to stop. Because we're not only sending them the money, we're sending them our sons.

FORMER DRUG ADDICT

I started off sniffing glue, and then I went on to the big stuff. I was writing bad checks, breaking into stores and apartments. Then I heard about Phoenix House. I went in, and I've been off drugs a few months now. Pretty soon I hope to go to high school.

VOICE OVER

Mayor Lindsay started the first comprehensive city program to fight drug addiction, because three years ago there was no place for a kid like this to go, except to jail.

• **[TRAIN] VOICE-OVER**

Every New Yorker should make this trip at least once before November 4—just across the river, to Newark. [Scenes of devastation] In order to see what's happened in New York since Mayor Lindsay took over, you have to see what hasn't happened.

VOICE-OVER

Commuters who use this town should help pay the cost of running it. Mayor Lindsay fought for and got a commuter tax. He figured if they paid their share, you wouldn't have to pay it for them.

Second Inaugural Address

December 31, 1969

After four years, Lindsay's second-term inaugural address was more sober than his first. Here are excerpts:

This is the last day of the decade and we have, all of us, been through much hope and sorrow. And if we have learned anything from these 10 turbulent, unsettling years, we have learned not to assume too much, because assumptions have a way of failing before the merciless assault of facts.

So it is best not to plan on promises and dreams. If we do all we hope to do in the next four years, there will still be too much of crime and poverty, too much of slums and pollution. There will still be a city that often seems to frustrate those who love it most.

But this does not mean that we must surrender to the pressures afflicting New York. It means only an understanding that we are all human, we are all fallible. The test for this administration and for this city is whether we have learned, both from mistakes and from the real and vital beginnings that have been made.

We have, I think, all learned that the lifeblood of New York is something more than the grandeur of its skyline and the richness of its commerce and art. The life of the mind has always flourished in New York, and, properly nourished, it always will.

But the future of our city is bound up inseparably in its neighborhoods, in the dozens of communities where the quality of life is set. For, together, these communities set the quality of life for us as a city.

Perhaps most important, we need the help of the men and women of our neighborhoods.

We intend to offer them the responsibility of charting the course of their communities. We ask their help. We offer our help.

And we will, despite all the setbacks and all of the obstacles, struggle against the vicious cycle of poverty and discrimination. To be condemned to suffering or powerlessness because you are the wrong color or speak the wrong language, or worship the wrong God, or come from the wrong country, is simply unjust.

These goals cannot be won if we are drained of our own resources, if the energy of this nation is thrown into the work of death abroad instead of the work of life at home, if the city continues as a stepchild of the state.

I know that we have been through a long—sometimes bitter—political campaign. And the differences among us will not disappear. Controversy is part of New York's vitality and none of us would have it any different. But we can at least recognize another loyalty beyond politics, and that is the loyalty to this city and to its future—our future.

With that kind of new loyalty, we can accomplish much together, not out of some magic affection for each other, but out of a simple honest recognition that it is the only way to achieve what each of us wants.

It is not easy to live with turmoil and difficulty. At times it is barely endurable. We remain New Yorkers not simply because we live here, but because we know the kind of city this can be at its best.

a vote for Lindsay was at best a possibility; one that required a rigorous courtship in the form of visits to synagogues and Jewish community centers of widely varying religiosity. (I have a vivid memory of visiting Brooklyn, along with a veritable *minyan* of highly secular, assimilated Jews, to participate in a Hasidic ceremony honoring one or another of the significant rabbinical figures, a ceremony whose length threatened to extend to the actual appearance of the Messiah). The courtship also required a heightened sensitivity to anything that might seem like a word or deed of disrespect. According to Vincent Cannato's *The Ungovernable City*, the mayor was walking through Fresh Meadows in Queens after that disastrous snowstorm when a woman called him "a wonderful man," prompting the mayor to respond, "And you're a wonderful woman, not like those fat Jewish broads up there," pointing to women in a nearby building who had criticized him. Cannato writes that three New York media outlets had or had heard a tape of this comment and chose not report it. (Lindsay aides say they have no knowledge of the remarks—the reporting of which would almost surely have doomed Lindsay's re-election chances). Of all the issues close to the heart of the middle-class Jewish voter outside Manhattan, none was dearer than the survival of the state of Israel (Lindsay, in Congress, had proved himself a staunch supporter). And this is where a visitor from far away played a pivotal role in Lindsay's re-election. But not just any visitor: Golda Meir, the Israeli prime minister, who was coming to the United States on a state visit. With a *haimisheh* demeanor that reminded countless Jews of their beloved grandmothers, with a background that included a childhood spent in the United States, Meir was as revered a figure as any in the Jewish community. So it was only natural that the City of New York threw a dinner in her honor. But her visit coincided with the holiday of Sukkot, a harvest holiday that features the building of an outdoor enclosed structure called a *sukkah*. What to do? Construct an enormous *sukkah* at the Brooklyn Museum and invite some 2,500 guests.

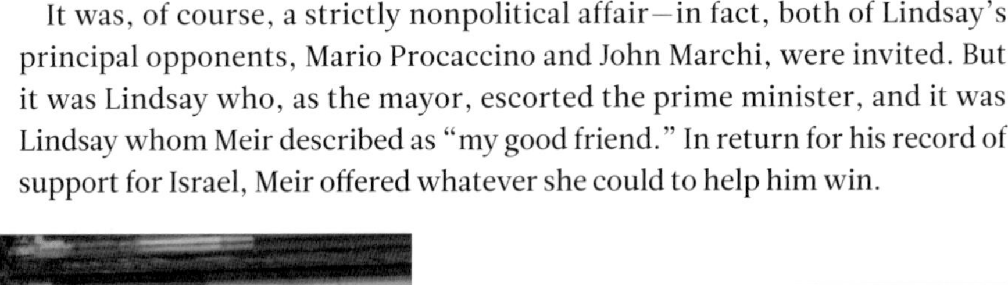

It was, of course, a strictly nonpolitical affair—in fact, both of Lindsay's principal opponents, Mario Procaccino and John Marchi, were invited. But it was Lindsay who, as the mayor, escorted the prime minister, and it was Lindsay whom Meir described as "my good friend." In return for his record of support for Israel, Meir offered whatever she could to help him win.

Assemblyman Charles B. Rangel of Harlem was among more than 40 Democratic elected officials who crossed party lines to endorse Lindsay in 1969. Rangel was elected to Congress the following year.

A Beatable Opponent

If Golda Meir was a huge asset to Lindsay's re-election—and she was—she was not as consequential an asset as Lindsay's Democratic opponent. In Mario Procaccino, for reasons good and not so good, Lindsay was blessed with the one opponent he was most likely to defeat. If Lindsay unwittingly won politically by losing the Republican

Reflection

JIMMY BRESLIN

In 1969, Norman Mailer ran for mayor in the Democratic primary. Jimmy Breslin, the columnist, was his running mate for City Council President. Their platform was to secede and establish New York City as the 51st state. Also, to sell more copies of their latest books. Their three-word campaign slogan—a vulgarization of "No More Bull"—was unprintable.

Breslin came in fifth in a field of six, with more than 75,000 votes, or 11 percent. He would later say he regretted having beaten the only black candidate in the race, Charles B. Rangel. But he was immediately remorseful for another reason. "I am mortified," he said, "to have taken part in a process that required bars to be closed," as they had to be on Election Day, Breslin wrote in *New York* magazine:

After Norman Mailer and I finished seven weeks of a mayoralty campaign adjudged unlikely, I still came away nervous and depressed by what I had seen of my city. I saw a sprawling, disjointed place which did not understand itself and was decaying physically and spiritually, decaying with these terrible little fires of rage flickering in the decay. Rage which, with heat and humidity and crowding and misery and misunderstanding and misused or misunderstood authority, could turn the city into a horror on any night soon. On top of the city was an almost unworkable form of government and a set of casually unknowing, unfeeling, uncaring men and institutions. The absence of communications in a city which is the communications center of the world is so bad that you are almost forced to believe the condition of the city is terminal.

"Lindsay?" we'd yell out in answer to a question. "Lindsay is too tall to be the mayor of New York."

That line was much more than a cute throwaway. It illustrated the great sense of the history of the city of New York which Norman and I brought to the campaign. For in the last 40 years of this city, John Lindsay is anywhere from five inches to almost an entire foot taller than anyone else who has held the office of mayor.

Our line about Lindsay being too tall was meant to say something important about his vulnerability in the election this fall. John Lindsay was a striking, handsome, cool, towering figure as he walked the streets of Harlem and was acclaimed across the country as future presidential material. But now, take Lindsay off the front pages of the *Washington Post* or *Los Angeles Times* or *Chicago Sun-Times* and put him on the Grand Concourse in the Bronx. Put him there with the schools closed and the garbage not picked up and the robberies and assaults way up. Put him there in a crowd of stumpy, bulging, balding Bronxites. Do this, and you do not have a towering figure anymore. You have a bony Protestant from Yale and Wall Street whose height makes him a conspicuous target for the stumpy little people who yell up at him, "Lindsay, make the robbers go away or you go away!"

"John Lindsay made us proud to be New Yorkers. He was and is the only Republican I have ever endorsed for public office."

–*Congressman* **Charles B. Rangel**

primary and shedding that party's baggage, he also won because more muscular potential rivals lost the Democratic primary. The governing assumption of Lindsay's campaign team was that it would be facing former Mayor Robert F. Wagner, who had declined to run in 1965, but who decided on a comeback when he saw how vulnerable Lindsay was. (In one of his primary ads, Wagner appeared at a Sanitation Department staging area and chuckled, "Mr. Mayor...I found your snowplows!") For his part, the mayor's advisers and strategists planned a fall campaign devoted to reminding New Yorkers about "the way it was" and how damaged a city Wagner had left the new mayor. (I wrote a brief comedic skit that was enacted during a preprimary fund-raiser. "I say Lindsay's done too much for whites!" said one. "I say he's done too much for the blacks!" "Confused?" said the announcer. "Then vote for Robert Wagner. He didn't do much for anybody." (Maybe you had to be there.) But on primary night, New York's Democrats delivered a shock. The comptroller, Mario Procaccino, loyal son of the Bronx Democratic organization, beat Wagner by some 31,000 votes, garnering a third of the total primary vote. Bronx Borough President Herman Badillo, the favorite of reform Democrats,finished 7,000 votes behind Wagner—and novelist Norman Mailer, running on a ticket with columnist Jimmy Breslin on a promise to make the city "the 51st state" won a surprising 41,000 votes. (The fractured result led to the passage of a municipal runoff election law—still in effect—providing that if no candidate for citywide office wins at least 40 percent of the primary vote, a second election must be held. Had that law been in effect in 1969, Wagner would almost surely have beaten Procaccino, giving Lindsay a significantly tougher opponent. And had Mailer not run, Badillo might have won the nomination and challenged Lindsay from the left.) The loss of the Republican line meant Lindsay would face two conservatives, Italians with drastically different demeanors—John Marchi was a tall, elegant, well-read, composed candidate; Procaccino was short, squat, bellicose, and rhetorically challenged—thus making it significantly easier for Lindsay to reach out to liberals. And with Procaccino, Democrats had given Lindsay a candidate with significant political and cultural liabilities. He was—there is no polite way to put this—a walking stereotype, who might have sprung full-blown from the old radio and TV show "Life With Luigi." Florid of face, expansive of gestures, sporting a thin mustache and suits that strained to fit his frame, Procaccino's physical appearance was only underlined by his use—or misuse—of language, which quickly became grist for the political mill." Did he really appear before a black audience and declare: "My heart is as black as yours!"? Did he really say of a one-time political ally: "Frank O'Connor grows on you—like cancer"? Did he

(From left) John Marchi, Mario Procaccino, and Lindsay debate on November 3, 1969. Again, Lindsay was lucky to be running against two more conservative candidates.

Probably no other mayor was featured on more magazine covers (left, *Life* May 24, 1968; right, *Time*, November 1, 1968.) He presided in the nation's media capital and was mentioned from Day One as a presidential prospect. Not all the publicity was positive.

really explain his public weeping by pointing out that Jesus Christ also wept? Indeed. And that mix was enough to make Procaccino the butt of mockery that not only came close to the line of cultural stereotyping—but sometimes leapt right over it. I remember listening to Woody Allen, at a Lindsay fund-raising gala, suggest that Procaccino was so confident of his election that he was having Gracie Mansion measured for linoleum (and offering up a silent prayer that Allen's zinger did not circulate too widely outside Manhattan). But Procaccino's weaknesses ran far beyond unfair stereotyping. In a city where liberalism was still a badge of honor—at least among a plurality of voters—Procaccino was simply too conservative for many Democrats to stomach. He was vociferously pro-Vietnam War, and equally militant in his opposition to affirmative action. (His most frequently broadcast primary TV commercial—maybe the only one—showed a burning building and declared that violence and lawlessness had to be stopped and that "discriminating quotas cannot be tolerated." In a city where Lindsay's visits to the most troubled streets of the ghettos were still regarded as acts of personal courage and peacekeeping, Procaccino's campaign was seen by many voters as a not-so-subtle promise to white ethnics that blacks would no longer have a receptive ear at City Hall. If that weren't enough to drive voters away, Procaccino was also emblematic of old-fashioned Democratic clubhouse politics that had fallen into disfavor with a range of middle- and upper-class New Yorkers. (In later years, revisionist analysts suggested that patronage and clubhouse politics had helped make for an efficiently run city. However that argument looks some decades out; it was definitely not the way machine politics appeared circa 1969. The consequence was a wholesale defection of Democrats to Lindsay, a defection made easier by the fact that he was not running as the nominee of the Republican

A Letter from David Halberstam

DAVID HALBERSTAM

May 21, 1970

Lindsay's short-lived presidential campaign ended with the Wisconsin primary in April 1972. He had switched parties the year before, but, after suffering his second decisive primary defeat (he finished fifth in Florida, then sixth in Wisconsin) he withdrew. A last-minute campaign slogan—"The Switch Is On"—apparently failed to persuade Wisconsin voters to switch to Lindsay.

This is an excerpt from a personal letter to the mayor dated May 21, 1970, from the author David Halberstam, who began "I do not know you personally, but most of what I know I like, and I know something about this country and what is happening, and most of what I know I don't like." He elaborated on why he believed President Nixon was vulnerable, particularly for his failure to end the war in Vietnam, and why Lindsay should abandon the Republican Party, become a Democrat and seek the presidency:

You are the most attractive figure in American politics today, certainly in a somewhat despairing nation, the most hopeful. In an age when television is for better or worse the vital political medium, you are now our most telegenic politician. You have talent, intelligence, good instincts, and a sense of the nation, and you bring together and symbolize most of what is best in this country. To be blunt, watching you on television in the last year, as opposed to watching you in 1964, I had a feeling that the baby fat was gone. For you not to run for president would be criminal, like a painter not painting, or a writer not writing.

You are already the chief national spokesman on what are essentially the Democratic issues: failed priorities, the military budget, dying cities, lack of generosity of sprit, racial failure.

I think you should run because it is the right thing, and that your chances of winning, and making a difference in our country are the best in the Democratic party; that for about 10 years now the American people have been responding better to events than their politicians, and I think they will respond to you.

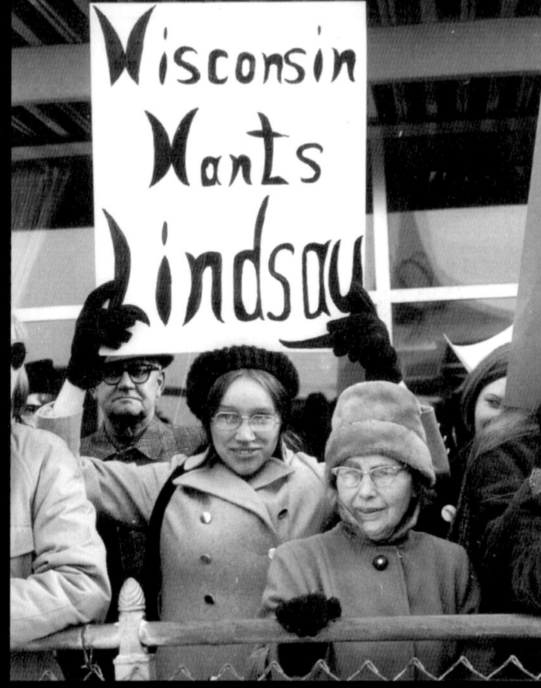

Not enough Wisconsonites wanted him, though. Lindsay left the 1972 presidential race after that state's Democratic primary.

Party. Manhattan reformers like Al Blumenthal and Manfred Ohrenstein, black leaders, including Congresswoman Shirley Chisholm of Brooklyn, and Badillo all endorsed Lindsay. Procaccino argued that this was yet more evidence of an unholy alliance between elitist affluent liberals and minorities; he called it "a Manhattan arrangement." He also provided an enduring addition to America's political vocabulary when he blasted his foes as "limousine liberals," a crew of the privileged who were insulated by their position from the real-life consequences of crime, quotas, and failing public schools. It would prove to be a powerful political message, helping to further fracture the one-time impregnable Democratic Party coalition—but Procaccino was simply an unconvincing messenger. All four of Procaccino's rivals for the Democratic nomination snubbed him in the general election (Wagner, after Election Day, admitted that he had voted for Lindsay).

Lindsay also benefited from the change of heart by many of the unions with which he had warred: District Council 37 of the municipal employees' union and the sanitation union endorsed the mayor, and the United Federation of Teachers remained neutral. Why? All three unions signed contracts with the city that could charitably be described as "generous."

A Boost from the Mets

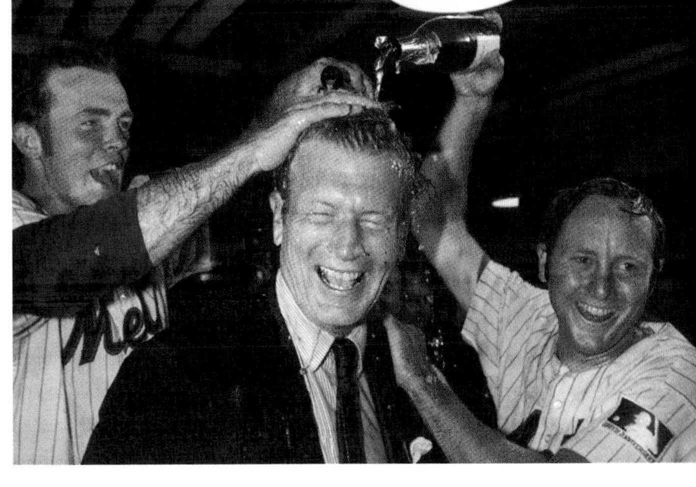

That championship season: Lindsay was doused with champagne in the clubhouse following the Mets' surprise 1969 World Series win at Shea Stadium. The victory created a euphoria that infused Lindsay's bid for reelection.

And then there were the Mets. The expansion team born after the flight of the Brooklyn Dodgers and New York Giants to California had begun play in 1962 and established a record of futility that still stands—120 losses in one season. Playing in Queens' Shea Stadium, they won the hearts of National League fans by not being the hated, more-or-less-perennial world champion Yankees—but they had staked a claim on last place for so long that their first manager, Casey Stengel, seemed to have summed up the Mets' entire existence when he asked: "Can't anybody here play this game?" But now, in 1969, in the season of the city's discontent, the Mets were winning; with a pitching staff that included Tom Seaver, Nolan Ryan, and Jerry Koosman, and under the managerial helm of the one-time Brooklyn Dodger first baseman Gil Hodges, they somehow, improbably won their division and were headed for the playoffs. And the Lindsay campaign was determined to join the mayor and the Mets at the hip. There was only one problem: John Lindsay knew nothing about baseball and cared less. The journalist Richard Reeves remembers Lindsay impatiently asking after every inning if it was time to leave; the concept of "extra innings" was completely alien to him. But when the Mets beat Atlanta and won the National League pennant, John Lindsay was at Shea. And then he was in the tumultuous clubhouse, where an aide, Shelley Brosoff, guided him

"I thought he did a lot of good things when he was Mayor of New York City. He tried to RUDY GIULIANIanize New York City government."

—Former mayor
Rudolph W. Giuliani

into the scrum, and more or less persuaded him to be part of the celebration The next morning, the front pages of New York papers featured the photo of two Mets players, Jerry Grote and Ron Gaspar, dousing the "delighted" mayor with champagne. And in that moment, the aristocratic, tennis-playing, sailboat-loving mayor became one of the guys. From that moment on, we never let up. The mayor was at La Guardia Airport to see the team off when it set out to confront the highly-favored Baltimore Orioles in the World Series. He even offered up a poem I composed, which went as follows:

> *Oh, the outlook isn't pretty for the Orioles today/ They may have won the pennant/ but the Mets are on the way/ And when Gil Hodges' supermen get through with Baltimore/ They'll be the champions of the world, they'll win it all in/ four....So good luck down in Baltimore, New Yorkers place your/ bets, We know we've got a winner—with our Amazin' Mets.*

(It is testament to my own superlative knowledge of the game that the poem listed just about every member of the team—but somehow left out Seaver, who won 25 games that year—and the Cy Young award as the best pitcher in the National League.)

When the Mets beat the Orioles—they won it in five, not four—the city exploded in joy. I took the subway back from Shea with some folks from out of town, and I learnedly explained how the city had gotten so used to World Series wins by the Yankees that it would never erupt in the kind of frenzy you would see in Pittsburgh or St. Louis. We then exited Grand Central to a sight right out of V-J Day—confetti, dancing in the streets, total, joyous gridlock. ("How long have you lived here, Jeff?" one of my companions asked.) It's impossible to measure the political impact of the ticker-tape parade or appearances at rallies and in TV commercials by the Mets. All we know is that the city got an enormous boost to its pride and happiness—and for a vulnerable incumbent mayor (even one who outspent his two rivals combined, by four-to-one), that's a pearl of great price.

Lindsay and his running mates in the 1969 election. Sanford Garelik (to left of Lindsay) won as City Council president, but Fioravante Perrotta lost for comptroller.

Lindsay won with 41.1 per cent of the vote, to Procaccino's 33.8 percent and Marchi's 22.1 percent. He carried some 85 percent of the black vote and 45 percent of the Jewish vote, and, most surprisingly, as much as 25 percent of the white Catholic vote. He even carried Queens.

It would be pleasant to recount a mayoral reelection that began the renaissance of a great city. But that was not the case. Two years later, he became a Democrat and then embarked on a short-lived run for the presidency. By 1973, he was a spent force, leaving after two terms to be succeeded by Abe Beame, 14 inches shorter and the mirror-opposite of Lindsay in other ways as well.

Lindsay for President

Campaign ads, 1972

In 1969, the Lindsay campaign again teamed up with political strategist David Garth to produce ads. Among them was the famous "mistakes" commercial in which Lindsay actually admitted to less than met the eye. Also, the message that the mayoralty was "the second toughest job in America" was a reminder to measure Lindsay against that standard and to suggest that his opponents fell short. Garth, an Adlai Stevenson Democrat, would go on to help elect Mayors Koch, Giuliani, and Bloomberg.

• **JOHN V. LINDSAY**

I spoke out against the war seven years ago because it was a senseless waste. On hot summer nights I walked the streets of New York, because we couldn't surrender to violence. I cut pollution by 30 percent because our lives were on the line. I won some, I lost some, and I learned. Maybe it's time we had a president who knows how to fight and what to fight for. That's why I want the job.

VOICE-OVER

Lindsay hasn't had the luxury of just talking about our problems. He's been too busy fighting them.

• **VOICE-OVER**

For six years, this man has had the second-toughest job in America, and when you're mayor of New York your problems don't happen quietly, they explode. And John Lindsay's had them all. Garbage strikes, City Hall protests—sometimes it seems like they never end.

But John Lindsay's learned how to fight like nobody else in this country. When there was a riot in the New York City prisons, and they took hostages, John Lindsay didn't send in troops, he walked in himself, and no prisoner or hostage was killed. And he's won some of the big ones: half-fare transportation for a million senior citizens, a free university education for every high school graduate, black and white, 4,000 more police to fight crime, cleaner air for the first time in a generation. And when cities all over America went up in flames, John Lindsay put his life on the line and walked the streets to hold New York together. After six years in the second- toughest job in America, John Lindsay is ready for the toughest.

"Remember Lindsay?"

SAM ROBERTS

The New York Times, September 26, 2009

It's the second toughest job in America. Again.

A new campaign commercial for Mayor Michael R. Bloomberg has unabashedly borrowed the slogan that helped get John V. Lindsay re-elected 40 years ago.

Unlike Mr. Bloomberg, Mr. Lindsay was the decided underdog, but won on the Liberal Party line after losing the Republican primary. He was regarded by some voters as an arrogant Manhattan-centric liberal out of touch with the middle class.

Mr. Lindsay's ubiquitous slogan, in effect, diminished his Democratic and Republican opponents by suggesting that they were unequal to the job. It was considered brilliant strategy, credited largely to Mr. Lindsay's campaign manager, Richard R. Aurelio, and his media consultant, David Garth.

"Rather than tear down the man we were running against, we built up the size of the job," said Tony Isidore, who was part of Mr. Lindsay's advertising team. Mr. Bloomberg's ad says: "This is New York City. It's a big, tough and complex place. To lead a city like this, we need a leader like this—independent." It concludes: "Running New York—it's the second toughest job in America."

A Bloomberg campaign spokeswoman said the ad was not inspired by the Lindsay slogan.

"We are flattered, because the campaign worked once, and they obviously feel he indeed has the credentials and record to live up to the size of the job," Mr. Isidore said.

At least one former Lindsay administration official, Warren Wechsler, was a bit taken aback. "Wouldn't it have been more accurate to say, 'Still the second toughest job in America after 40 years?' " he said.

November 30, 1970: The mayor opens a methadone clinic in Washington Heights in upper Manhattan, part of a project that expanded drug treatment.

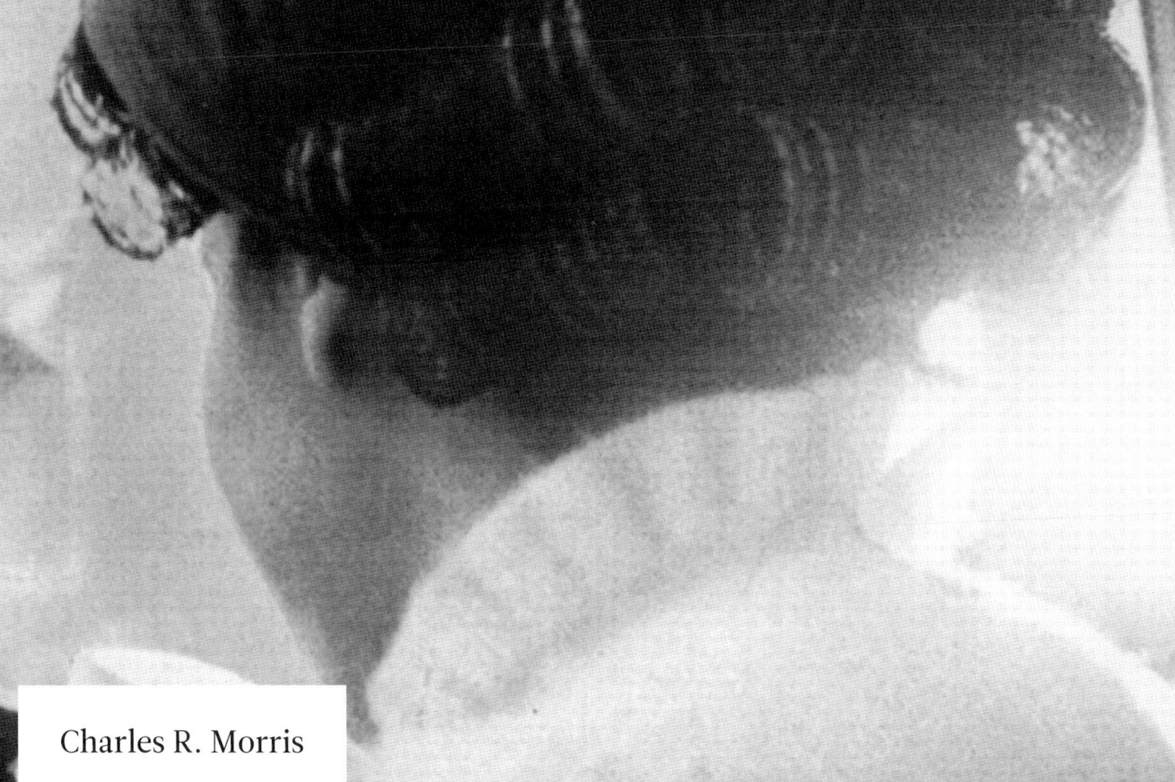

Charles R. Morris

New York's Great Society

When I was a teenager, in 1956, I stayed for a couple of weeks with the family of a distant uncle in Brooklyn. On one of my first nights there, I went to a party, came home late, and got confused by the look-alike brownstones. I went into two houses by mistake (tiptoeing gingerly out) before I found the right one. It seemed perfectly natural that none of the doors was locked. It had never crossed my mind to ask for a key.

CHARLES R. MORRIS, a lawyer and former banker, was New York City's assistant budget director and director of welfare and Medicaid programs from 1969 to 1973. He has written a dozen books, including *The Cost of Good Intentions: New York City and the Liberal Experiment, 1960–1975* and *The Trillion Dollar Meltdown*. His articles and reviews have appeared in *The Atlantic Monthly*, *The Harvard Business Review*, and many other publications.

Although Mayor Lindsay was a Republican and Senator Robert F. Kennedy a Democrat, they shared a commitment to civil rights and to improving the lot of the poor.

The 1950s was a golden age in New York City. The rich archipelago of Manhattan skyscrapers, headquarters for almost every big American company, was a reliable source of high-cholesterol taxes, but there was also a solid manufacturing base—printing, light electrical machinery, and consumer goods. Iron foundries lined the East River, and the port was among the world's busiest.

My uncle was an Irish Catholic, a union plumber, and his neighborhood was typical of New York's tightly drawn ethnic and religious map. Everybody knew each other. On sweltering nights, families slept on the fire escape or toted their blankets to the park. There was a lavish menu of services—the nickel subway and bus ride, decent schools, free tuition at city colleges for top high school graduates, even free hospitals.

The dearth of physical investment in the 1930s and 1940s had left serious infrastructure deficits, made all the worse by the postwar birth surge. By the 1950s, city-sponsored construction went into overdrive. Squalid old-law tenements were ripped down and replaced by public housing projects; critics gasped at their megalithic ugliness, but for working families they looked like spacious Edens. Hastily planned schools and sewers, police stations and firehouses, sanitation and highway garages, chased frantically after the residential sprawl in the boroughs outside Manhattan. New parks and trains and buses softened some of the city's sharper edges.

While Robert Moses played the heroic figure, much of the credit belonged to Robert F. Wagner, whose second term as mayor (1958–1961) was among the city's more distinguished. His signal achievements were to engineer the massive expansion of physical plant without giving the city away to unions and contractors, and to expand the city work force and to embrace municipal unionism without losing control of the budget. His biggest mistake was to run for a third term.

And Then It Changed

There was no diminution of Wagner's political skills in his third term; his problem was that the city shifted away beneath him. Blue-collar workers did very well in the 1950s, and as their incomes rose, they were drawn to the greater space and apparent freedom of the suburbs. Rural migrants from the Southern black belt and Puerto Rico poured in to take their place. "Blockbusting" realtors exploited the fears of left-behind whites, and the racial/economic demography of large swaths of the city seemed to flip overnight.

The demographic transition coincided with a national rise in social militancy, inspired by the epochal civil rights confrontations in the South. Northern blacks and Puerto Ricans, city unions and welfare clients, even college students, emulated tactics that had worked so dramatically in Selma and Birmingham. In New York, welfare-rights groups mounted noisy challenges to the city's system. For the first time, unions succeeded in organizing large blocs of citywide workers, like clerks, and gained the power to shut down the government. There was a serious riot in Harlem in 1964.

Wagner's reflexive strategy was to temporize: while he greatly increased social spending, his instinct was to muffle controversies. But his gray blandness and imperturbability seemed to infuriate radicals, even as the new spending destabilized the city budget. In short, he looked rather like Eisenhower, when the times appeared to call for a man on a white horse.

"From the outset, it was Lindsay's presence and his star-like quality that helped bring attention to the press and state leaders that cities were in dire need.…Though attention from the press at the meetings generally gravitated to him, never once did he plead solely for the City of New York. He included all of us, and our cities. Revenue-sharing was ultimately approved by the State of New York, due in large part to Lindsay's personal appeal."

–Alfred DelBello *was mayor of Yonkers when he joined with Lindsay and the chief executives of New York's four other biggest cities to form the big-six mayors' coalition. He later became lieutenant governor*

Enter Lindsay

John Vliet Lindsay came to office with no experience in the gritty politics of running a city. His Congressional record was superb, but his career was in a blind alley. That left the mayoralty.

Some four decades later, the two Lindsay mayoralties are still controversial. They are a prime exhibit for the overreaching of the 1960s "War on Poverty" and "Great Society" that helped drive national politics toward the antigovernment conservatism of Ronald Reagan. But they were also years of substantial achievements in applying modern management technology to city government. And then, of course, there is the fiscal crisis that exploded two years after Lindsay left office (and which is not considered in this essay). Finally, and perhaps surprisingly, a comparative summary of national major-city spending and social trends during the Lindsay years suggests that New York City was not nearly the special case that its advocates and detractors like to believe.

In his accession to the mayoralty, Lindsay self-consciously positioned himself as a countercultural force—implicitly in opposition to the traditional civil service, the city union leadership—especially in the police force—and the city's white middle class—especially in the outer boroughs. One way or the other, the most neuralgic issues tended to center around race.

Early in his first term, Lindsay accepted an appointment as vice chairman of the Kerner Commission, which was created to draft a national response to the wave of urban riots that swept the country in the last half of the decade. He was a forceful advocate for the strong positions taken in the final report: "[T]he Negro can never forget…that white society is deeply implicated in the ghetto. White institutions created it, white institutions maintain it, and white society condones it.…[Solutions] will require unprecedented levels

"John Lindsay didn't cause the snowstorm, but he sent a message, I'm sure inadvertent, to the people who lived outside of the center city, to the middle class in Queens and Brooklyn and the Bronx, where there were also problems—although it may have been worse in Queens, because it's more rural, or was—that they didn't matter as much. They didn't matter, you know? They just didn't matter."

—Joyce Purnick, *former New York Times reporter and author of* Mike Bloomberg: Money, Power, Politics

of funding and performance, but…there can be no higher priority for national action and no higher claim on the nation's conscience."

However true that may have been, it rankled white city voters, many of whom had only precarious perches in the middle class, and who were terrified that black street crime, school disruption, littered streets and parks, and wrecked housing stock were putting their hard-won gains at risk. The Police and Fire Departments were badly strained—an epidemic of false alarms in poor neighborhoods was driving firefighters to distraction—while pressure for more welfare, housing support, special education, and antiriot task forces was pushing taxes sharply upward.

During Lindsay's first years as mayor, the social-program pressures were concentrated on the welfare system and the new antipoverty programs. Welfare administration had become a focus of militant community organizers in the last year of the Wagner administration. Mobilization for Youth and Harlem's Haryou-Act (one of the models for the national anti-poverty program) played headline roles.

Two radical New York professors, Richard Cloward and Frances Fox Piven, co-founded the National Welfare Rights Organization shortly after Lindsay took office. Their avowed strategy, set out in a famous *Nation* article, was to force welfare federalization by bankrupting local operations.

Lindsay's first welfare commissioner, Mitchell Ginsberg, was sympathetic to such views, as were many federal welfare and antipoverty officials. Ginsberg stressed to caseworkers that welfare-eligible New Yorkers *not* receiving assistance outnumbered the people on the welfare rolls. Although welfare caseloads started rising rapidly during Wagner's last years in office, the system was still notably stingy, and caseloads had clearly not kept pace with the influx of poor blacks and Puerto Ricans. Case-rejection rates were high, and applications were discouraged by onerous and intrusive eligibility reviews. Caseworkers also had substantial authority in setting case budgets. The welfare rights organizations' strategy was to use legal appeals and protest demonstrations to force higher acceptance rates and better budgets.

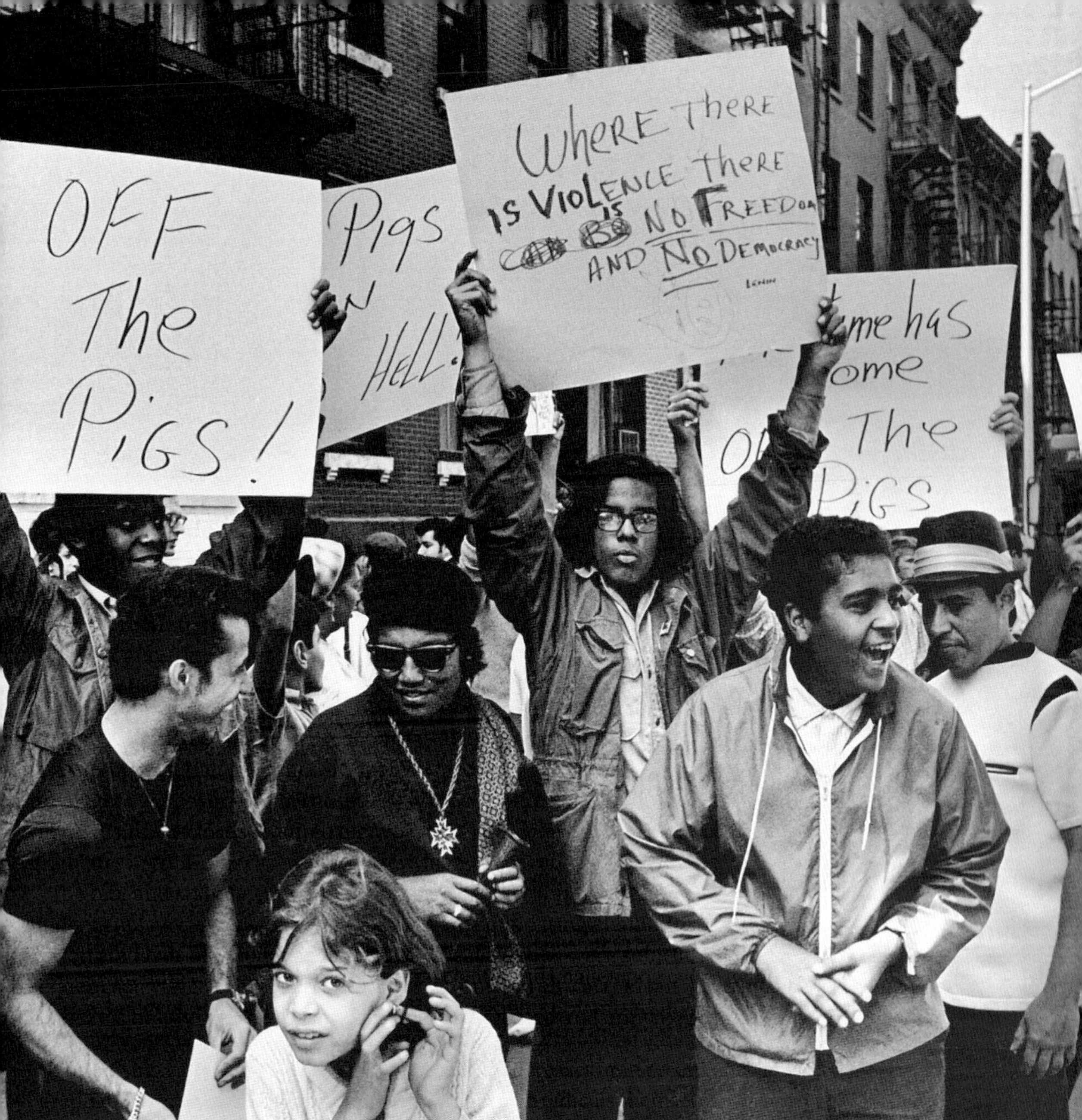
OFF The Pigs!
Pigs
Hell!
Where there is Violence there is No Freedo
And No Democracy
The Pigs

Social unrest was common in the fall of 1969. Here, New Yorkers stage a protest in front of P.S. 15 in Manhattan.

Within a year or two, welfare rights organizers had brought the system to its knees, flooding the centers with potential clients and challenging every detail of case budgets. Half of all the National Welfare Rights Organization's national organizers were working in the city, with caseworkers often right alongside them. Rising caseloads required big welfare staff increases, and recent college graduates recruited as caseworkers were likely to be radicals themselves.

The city and state finessed the bottlenecks by scrapping the detailed case budgets in favor of mostly flat grants, and by eliminating eligibility investigations in favor of income declarations. (Declarations were subject to subsequent selective verifications, which were only rarely carried out.) During Lindsay's first term, the caseload more than doubled and annual spending

From "A Strategy to End Poverty"

RICHARD A. CLOWARD AND FRANCES FOX PIVEN

The Nation, May 2, 1966

Professors Richard Cloward and Frances Fox Piven co-founded the National Welfare Rights Organization shortly after Lindsay took office. Their Strategy, outlined in this article excerpted from *The Nation*, was to get everyone who was eligible to sign up for benefits, thereby bankrupting local operations and forcing federalization of welfare.

How can the poor be organized to press for relief from poverty? How can a broad-based movement be developed and the current disarray of activist forces be halted? It is our purpose to advance a strategy which affords the basis for a convergence of civil rights organizations, militant antipoverty groups and the poor. If this strategy were implemented, a political crisis would result that could lead to legislation for a guaranteed annual income and thus an end to poverty.

The strategy is based on the fact that a vast discrepancy exists between the benefits to which people are entitled under public welfare programs and the sums which they actually receive. This gulf is not recognized in a society that is wholly and self-righteously oriented toward getting people OFF the welfare rolls. It is widely known, for example, that nearly eight million persons (half of them white) do subsist on welfare, but it is not generally known that for every person on the rolls at least one more probably meets existing criteria of eligibility.

The discrepancy is not an accident stemming from bureaucratic inefficiency; rather, it is an integral feature of the welfare system which, if challenged, would precipitate a profound financial and political crisis. The force for that challenge, and the strategy we propose, is a massive drive to recruit the poor ONTO the welfare rolls.

A series of welfare drives in large cities would, we believe, impel action on a new federal program to distribute income, eliminating the present public welfare system and alleviating the abject poverty which it perpetrates. Widespread campaigns to register the eligible poor for welfare aid, and to help existing recipients obtain their full benefits, would produce bureaucratic disruption in welfare agencies and fiscal disruption in local and state governments. These disruptions would generate severe political strains and deepen existing divisions among elements in the big-city Democratic coalition: the remaining white middle class, the white working-class ethnic groups and the growing minority poor. To avoid a further weakening of that historic coalition, a national Democratic administration would be constrained to advance a federal solution to poverty that would override local welfare failures, local class and racial conflicts and local revenue dilemmas. By the internal disruption of local bureaucratic practices, by the furor over public welfare poverty and by the collapse of current financing arrangements, powerful forces can be generated for major economic reforms at the national level.

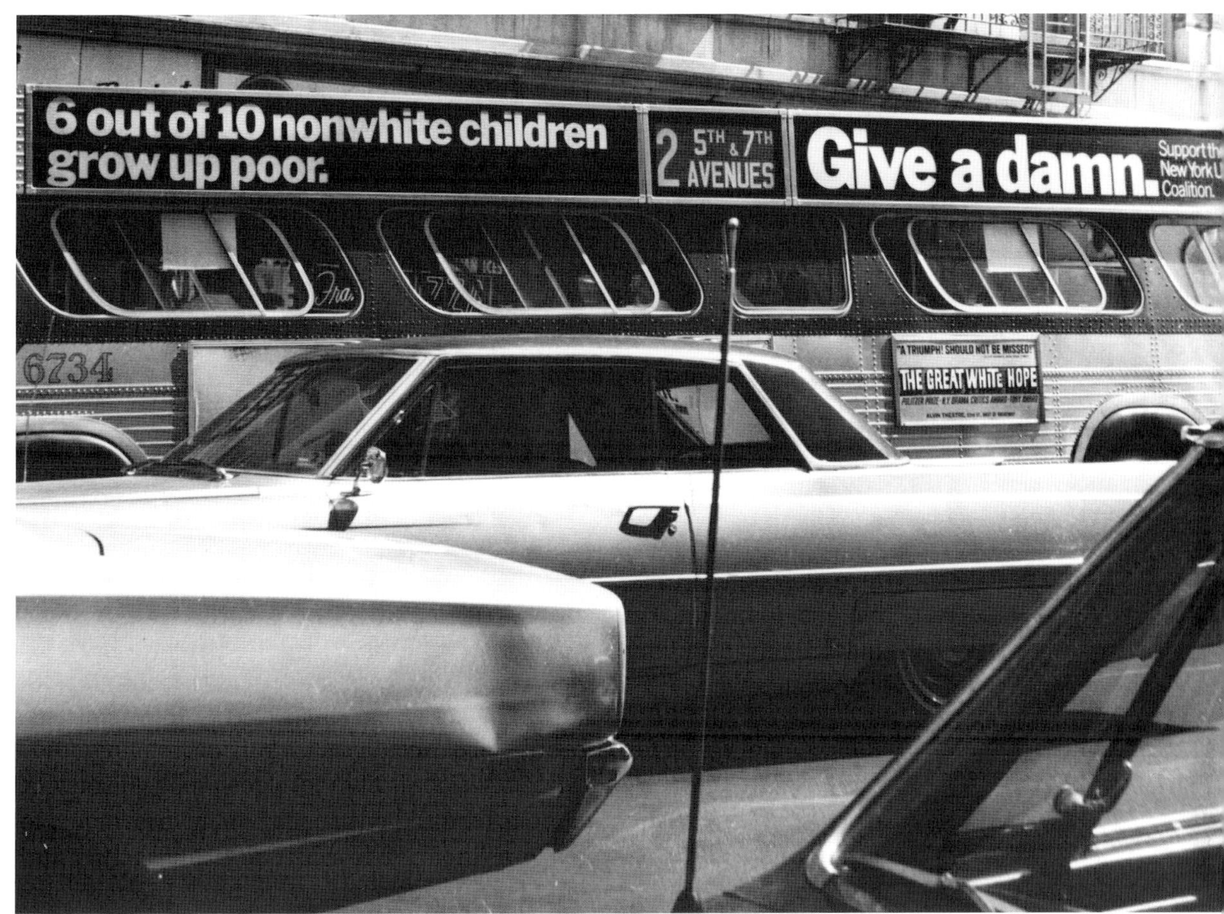
6 out of 10 nonwhite children grow up poor.
2 5TH & 7TH AVENUES
Give a damn.
6734
"A TRIUMPH! SHOULD NOT BE MISSED!"
THE GREAT WHITE HOPE

Getting people to care: the Urban Coalition raised millions of dollars from corporations for summer youth programs and appealed to the public with its award-winning "Give a Damn" campaign in 1968.

increased from $400 million to $1 billion. Medicaid spending, which was tied to welfare eligibility, and cost roughly the same, rose right alongside. Total welfare and social-service spending rose from 20 percent to 30 percent of the city budget, with about a third of it financed from the city tax base.

Compared to welfare, the official city antipoverty efforts had minimal budget impact—it was almost all federal money, not the city's—and delivered far fewer resources to the poor. But they were far noisier and even more controversial. Like the national initiative, the city's programs were an impossible jumble—an olio of space-age systems engineering, Alinsky-style radical community organizing (Chicago-born Saul Alinsky spent nearly four decades galvanizing poor people for radical social causes), and Fanon-rooted theories of empowerment and alienation (Frantz Fanon, born in Martinique, was an influential thinker on issues of decolonization and the psychopathology of colonization). Lindsay's early antipoverty appointees were intelligent and well-intentioned. But the programs were a mess—victims of flamboyant community politics, the scrambling after sudden showers of federal money, sheer administrative snarl, and their own incoherence.

Some programs were undoubtedly helpful—Head Start and summer jobs for poor kids among others—but in another era they would have been implemented without the wearying theatrics. On the bright side, locally financed antipoverty spending under Lindsay was actually lower than under Wagner.

Days of rage: protesters and police clash at the 1968 Democratic National Convention in Chicago.

The Police

The more important theater for racial politics was the administration's relations with the police. Jay Kriegel, one of the mayor's closest aides, said that, "In a real sense, the 1965 campaign was run against the police force." Besides the force's being "old and tired," Kriegel went on, "institutionalized racism *was* an important issue—the problem of brutality and the lack of minorities on the force."

Creating a civilian review board for complaints about police officers was one of Lindsay's first legislative initiatives, and when the City Council refused to do so, his police commissioner instituted it. The police union responded with a "Don't Handcuff the Police" referendum for the following November's election. The union referendum won by a crushing two-to-one margin. "We were simply mauled," said Kriegel. "It was one of the worst political defeats we could have taken. It was early, it was racial, and it was overwhelming."

The most visible stage for working through administration-police relations was the management of civil disorder, which is justly remembered as one of the most important achievements of the Lindsay era.

For much of the 1960s, riots in black urban neighborhoods were endemic, affecting almost every medium-sized American city. While the Kerner Commission rationalized urban riots as civil rights protests, cynics, and future neo-conservatives, saw them as rioting "for fun and profit." Liberal intellectuals also tended to link black inner-city rioting with student protests against the war in Vietnam, and they made media stars of groups like the radical, and murderous, Black Panthers.

The Lindsay response emerged spontaneously. The first disturbance was in East New York in 1966, a confrontation between a group of white provocateurs (SPONGE, the Society for Preventing Niggers from Getting Everything) and local blacks, during which a black child was killed by a sniper. The instinctive response from Lindsay's young aides—Kriegel, Barry Gottehrer, and Sid Davidoff—was to rush to the scene, where the police responded with a strong presence. But instead of breaking up the confrontation with force, they mediated a mutual stand-down. The Lindsay administration's success in East New York was transformed into a conscious and controversial strategy: restraint in the use of force. A core of City Hall assistants under Gottehrer built lines of communication throughout combustible neighborhoods—along the way working with a number of underworld figures, both black and white.

Early warnings of trouble often allowed "cool-down" interventions—like buses to take black youths to the beach—but the critical change was in police strategy. New York was probably the first city to drop the established "tactical-patrol" approach to civil disturbance—coming "dripping to your ankles with metal to overawe people," one police veteran put it. (Even smaller cities were buying half-tracks and machine guns in anticipation of riots.) Instead, the area was flooded with blue uniforms, with a strong on-site command presence. The emphasis was first to isolate the trouble spot, keep disturbances from spreading, then to fragment and arrest the incendiaries. That was hard for cops to swallow, for it often required leaving looters alone at first until a tactical area was secured.

But on any fair judgment, the strategy mostly worked. New York City had multiple dangerous flare-ups, but they never degenerated into the all-out police-ghetto warfare, with the shocking death tolls, that were seen in Los Angeles, Detroit, and Newark.

Lindsay's success in calming New York drew wide attention, especially by contrast with the police-against-the-radicals free-for-all during the 1968 Chicago Democratic convention. For a brief period, Lindsay was "America's Mayor," and other mayors began consciously to pattern their policies after his. Over the next decade or so, the New York police tactics became standard practice in almost all major cities.

There were costs. Relations between the police and City Hall were sullen for much of the Lindsay tenure, and they became poisonous when four cops were killed in isolated attacks during 1968. The police unleashed their frustration on the radical students who took over Columbia University that same year. The college had dithered for days before allowing the police on campus. The students had time to build barricades, and then went to extremes to provoke the police. When the police were finally ordered to clear the buildings, a virtual police riot ensued.

A more measurable cost was the very large collective bargaining settlements the police union extracted to assuage the rank-and-file's sense of grievance. Those agreements naturally flowed over into the contracts for firefighters and sanitation workers, who were nearly as disaffected. Edward Kiernan, the police union leader, said that the uniformed services did very well financially under Lindsay, "but as far as the men were concerned, it made no difference at all. In fact, at one negotiating session, the mayor asked me if it would help sell the contract if he laid in the street and had his picture taken with my foot on his neck. I said, 'Hell no. The men would scalp me for not killing you.'"

The End of Race-Driven Politics

Lindsay's first-term approach to improving the lot of New York's blacks and other minorities was filtered through a civil rights lens. Through that lens, blacks in New York were understood as an oppressed people, who needed to take control of their own neighborhoods and destinies. The changes required might be traumatic or even revolutionary, but a mayor's job was to prod and to facilitate the process as best he could. It was a perspective that contained much truth, and was widely held by the intellectual elite.

But it was not an adequate premise for governing. It perpetuated the confusion between problems of class and problems of discrimination; it ignored the progress of the black middle class, and their need for peaceful schools, decent neighborhoods, and protection from black crime; and it disenfranchised the respectable black majority in favor of leaders who specialized in outrageous display. At its worst, it was self-righteous and polarizing—as in a 1967 draft of a City Planning Commission master plan that blamed black problems on "the callous disinterest of the white middle class."

That simplistic civil rights paradigm confronted bitter reality during the 1968 school strike, and reality won. School decentralization had been a New York reform priority for years, favored by administrators and the union alike, as a way around the impossible bureaucratic clog at central headquarters. The state legislature agreed to a decentralization push in 1967—it would improve the state aid formula for the city schools—but asked for a detailed plan. Lindsay convened a planning panel chaired by McGeorge Bundy, president of the Ford Foundation, that had no teacher or union representatives.

The choice of Bundy to head the panel, as Lindsay surely knew, tilted the outcome away from a traditional understanding of administrative decentralization and toward "community control." The Bundy plan sailed through the mayor's office and the State Board of Regents with only minor changes. The teachers' union, the United Federation of Teachers, was largely excluded from the process, although decentralization arguably put into jeopardy hard-won appointment, seniority, and transfer rights.

In the meantime, the teachers' union had been working with local parent groups on decentralization experiments. (The union and its leadership, most particularly its president, Albert Shanker, had a long and honorable history in the civil rights struggle.) One of the experiments was in Ocean Hill-Brownsville, a drearily impoverished Brooklyn neighborhood. The Ford Foundation was interested in financing decentralization experiments, and with the union's assistance, a grant was funneled to the parents' group through the central Board of Education.

Without waiting for guidance from the central board, the Ocean-Hill Brownsville group held an election for a district board and hired an administrator, a black school-system veteran, Rhody McCoy. Teachers went on strike throughout the city over pay and classroom conditions at the beginning of the 1967–68 school year—a strike that Shanker blamed on Lindsay's tin ear for bargaining nuance. McCoy tried to keep his schools open with nonunion substitutes, and the union broke off its relations with the district. The following spring, McCoy summarily dismissed 19 teachers and principals. The district's 350 union teachers walked off the job, McCoy suspended them all, and the school year closed with the impasse unresolved.

The state Legislature decided to postpone decentralization for another year, and charged the school board to come up with a revised plan. The Legislature also expanded the Board of Education by seven new mayoral appointments, assuring City Hall of a majority to drive the planning process. As if to quell any doubts on the nature of the changes afoot, six of Lindsay's seven new members were prominently associated with the civil rights and antipoverty movements.

The union took a strike vote in late summer to force the Board of Education to deal with its decentralization concerns, and to override McCoy's springtime

"I think that Lindsay was dealt a very bad hand. His administration—administrations, really, but certainly the first—was crisis-driven. There's no question there was one crisis after another. He didn't cause those crises, but he didn't deal with them as I think—as many of us think—he should have, and he has to take responsibility for that. I think the transit strike is one example.... I cannot imagine a strong, willful mayor allowing a school strike to go on for almost three months. I cannot imagine that happening today."

–Joyce Purnick,
former New York Times *reporter and author of* Mike Bloomberg: Money, Power, Politics

Lindsay with his consumer affairs commissioner, Bess Myerson, at a legislative hearing in December 1969. Lindsay created the nation's first Consumer Affairs Department.

dismissals, which were illegal. The board quickly capitulated, although the schools opened late for the second straight year.

When the suspended teachers showed up for work, McCoy instructed them to report to an auditorium where they were terrorized—surrounded by shouting militants, some apparently armed. Shanker called another strike.

The second strike lasted through September, until the Board of Education promised that the fired teachers would be returned to work, and monitors would be on hand to ensure that McCoy and his local board would comply with the understandings. McCoy promptly violated the agreement, and Shanker called another strike.

The third strike shut down the entire system through November, and suffused the city with hatred—hatred of all against all. Blacks against teachers and Jews. Strikers against strikebreakers. Almost everybody against the Board of Education and especially against Lindsay, who had looked wobbly throughout the crisis.

When the strike finally ended, it was more from exhaustion than from any bargaining breakthroughs. The teachers returned to their schools—in Ocean Hill-Brownsville, with the assistance of 1,000 police officers. Decentralization was dead, as were romantic notions of "community control."

Thoroughly quashed as well was any illusion that the governance of a major city could be subordinated to a civil rights and antipoverty agenda. Running a city, after all, is mostly a dull business—picking up garbage, fixing sewers, inspecting buildings, collecting taxes, operating schools, maintaining a peaceful space for citizens to carry on their private lives—an altogether poor environment for sweeping social experiments. Judging by his 1969 campaign for re-election, and his second term, Lindsay thoroughly internalized that lesson.

Back to Basics

Early in his first administration, Lindsay and his budget director, Frederick O'R. Hayes, instituted a citywide "Operations Improvement" management program jointly spearheaded by City Hall and the budget bureau. The program's staff were new employees, most of them young, many from graduate schools of business, and heavily supported by business consultants, especially from McKinsey & Co. Andrew Kerr, a former Booz Allen consultant, and later the administrator of the housing and development agency, ran the inside implementation teams.

The initiatives generally got off to a rocky start. The agencies had strong antibodies against outsiders, and the "project management staff" as it was called, was sometimes arrogant and callow. New York City, in fact, had for many years been known for its outstanding management systems. But they were paper-based, and they were breaking down under the double whammy of heavy new demands and the declining quality of entry-level clerical workers. The elegant Fire Department dispatching system was overwhelmed by the sudden flood of false alarms and real fires, while the huge upsurge of welfare clients and disruptions in t he welfare centers had left the system in near-chaos.

By the end of Lindsay's first term, however, the project-management staff had developed a deep knowledge base of the city's internal operations, and the best of them had been absorbed into the agencies to work as change agents from within. When Edward K. Hamilton, Hayes's successor at the budget bureau, moved over to City Hall as deputy mayor, he elevated the program's public profile by renaming it "productivity" and establishing detailed objectives for each agency. Tracking systems issued well-publicized reports on successes and failures. The concept caught on around the country. The federal government created a National Commission on Productivity, and in 1973 there was a national productivity conference for state and local governments at which the New York City programs were a prime exhibit.

Some of most striking successes were in the Sanitation Department, long one of the least malleable of city agencies. Jerome Kretchmer and Herbert Elish applied standard industrial processes to the maintenance and deployment of sanitation trucks—it took years of slogging work—and dramatically improved equipment availability and collection results. Truck downtime was reduced from 38 percent to less than 10 percent, the equivalent of 450 more trucks on the street each day. By 1973, the number of missed collections dropped to virtually zero. Improved street-sweeper maintenance doubled effective sweeping miles. Hundreds of workers were freed to improve business-district cleanliness or for cleanup blitzes in poorer neighborhoods.

March 26, 1967: Thousands gather for the first "be-in" at Central Park's Great Lawn, part protest against racism and war, part happening.

"At a time when conventional wisdom said that cities were dying, he injected a spirit of life and hope into urban America."

–Vernon E. Jordan Jr. *was president of the National Urban League from 1971 to 1981*

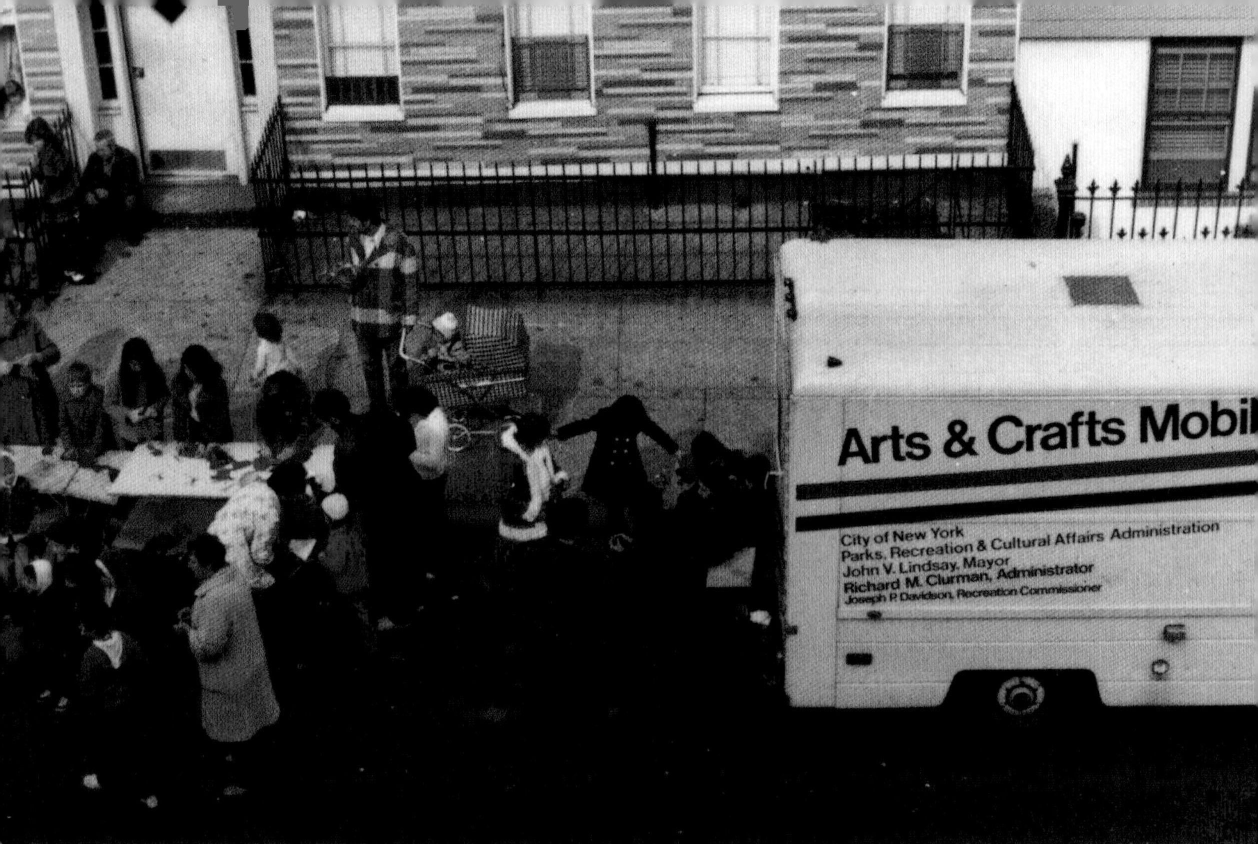

Bringing culture to the crowd in 1973: This mobile arts and crafts center was part of the Lindsay administration's outreach to youngsters through privately funded summer programs.

"Operation Scorecard" was a new system for measuring and reporting street cleanliness; it was housed in an outside foundation to produce objective reports on the department's progress. It is still in effect 36 years later.

One constant was steady success in upgrading the city's use of modern computers. At the Health Department, long one of the least responsive of agencies, beginning in Lindsay's first term Gordon Chase used computerized tracking and management systems to mount a citywide lead paint inspection and follow-up program that cut excessive childhood lead levels by two-thirds within just a few years. Weekly tracking of individual inspectors' performance increased each one's apartment inspections from an average of one a week to four a day. The same techniques were applied to rat control, birth-certificate issuance, and gearing up a methadone-maintenance program.

Similar methods greatly improved issuing annual rent notices from the housing department, while computer tracking of scheduled capital improvements, from new schools to highway repair, notably accelerated delivery schedules. And at the welfare department, a Babel of dozens of computer systems and languages was painfully re-engineered into a modern unified processing environment. One early dividend was that case closings could be managed centrally; as a huge backlog was worked off, welfare rolls actually dropped. Over the next decade, as virtually all transactional work was removed from the centers, error rates and client traffic dropped substantially.

The outstanding management achievement, however, may have been at the Police Department. The commissioner for most of Lindsay's second term was Patrick V. Murphy, a second-generation New York police officer. Murphy had risen through the ranks to deputy commissioner before taking commissioner jobs in Syracuse, N.Y. and Washington. He went hammer-and-tong after the force's long-ingrained complacency and corruption, which had been left undisturbed during the focus on civil disorders. Murphy engineered a virtually complete turnover in the department's senior management ranks, redistributed precincts and manpower to match demand, and attacked lackadaisical precinct command with tight reporting and accountability systems. He also pioneered a number of new policing approaches, like focusing on high-crime areas and community policing, that were emulated and enhanced by subsequent New York administrations, and by most other major cities. Murphy later became a senior federal law enforcement administrator and head of the Police Foundation. On his retirement, the F.B.I. declared that his "long-range impact on American policing nationally [may be]...as significant as that of J. Edgar Hoover."

Lindsay's nose-to-the-grindstone performance at the outset of his second term earned him much goodwill, but he threw it away with a dreadfully misadvised presidential run in 1972. Humiliated in the early primaries, he returned, repentant again, and quietly served out the remainder of his term.

Finally, everything broke right. Wall Street did well during his second term and tax collections rose, while national wage and price controls finally put a lid on bargaining agreements. City finances improved, and the city's bond ratings were upgraded. Banks and rating agencies were impressed by the new computer centers and the results from the management improvements. Even Comptroller Abraham D. Beame said "Lindsay could go anywhere if he'd do the kind of job he's been doing for the last eight months." John Lindsay could go out on a high note.

How Different Was New York?

New Yorkers take perverse pride in the outsized scale of their city—its great skyscrapers, museums, and parks, of course, but also in its unruliness, its unmanageability, its financial disasters. New York City is unique, too, in the breadth of its government's responsibilities. Nowhere else were police, sanitation, schools, welfare, Medicaid, a college system, a full-blown hospital chain, all operated or financed out of City Hall. The city also bears special costs for the hordes of tourists, the public events, and the parades that come with the role of cultural and financial capital.

The scale of the city's undertakings complicates financial comparisons with other cities. The federal government, however, does track urban spending by "common municipal functions"—things almost all cities provide, like police and fire collection, sanitation services and parks—which permit suggestive comparisons. The data confirm that among the ranks of the biggest cities, New York has always been one of the bigger spenders, and, by the standards of previous administrations, there was nothing remarkable in the spending of the Lindsay years.

"I think he ducked. I think he was genuinely confused. I think he idealistically wanted community control to work. I think he saw a lot of justice in blacks' claims that they should control more of the resources. But he wound up indulging people who weren't ready to do it. There's a famous quote from Thucydides, the Greek historian. He says, 'You shouldn't put brilliant and privileged men in charge of public affairs, because they're prone to think that everyone else is brilliant and privileged too.'"

–**Jim Sleeper**, *a lecturer at Yale and the author of* The Closest of Strangers: Liberalism and the Politics of Race in New York,

Measured by per capita spending for all common functions, New York ranked second among the biggest cities when Lindsay took office, and third when he left. The growth rate in spending was in the middle of the pack. Average salaries in common functions slipped from second to fifth, and the spending growth rate was only fifth highest. New York City employees, indeed, fared less-well financially than their peers in other cities when local cost of living is taken into account. Pension benefits were high in New York City, but the comparisons suggest again that employees lost ground during the Lindsay years. (Several of the comparison cities also provided post-retirement cost of living adjustments, which New York did not.) Total fringe benefits do look higher than anywhere else at the close of the Lindsay years—the data is murky—but that may also have been true when Lindsay took office. Educational spending (using counties that include other big cities as the comparison) did grow faster than elsewhere during the Lindsay years, and the city's rank rose from fourth to second. Spending in New York on comparable functions was not much different from anywhere else.

The welfare caseload's growth shows much the same picture. The growth in New York City happened sooner than in the rest of the country, but over a longer time frame growth rates were much the same. The most rapid relative growth in New York—about twice as fast as in the rest of the country—occurred at the end of the Wagner administration and in the first year or two of Lindsay's. The fastest absolute rate of growth in New York—16.4 percent a year—came largely in Lindsay's first term; but growth rates in the rest of the country, at 15.8 percent, were almost as high. Comparing New York City with the rest of the state produces a similar picture. In the seven years from 1961 through 1968, the city's caseload grew by 275 percent, while the rest of the state's grew only by 94 percent. But the situation reversed during the next seven years: growth of 254 percent in the rest of the state, and only 109 percent in the city. Finally, when the state carried out a careful audit of welfare ineligibility in 1973, Lindsay's last year in office, it turned out that the rates in the city and elsewhere in the state were identical.

New York City, however, was unique in its commitment to hospital services and higher education. A number of major American cities operated a municipal hospital or two. But none, on any scale of proportionality, had anything approaching New York's massive 18-hospital network. Similarly, a few municipalities operate a community college, but New York's extensive system of higher education, from community colleges through graduate school, and with some of the highest-paid faculty in the country, was *sui generis*. Both received major financial infusions during the Lindsay years and were important contributors to the eventual financial crisis.

The expansion of hospital spending was arguably the more defensible. The system was in a state of collapse when Lindsay took office, plans for major upgrades had long been in the works, and the critical decisions were made before the extent of the city's financial difficulties was broadly understood. The spending increases, moreover, were tied to a planned privatization of the system intended to reduce the city's financial commitment over the longer term.

Cartoon by Gib Crockett, 1966. Lindsay often faced a recalcitrant City Council, but won some fights.

The second-term surge in higher education spending, by contrast, was purely policy-driven. In the run-up to the 1969 election, the administration chose to guarantee a place in the city college system for every city high school graduate. Enrollment in the city's colleges had been growing rapidly for many years, and "open enrollment" had long been a cherished objective. But the decision to press ahead with full and immediate implementation was taken in the face of a dangerously worsening fiscal position. Enrollment jumped by 45,000 students in two years, placing the system under enormous stress, more so since so many of the students were woefully unprepared for college-level work.

Reflection

Professor **STAN ALTMAN** of Baruch College was a consultant to the Sanitation Department under Lindsay and later served as dean of the college's School of Public Affairs and interim president of the college.

The field of modern public management really dates from the shock of the Sputnik launch in 1957, which produced a massive increase in federal funds for science and technology and all the related fields of engineering and systems operations.

The election of John F. Kennedy in 1960 and his appointment of Robert S. McNamara as Defense Secretary brought in legions of business whiz kids who introduced new approaches like systems analysis and program planning and budgeting. At the same time, the Rand Institute's research and development activities expanded beyond strategic analysis for the Air Force and influenced the national Aeronautics and Space Administration's development of project-management systems to monitor its incredibly complex work flows. For the next few years, this explosion of new techniques was the sole province of the federal government.

Then in 1966, John Lindsay determined to import these modern approaches to New York's creaky government. He recruited a leading federal budget and management expert in Fred Hayes, who brought to New York a cadre of experienced aides who invaded the city's aged Budget Bureau. From there, these new program planners—a position previously unknown to City government—began to scrutinize and probe every area of the city's operations.

They launched a massive effort to gather data on every city function, to standardize its collection, and to measure performance. They built an unprecedented body of statistical data for everything from fire-alarm response times to sanitation truckloads and miles covered, from police manning levels to building and health inspections per employee.

Lindsay and Hayes also brought Rand to New York for its first immersion in urban affairs, using the same strategic analysis it did for the Defense Department, as well as bringing in McKinsey, the consulting firm, to bring the most advanced techniques of project management.

Over the next few years, Hayes's new urban management experts moved directly into the operating agencies creating in each a capacity for planning, budgeting, and analysis never before seen and who were able to change the way virtually every city agency functioned—and thought about its work.

Aside from the Feds, no other government in America had anything like this massive effort. And when New York leveraged these efforts in 1970 into its pioneering Productivity Program, the tables were turned and Washington now followed New York's lead with the Federal Productivity Commission, created in 1972.

Lindsay's massive investment in talent and resources, and the patience to learn and nurture and build these databases and systems, was the beginning of the modern discipline of public management that has altered the curriculum of every school of public affairs, the training of every government manager at any level, and the way every government and the public measures its performance. That legacy has been profound and it is unknowingly carried forward every day by government officials, not just in every agency of New York City, but in virtually every major city and state in the nation.

JAY L. KRIEGEL was Lindsay's special counsel and chief of staff

Howard Leary, Lindsay's first police commissioner, was not just an outsider from Philadelphia but a loner—a cunning, distrustful survivor who demonstrated extraordinary skill, flexibility and instincts. In his first year, Leary faced the titanic political battle over the Civilian Complaint Review Board, where the PBA triumphed over the Mayor and assumed a political status never before achieved by a municipal union. From then on, Leary was caught in the middle of one heated public battle after another between the Mayor and the union.

Yet Leary, alone in American policing in the face of the greatest challenge to civil peace in a hundred years, was able to not just adopt but rapidly and thoroughly implement Lindsay's revolutionary policy of police restraint in the use of force. This was truly an extraordinary management achievement that virtually overnight altered the behavior of a 30,000-member old-guard urban police department, and sustained it, even in the face of the most severe verbal and physical provocation.

Lindsay used to say he never trusted air he couldn't see.
From the roof of the Statler Hilton in 1967, he could see plenty. In addition to establishing the Department of Consumer Affairs in 1969, Lindsay created the nation's first Department of Environmental Protection in 1969 and was a leader of the first Earth Day in 1970.

Summing Up the Lindsay Record

Even with some four decades' perspective, the Lindsay record remains controversial—and will doubtless remain so, for the contrasts between the successes and failures are so stark.

Lindsay can fairly be credited with two exemplary policy innovations that changed the face of local government throughout the country. The first was the strategy of a nonmilitarized response to civil unrest—talking rather than shooting, while building a massive police presence to suppress disturbances by sheer weight of numbers. It was a tactic that implicitly accepted some property damage in the early stages of a disturbance, but avoided the all-out warfare that occurred in some other large cities.

The other was the second term's greater focus on productivity, which has become an enduring feature of governments.

But the other side of the balance sheet is as imposing. Policy making in the first administration tended to be moralizing and racially polarizing, and, intentionally or not, often communicated disdain for the city work force. Major policy shifts, like the welfare-declaration system and open enrollment at the City University, were taken with minimal regard to the capacity of the system to carry them out.

The administration's openhanded spending practices were a major contributor to the fiscal collapse of 1975. In fairness, the most egregious budget gimmickry was invented and nurtured by Governor Nelson A. Rockefeller's state administration and implemented by Beame, who as comptroller was an independently elected city official.

But Lindsay's annual crusades for expanded services and more state aid maintained unrelenting spending pressure. And since Lindsay and his top aides regularly boasted of the city's superior financial and managerial talent, they can hardly escape blame for the ultimate financial debacle.

The fiscal headaches began early as Lindsay inherited debt from the Wagner administration. Here, the mayor at a public hearing on the capital budget in February 1966.

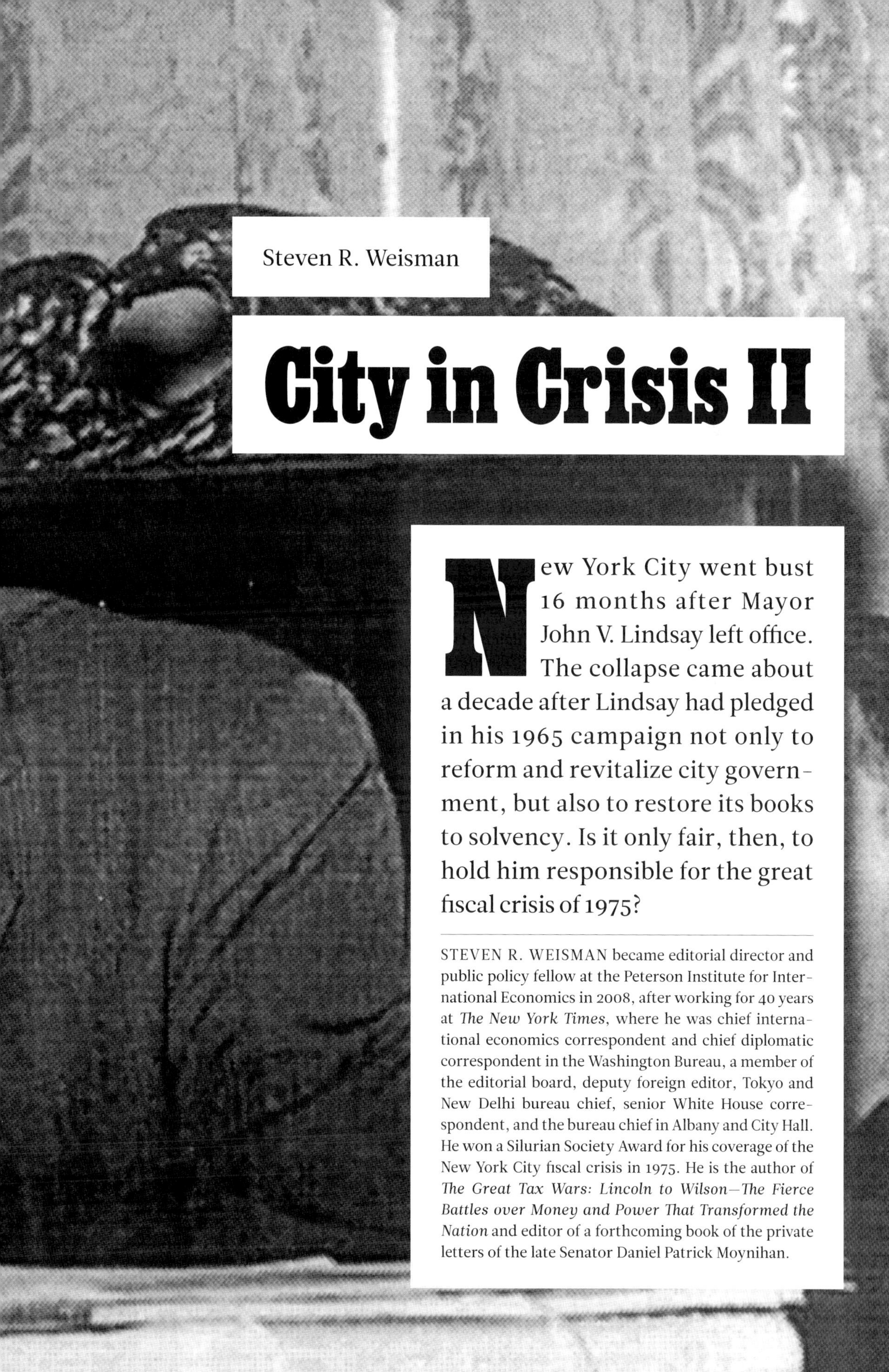

Steven R. Weisman

City in Crisis II

New York City went bust 16 months after Mayor John V. Lindsay left office. The collapse came about a decade after Lindsay had pledged in his 1965 campaign not only to reform and revitalize city government, but also to restore its books to solvency. Is it only fair, then, to hold him responsible for the great fiscal crisis of 1975?

STEVEN R. WEISMAN became editorial director and public policy fellow at the Peterson Institute for International Economics in 2008, after working for 40 years at *The New York Times*, where he was chief international economics correspondent and chief diplomatic correspondent in the Washington Bureau, a member of the editorial board, deputy foreign editor, Tokyo and New Delhi bureau chief, senior White House correspondent, and the bureau chief in Albany and City Hall. He won a Silurian Society Award for his coverage of the New York City fiscal crisis in 1975. He is the author of *The Great Tax Wars: Lincoln to Wilson—The Fierce Battles over Money and Power That Transformed the Nation* and editor of a forthcoming book of the private letters of the late Senator Daniel Patrick Moynihan.

Yes, it is—but he shares that responsibility with many others.

Mayor Lindsay steered New York City through gale-force winds of change: a collapsing economy and tax-revenue base; rising social unrest, racial polarization and crime; increasing labor union militancy; growing public demands for services—and many other factors at least partly beyond his control. These forces pushed city budgets ever deeper into the red. But Lindsay and others at City Hall and Albany never proclaimed themselves to be helpless pawns, and neither should they be judged that way. They all fell short in coping with the crushing fiscal realities of the era and engaged in, implicitly accepted—or did not aggressively enough denounce—a multitude of accounting gimmicks to paper over these budget deficits, especially in Lindsay's second term.

Though poorly understood at the time, these bookkeeping devices—like artificially deferring costs or borrowing against dubious or non-existent receivables—produced hidden deficits that drove up the city's short-term borrowing from a negligible amount in 1970 to more than $6 billion in 1975. The day of reckoning came when the market for city debt slammed shut in the spring of 1975, ushering in a six-month drama of confrontations, threats of default, and talk of bankruptcy. By the end of the year, with federal help, city and state officials and unions averted an outright collapse by making the cost-cutting decisions they had failed to make in the previous 15 years.

The backdrop of the crisis was, of course, one of soaring city spending, taxing, and borrowing. Under Lindsay, the municipal budget nearly tripled in size from $2.6 billion in 1969 to more than $10.2 billion eight years later, while the municipal work force grew from 247,000 to 291,000 over the same period. The budgets reflected a dramatic expansion of municipal services, especially for the poor and in health care and higher education. Wages, fringe benefits, and pension costs for the city's growing work force (accounting for half or more of the budget) also exploded in size, from $2.1 billion in 1966 to nearly $5.2 billion in 1974.

Other cities, and indeed many of the suburban communities surrounding New York City, were undergoing similar trends in their services for the poor and in the cost of their work force. In addition, the pattern of escalating budgets was set by Lindsay's predecessor, Mayor Robert F. Wagner, in his last term, and many of the costs were foisted on the city by state and federal mandates and the success of unions in circumventing City Hall and winning legislative approval in Albany for pension and wage deals. But these costs were also undeniably beyond what Lindsay and other political leaders were willing or able to pay for. Hence the resorting to debt that led to a downfall.

Was it mayors, governors, lawmakers, and comptrollers who were at fault, or was it the political system itself? In the 1960s, the most respected scholarly work on public affairs in New York was *Governing New York City*, by Wallace Sayre of Columbia University and Herbert Kaufman of Yale. The authors studied the variety of political forces in the city and concluded that they had helped make the city open, democratic, and soundly run. "What other American city is as democratically and as well governed?" Sayre and Kaufman famously asked at the end of their 744-page study. But by the end of the fiscal crisis, a new conventional wisdom took root: that the city's political institutions did not lend themselves to sound government, or to sound finance of government. Two important books since the crisis argued instead that New York's system of interests and alliances, in navigating the economic and political pressures of the era, produced bad government and worse budgets. "The result of this type of political coalition is a fiscal crisis in which the city commits to more expenditures than it can raise in taxes or borrowing," wrote Charles Brecher and Raymond D. Horton in their book *Power Failure*, about New York City government after 1960. Or as the political scientist Martin Shefter put it in *Political Crisis Fiscal Crisis*, "Fiscal crises should be regarded not as aberrations but as an integral part of urban politics."

A Tale of Two Terms

Whether the system or individuals were to blame, the story of Lindsay's coping with these problems can be divided into two parts. In his first term, Lindsay paid for the city's soaring costs by landing impressive increases in state and federal aid, and with a variety of tax increases, including taxes on income from city residents and commuters alike. He also introduced productivity reforms that in the second term improved the city's ability to keep track of its budgets. The commuter tax, repealed in 1999, was one of Lindsay's most extraordinary political achievements. Undeniably, his achievements in these areas resulted from his leadership skills—his empathy for the poor and minorities and his ability to dramatize the crisis of the cities as a moral issue.

The mayor unveils his proposed budget in March 1967.

Virtually all accounts of the Lindsay years agree that his first-term budgetary success was real. For example, in his otherwise critical book on the Lindsay record, *The Ungovernable City: John Lindsay and His Struggle to Save New York*, the conservative historian Vincent J. Cannato notes that Lindsay's first-term budgets "were fairly successful attempts at responsible fiscal policy," and that "Lindsay deserves credit for cajoling more money for the city, especially from the state." Indeed, despite the racial polarization, strikes, protests, and discord among the white working class over programs for the poor and the quality of services in their neighborhoods, Lindsay won re-election in 1969 at least partly on the claim that he had kept the city together—and kept it solvent.

In fiscal terms, Lindsay's second term was different. After 1970, and the onset of a nationwide recession that hit New York City especially hard, aid from Washington and Albany began to dry up. So did the appetite for more taxes. Yet any fair judgment of culpability for the borrowing to which the city resorted has to place responsibility with others as well as Lindsay—most especially Abraham D. Beame, his pugnacious successor as mayor and his rival, as comptroller, in the second term.

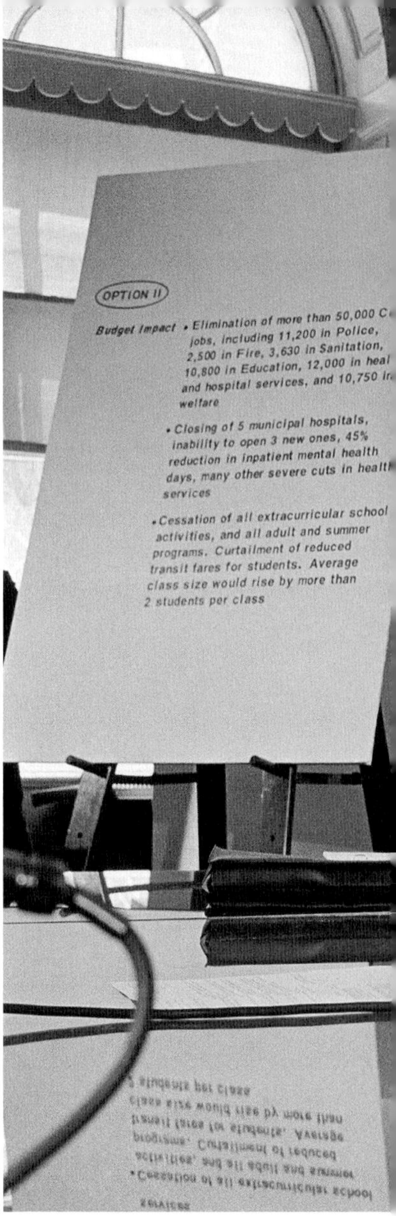

Indeed, Beame, often portraying himself as a fiscal savior determined to rescue the city from layoffs and service cutbacks, pressed many of the accounting devices (such as deferring payroll dates or revising revenue estimates) on Lindsay and on the rest of the Board of Estimate, which was eager to find ways to avoid spending cuts. Two of the four budgets during Lindsay's second term were adopted by the board over Lindsay's formal objections. No other no votes were recorded in any of these four spending plans. Lindsay's dissents, on the other hand, were largely academic, and he effectively went along with the revised budgets, pledging to retool spending on the margins during the course of each year. (Perhaps he could have warned more vociferously of impending catastrophe, but politically and legally, facing a recalcitrant Board of Estimate and City Council united against him, it is uncertain how he could have pursued fiscal restraint more aggressively.)

There were other partners, meanwhile, in the city's record of producing misleading budgets. The accounting gimmicks and short-term borrowing employed to masquerade deficits often required the approval (and, in 1971, the instigation) of Governor Nelson A. Rockefeller and his successor, Malcolm Wilson, as well as the state legislature. Beame's own technical advisory committee on city debt went along with approving the use of short-term notes, as did various rating agencies. Crucially, the major banks and investment firms, which could have asked questions about the city's underlying solvency, were instead happy to profit from underwriting city debt and marketing it to their customers.

Looking back in 2003 at the causes of the collapse, Felix G. Rohatyn, the investment banker who helped design the city's rescue in 1975, faulted, among other players in the city's landscape, unions for driving up costs and banks for looking the other way as debts mounted. But most of his blame was focused on "New York mayors from Lindsay to Beame and governors from Rockefeller to Wilson" for the epidemic of "deficits over expenditure cuts and borrowing in lieu of tax increases" that characterized the 1970s.

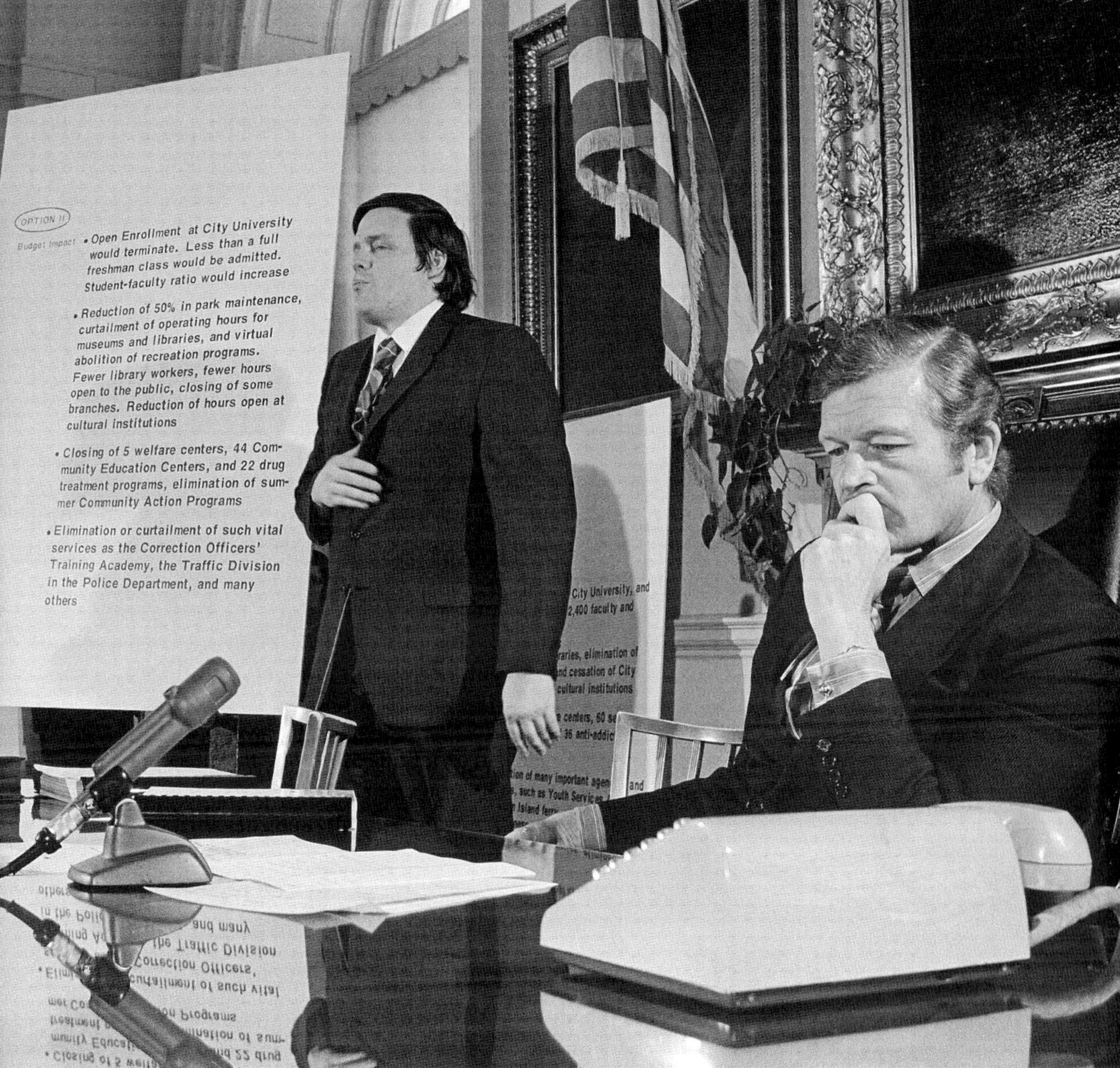

OPTION II
Budget Impact
• Open Enrollment at City University would terminate. Less than a full freshman class would be admitted. Student-faculty ratio would increase
• Reduction of 50% in park maintenance, curtailment of operating hours for museums and libraries, and virtual abolition of recreation programs. Fewer library workers, fewer hours open to the public, closing of some branches. Reduction of hours open at cultural institutions
• Closing of 5 welfare centers, 44 Community Education Centers, and 22 drug treatment programs, elimination of summer Community Action Programs
• Elimination or curtailment of such vital services as the Correction Officers' Training Academy, the Traffic Division in the Police Department, and many others

Edward K. Hamilton, then the budget director and later deputy mayor, briefs reporters on budget alternatives in 1971 as Lindsay glumly looks on.

Averting Bankruptcy

The New York City fiscal crisis seemed at the time like a unique interplay of disparate forces, but it was quite similar to other modern debt crises. Like Latin America in the 1980s and Asian countries in the 1990s, and European and American banks in 2008, the city courted disaster by financing ongoing expenses with short-term debt. A reckoning almost always comes in such circumstances. It came in 1975, first with the default of the New York State Urban Development Corporation and then when the city's most powerful banks stopped purchasing or underwriting short-term city notes, which were being marketed at a rate of $600 million a month.

Bankruptcy was averted in stages over the following six months, finally with President Gerald Ford and Congress agreeing to participate with a package of short-term "seasonal" loans. Governor Hugh L. Carey—like Beame, a product of Brooklyn Democratic clubhouse politics—led the city back from the brink by bringing unions, banks, and political figures together to accept a package of shared sacrifices, including tax and fee increases (tuition at the City University, for example), a moratorium on $1.6 billion in notes, an agreement to reduce the city's work force by 60,000 over three years, and an agreement by unions to limit wage increases and buy city debt for their pension funds. A Municipal Assistance Corporation was established to refinance the city's debt, and an Emergency Financial Control Board, headed by Carey, effectively wrested the city's fiscal functions from a hapless Beame administration.

Could these steps have been taken in the absence of a crisis? That is highly doubtful. But the austerity and decline in city services (and quality of life) ushered in by the actions under Governor Carey probably contributed to the tarnishing of Lindsay's image in the eyes of New Yorkers, who also generally became disenchanted with his form of liberalism in later years.

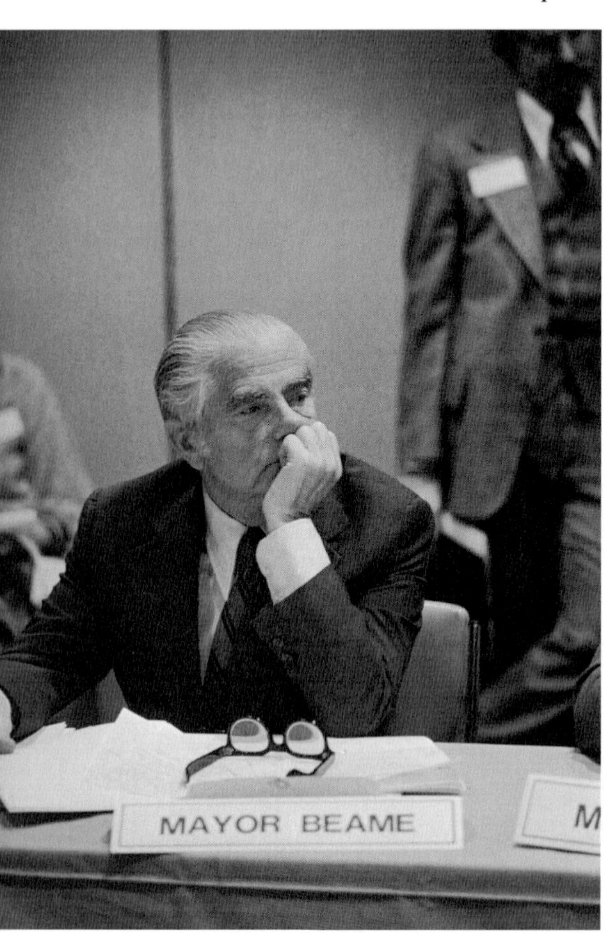

Abraham D. Beame, seen here as mayor in October 1975, campaigned as the comptroller who "knows the buck." As mayor, he presided over the fiscal crisis.

The fiscal crisis certainly contrasted dramatically with the hopeful moment that Lindsay represented when he ran for office in 1965 to rescue New York from what was described by *The New York Herald Tribune* as a "City in Crisis." A fiscal chronology of this period illustrates how the city slipped steadily into trouble.

To begin with, Lindsay did not invent deficit-financing. Lindsay, a Republican congressman from the East Side of Manhattan, and Beame, the city comptroller, ran against each other to succeed Wagner, and both denounced a debt scheme proposed by Wagner in his final year. Once in office, Lindsay was able to balance the city's books and repay Wagner's borrowing.

But soon the new mayor was engulfed by larger economic forces. After World War II, a million poor migrants, blacks and Puerto Ricans, moved to New York City and at least as many (largely white) middle-class New Yorkers moved out, many to the suburbs. The city's tax base weakened at a time of rising demands for racial justice and poverty alleviation and of spreading crime and drug use. Labor unions, granted the right to collective bargaining by Wagner, grew increasingly militant and resentful of Lindsay, and the feeling was mutual after the bitter transit strike that rang in his term on New Year's Day.

Turning to Albany, Lindsay won successive packages of new state aid and tax increases, which under state law had to be approved by the state legislature. These included an income tax, new ways of calculating business taxes, a stock-transfer tax, increased water charges, a gross receipts tax on utilities, and even an income tax on commuters. Rockefeller at first sought to help Lindsay, whom he had supported for mayor in 1965, by championing various forms of aid, including new school-aid formulas, even as his relations with Lindsay soured. Thanks to the War on Poverty, funds also flowed from Washington.

What was poorly realized in retrospect, however, was that federal and state aid often came with spending mandates for the city—reinforced by burdensome cost-sharing formulas dictated by Albany—and that construction of new schools, colleges, and hospitals meant increased need to pay teachers, professors, doctors, and nurses. In 1970, the City University—with Lindsay's active support—inaugurated "open enrollment," springing open the gates to a generation of new students—and spending on higher education doubled nearly every four years.

Though much of the rancor over Lindsay's leadership was stirred by poverty programs, funds for most of them came from Washington. But the expansion of welfare took a major toll on the city's budget, even though its share was only about a third of the total cost. Welfare rolls doubled during Lindsay's first term alone, and the city had to pay a hefty portion of the new Medicaid program. The total cost soared into the hundreds of millions.

President Lyndon B. Johnson's War on Poverty legislation, signed into law in August 1964, provided much of the funding for Lindsay's anti-poverty programs.

And then there was the cost of labor agreements. Personnel costs grew 250 percent as Lindsay tried to hold down the size of wage and benefit packages, only to be hit with strikes by virtually every group of employees, from nurses and doctors to teachers and sanitation workers. Jockeying by police, fire, and sanitation workers over pay ratios among them, and among officers and unionized supervisors, almost always produced increased pay and benefit packages for everyone.

Even so, Lindsay kept spending and revenues in balance during his first four years. That achievement unraveled with a recession in 1969 that cut deeper and lasted many years longer in New York City than elsewhere. Suddenly the city's unemployment rate, which had been below the national average, soared as the manufacturing sector collapsed. Wall Street suffered the bursting of its speculative bubble in technology stocks and so-called growth stocks. Business deals sputtered. More than 100 investment firms, including several major ones, closed down. The downturn spread to construction and the service sector, from insurance to advertising. At the same time, inflation roared ahead, driving up the cost of city government across the board.

In Albany, Rockefeller cut back aid to the city and its programs. Lindsay was running for re-election, on the other hand, with little room to abandon his promises to add to police, sanitation, and other services. His budget scraped by that year but he did begin, in a small way, the fateful practice of "balancing" the budget by overstating revenue and understating costs, only to end up with budgets in the red at the end of the fiscal year. The practice began as credit rating agencies and banks continued to declare that the city's books were basically sound.

Graffiti-covered subway cars were a visible symbol of a city growing out of control in the early 1970s.

Don't bet on it: In 1970, the State Legislature authorized the creation of Off-Track Betting. Here, Lindsay opens the city's first Off-Track Betting parlor in Grand Central Terminal on May 15, 1971 with OTB's first chairman, businessman Howard Samuels. By 1974, more than 130 parlors were generating over $40 million in revenue for the city.

The following year, 1970, was also a state election year, and Lindsay, while refusing to endorse Rockefeller for a new term, had learned how to maximize his leverage with the governor and state lawmakers running for re-election to get some increased help from Albany, including establishment of off-track betting. But the new aid fell short of what was needed. In late 1970, the city budget director, Frederick O'R. Hayes, resigned after four grueling years at the job and left a memo to the mayor, declaring in its first sentence: "We're in trouble."

As the memo made clear, there was no end in sight for the basic structural problem of costs outstripping revenue year after year. The limits on Lindsay's ability to control spending were also increasingly obvious. The city school system's budget was set by the mayor with the approval of the Board of Estimate and City Council, but the system itself was managed by a semi-independent Board of Education, for example. The hospitals were run by a semi-independent Health and Hospitals Corporation, ironically a Lindsay administration creation designed to increase the hospital system's control over its revenues and costs. Reimbursement rates for welfare and Medicaid were controlled by Albany. Everyone understood that 1971 was going to be a year of terrible budget choices.

Lindsay and his staff dealt with the problem by employing a fateful new tactic. Instead of presenting one spending plan, the mayor laid out four "options." The most drastic assumed no new taxes or aid, and it contemplated as many as 90,000 jobs eliminated, including massive layoffs of police officers and teachers.

Eventually, city and state negotiators agreed to a package of taxes and new aid that met some of the problem. But in reality the budget was also closed by what Charles Morris, in *The Cost of Good Intentions*, estimated was $700 million in "gimmicks and questionable borrowings" that marked "a critical turning point" in the city's slide toward dubious accounting. Nearly half of this amount consisted of higher revenue estimates proposed by Beame, denounced by Lindsay's office as reckless. That budget was adopted over Lindsay's dissent.

The budget also had a disastrous public relations side effect. Although Lindsay's confrontational approach worked on one level, it deepened a widespread perception—aided and abetted by media coverage—that Lindsay's threats had been false alarms and that a budget crisis had been averted by last-minute "found money" that may have been there all along.

"Did we cry 'wolf'?" the mayor's press secretary, Thomas P. Morgan, asked rhetorically in June of 1971, after the budget was adopted, for example. He and other city officials denied that they had misled the public, asserting that without their dramatic warnings, the city would not have received help from Albany. But fairly or not, the credibility of budget-making was widely seen as in tatters. A prominent City Councilman denounced Lindsay's budget theatrics as "a cruel hoax," and *The New York Times's* City Hall bureau chief, Martin Tolchin, cited the mayor's "long record of forecasting municipal disasters that have not materialized."

Virtually all of these criticisms overlooked the essentially fraudulent nature of the way the budget was balanced. Morris, a former assistant budget director under Lindsay, writes that the mayor's original budget options had been a correct forecast of what would happen if the city did not get additional aid. The mayor's success with Albany ironically came at the price of accepting other dubious means to balance the budget. As Morris points out, a threshold was crossed that "seemed to break, once and for all, any hard-and-fast relationship between the city's ability to raise revenues and its ability to spend." He concludes that in 1971, "the thoroughness with which the Albany legislative leadership and city budget officials began to mine the seemingly endless store of new budget-balancing devices was a whole new departure in itself. Over the next several years, budget gimmicking was raised from the level of haphazard expedient to an arcane art form, and the practical limits of irresponsibility were pushed further and further out on the horizon."

The gimmicks came to include shifting costs into the capital budget, which is financed by long-term borrowing, and intended to pay for major projects, not day-to-day operating expenses, as well as a bewildering raft of deliberate underestimations of spending, overstatement of revenues, suspension of payments to various reserve funds, shifting of payments (like the teachers' payroll) from one fiscal year to the next, and recognition of revenues on the books well before they would come in. City Hall and Albany cooperated in some of these schemes, most notably what came to be known as the "magic window" of state aid. The city would borrow at the beginning of its fiscal year, starting July 1, against revenues due in the last quarter of its fiscal year (April 1 to June 30). That quarter was the first quarter of the state's next fiscal year. So the state would borrow against revenues it expected to receive in the last quarter of its year in order to make a payment that was recognized as real a year earlier.

Labor Costs in the City of New York: Fiscal Years 1961–1975

Total Labor Costs[1]
($ in millions)

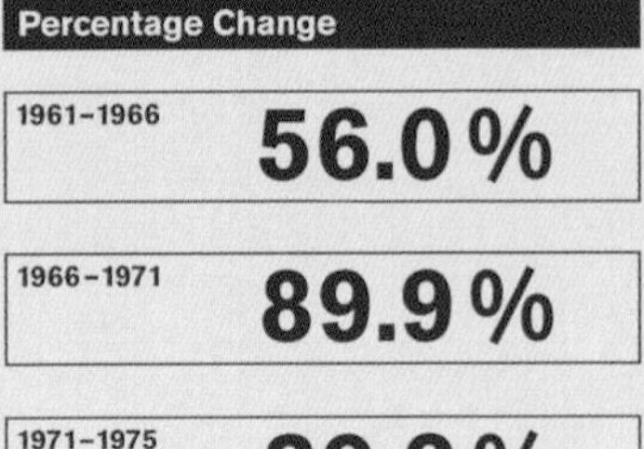

Total Labor Costs Percentage Change	
1961–1966	56.0 %
1966–1971	89.9 %
1971–1975	39.2 %
1961–1975	312.3 %

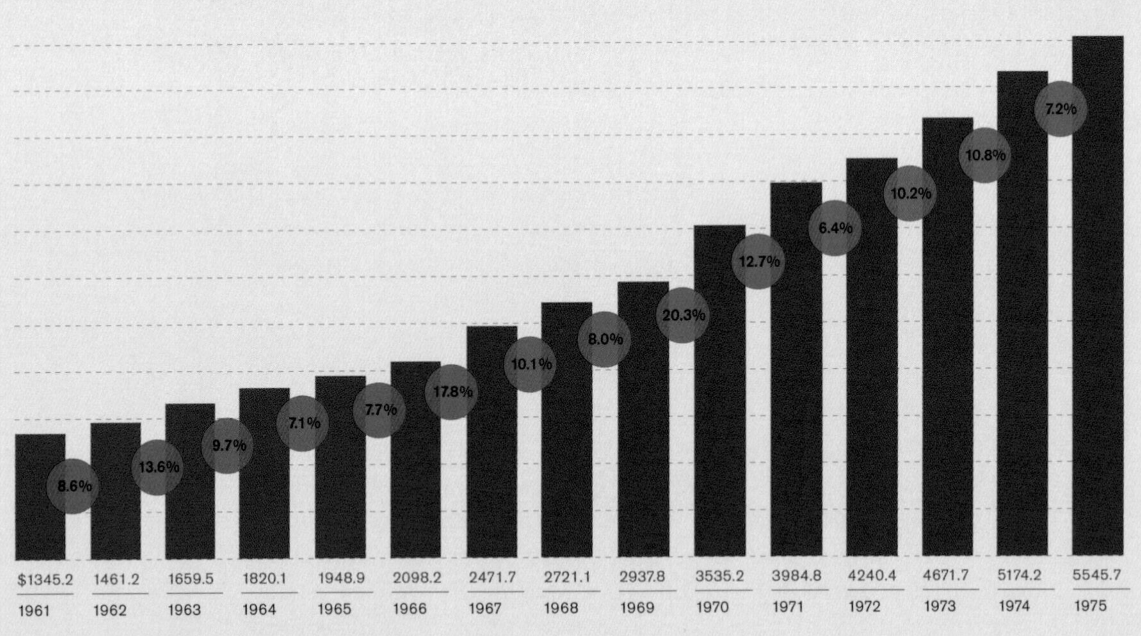

1 Employment data as of December 31 of each fiscal year

SOURCE
'The City in Transition: Prospects and Policies for New York," *Final Report of the Temporary Commission on City Finances*, June 1977, pp. 85–87.

Labor Costs[1]
(Constant $)[2]
($ in millions)

Total Labor Costs Percentage Change

Period	Change
1961–1966	43.0 %
1966–1971	48.3 %
1971–1975	5.8 %
1961–1975	124.3 %

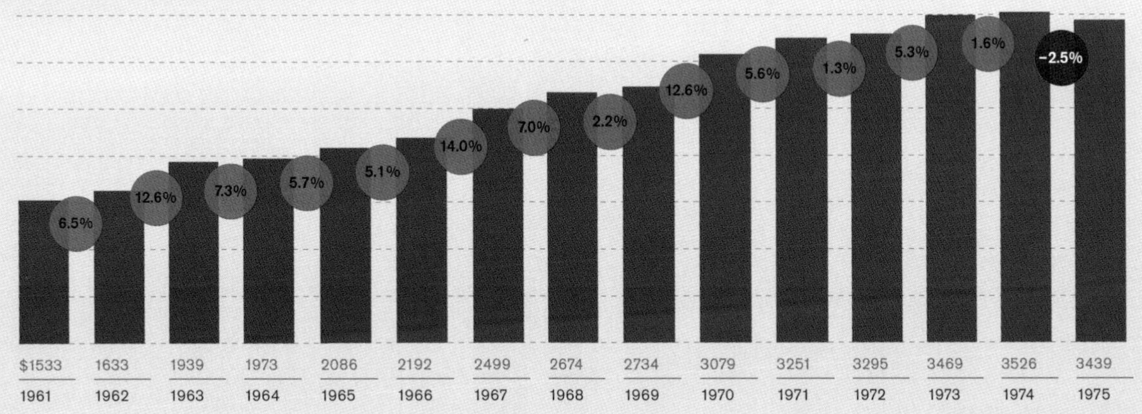

1961	1962	1963	1964	1965	1966	1967	1968	1969	1970	1971	1972	1973	1974	1975
$1533	1633	1939	1973	2086	2192	2499	2674	2734	3079	3251	3295	3469	3526	3439

1 Employment data as of December 31 of each fiscal year

2 Adjustments to fiscal year constant dollars are based on U.S., Department of Labor. Bureau of Labor Statistics Consumer Price Indexes

Employment Changes in Selected Service Areas: 1961–1975

Police[1]

Aggregate Change

1961–1975

38.3%

9,807

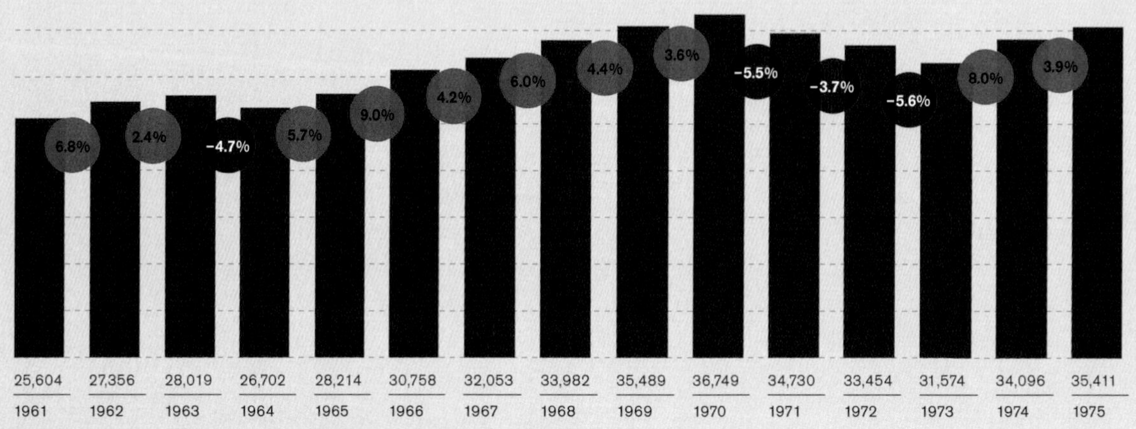

1 Employment data as of December 31 of each fiscal year

Education[1]

Aggregate Change

1961–1975

43.6%

24,264

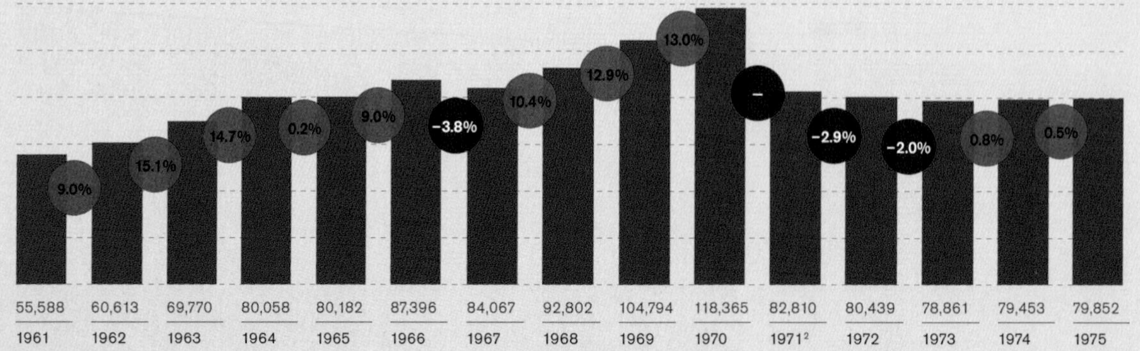

1 Employment data as of December 31 of each fiscal year

2 1971 numbers reflect a change in accounting procedures that altered the method of counting full-time employees.

Welfare[1]

Aggregate Change

1961–1975

213.3%

18,225

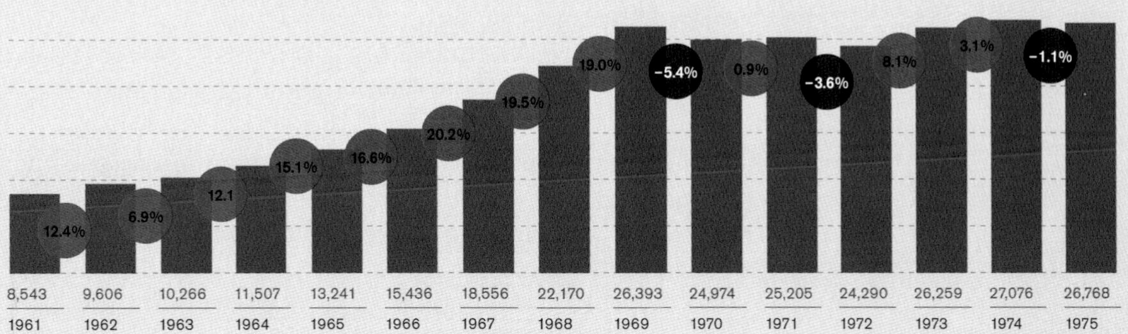

1 Employment data as of December 31 of each fiscal year

Higher Education[1]

Aggregate Change

1961–1975

365.0%

15,706

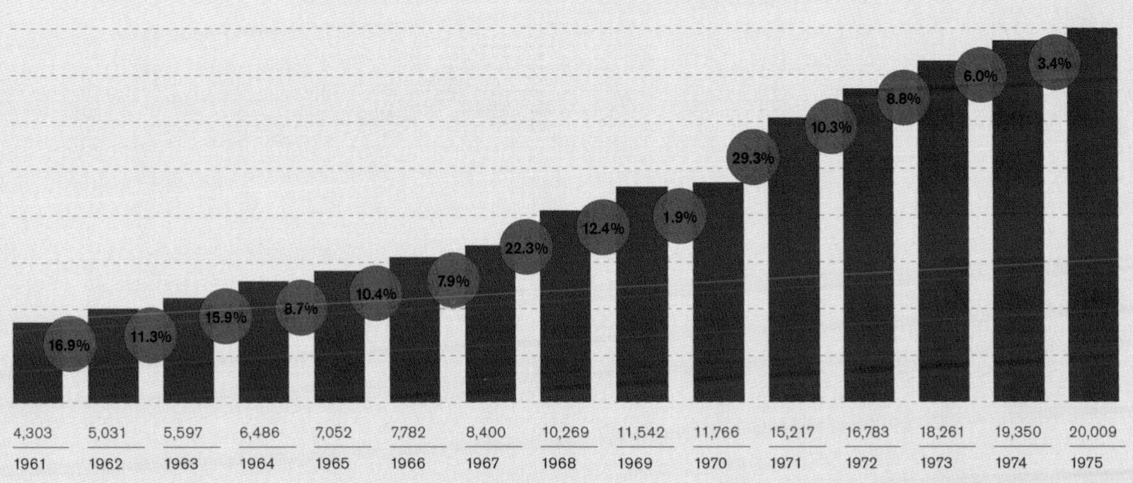

1 Employment data as of December 31 of each fiscal year

Still another fatally flawed bookkeeping and financial practice—supported in the early 1970s by Lindsay, Beame, the Board of Estimate, and the State Legislature—allowed the city to finance most of its network of 123 middle-income housing projects in the so-called Mitchell-Lama program by issuing short-term notes rather than long-term bonds, as the law required. Each year the Legislature waived the law's constraint so the city could take advantage of lower interest rates available when short-term notes are rolled over every six months or year. Lower interest rates helped keep rents low for the projects' tens of thousands of tenants. Not until the fiscal crisis hit in 1975 did the practice catch up to the city, as it realized to its dismay that these $1.1 billion in notes made up more than a sixth of its short-term debt, just as that debt got shut out of the market.

As short-term debts mounted, city and state auditors failed to sound the alarm over what was behind that trend. Indeed, all the city's fiscal officers certified each year that the city's fiscal situation was sound enough for it to keep borrowing. Equally important, the banks and investment firms that raked in profits from underwriting the city's notes showed little interest in looking carefully at the way the city had come to rely on borrowing short-term when cash fell short, and rolling over the notes when they came due.

The pattern of the city falling back on short-term debt continued for the next two years, but whatever leverage the mayor could wield to halt the practice was fatally weakened by perhaps the biggest political miscalculation of his time at City Hall: the decision at the end of 1971 to run for the Democratic nomination for president in 1972. Shortly after his campaign crashed and burned, he returned to work at home, with less influence than ever. Beame, meanwhile, geared up to run for mayor in 1973, eager to show his skills as a fiscal magician. In the public's eye, Beame had the credentials to call the shots on budgets, having served not only as comptroller in Lindsay's second term but also four years as comptroller in Wagner's last term and, before that, as Wagner's budget director for eight years. He used his clout generally to support bookkeeping acrobatics, although in at least one case, in 1972, he criticized Lindsay for the kind of thing he often advocated himself—deferring the cost of police pay raises after the police union rejected a pending contract.

Two years after the fiscal crisis, in 1977, the Securities and Exchange Commission staff looked back on these years of practices and concluded that both Mayor Beame and the city comptroller during his mayoralty, Harrison J. Goldin, "misled public investors" with false reassurances about municipal finances in 1974 and 1975 (after Lindsay had left office) while tolerating bogus bookkeeping devices that covered up deficits. Investors in city securities, it added, "were injured by these practices." Without saying so explicitly, the commission staff suggested that such conduct would have been deemed criminal in the corporate securities world. But although the staff focused nearly all its attention on 1974 and 1975, it pointedly cited one instance in which it said Beame was guilty of engaging in unsound practices while he was comptroller during the Lindsay years—by shifting the pay date of teachers from June 30 to July 1 so the cost could be deferred to a new fiscal year. The pay date may have shifted by a day, but like other moves, this one necessitated borrowing

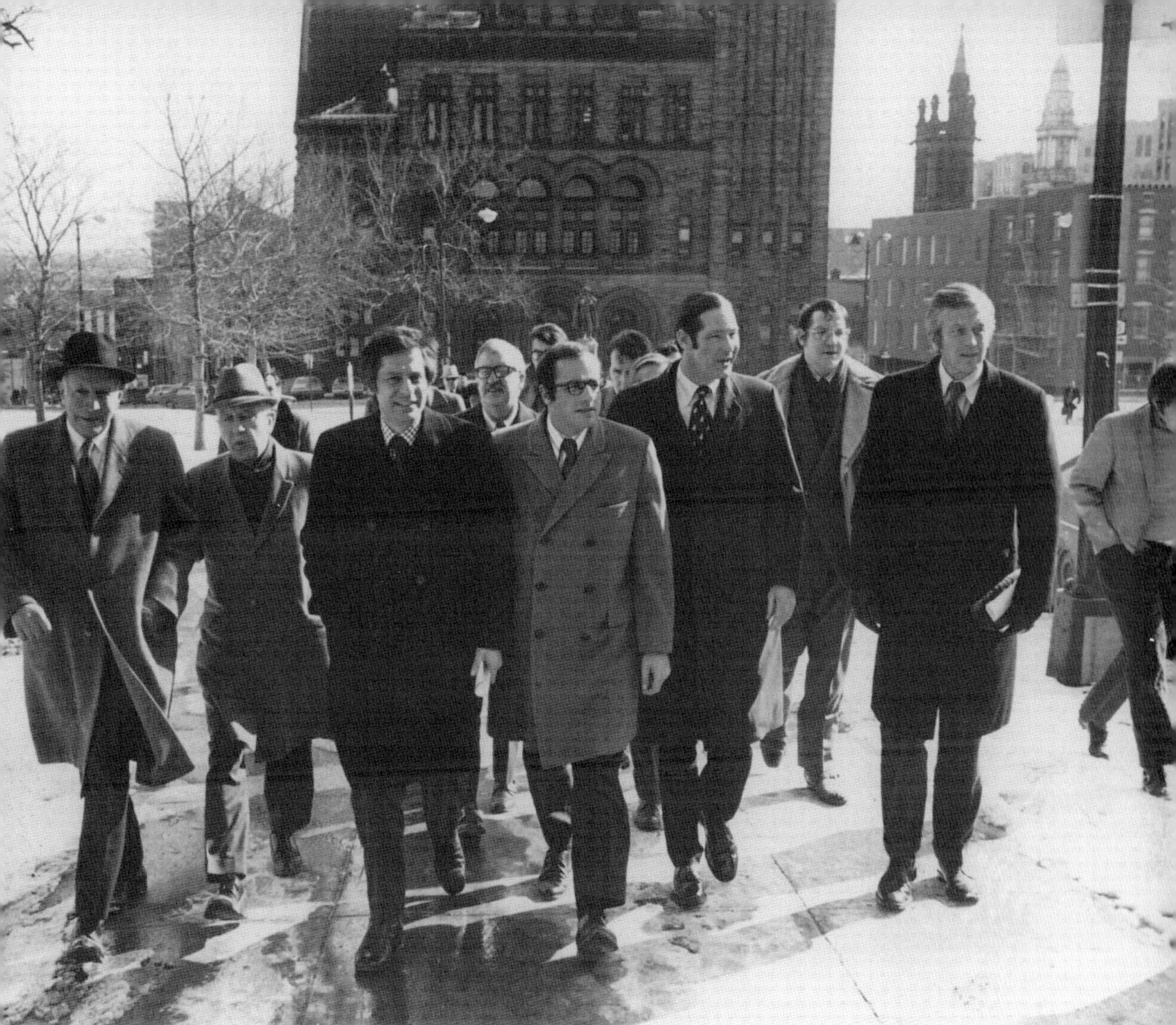

to meet the needs of cash flow. The Securities and Exchange Commission staff noted approvingly that Lindsay had denounced that stratagem as "stopgap financial juggling" that "merely puts off today's pain until tomorrow."

Why didn't Lindsay buck the gimmicks that he so readily criticized? First, it must be said again that Lindsay did vote no on the budgets adopted in June 1971 and June 1972. But for political and legal reasons, he lived with them and chose not to make his concerns into a passionate cause. There were times when he dissented loudly and other times when he readily accepted bogus budget-balancing proposals from Beame, apparently seeing nothing morally objectionable and certainly no other legal recourse. He understood, as many of his former aides recall, that Beame, as leader of the opposition, had the ability to override Lindsay's objections by rallying other city and state politicians and the authority to decide some matters on his own, such as when to issue paychecks. The courts, moreover, were loath to step into the recurrent city budget squabbles. Most important, the public discussion in these years focused more on the dire consequences of closing schools and hospitals and laying off police officers, firefighters, and sanitation workers—and decidedly not on the arcane budgeting arts employed to avert disaster.

Lindsay organized New York State's "Big Six" mayors to lobby for state aid in Albany and won a valuable state revenue sharing program in 1970. He also rallied 17 mayors across the country to win federal revenue sharing in 1971. Here, the "Big Six" return to Albany in 1972. From left: Erastus Corning II of Albany; Frank Sedita, Buffalo; Lee Alexander, Syracuse; Alfred DelBello, Yonkers; Stephen May, Rochester; and John Lindsay.

Dejected campaign workers in Wisconsin after Lindsay withdrew from the presidential race in April 1972.

HE S
IS
TO
LI

Mayor Abraham Beame (right) testified before the Senate Banking Committee on the city's financial situation in May 1977. Here he is with Committee Chairman Senator William Proxmire, (D-Wis.); in the center are New York's Senators Daniel Patrick Moynihan and Jacob K. Javits.

Edward K. Hamilton, Hayes's successor as budget director and later Lindsay's deputy mayor, notes that the pressures on Lindsay to accept flawed budgets are a feature of city, state, and federal government leadership during hard times. "The thing that may be hard to understand from the outside," he said, "is that once you have told everybody you have squeezed, shrunk, and beaten yourself up to get expenditures down, and then the comptroller comes in with proposals to avoid taxes or spending cuts, the mayor is absolutely defenseless. In that situation, the mayor turns to his budget director and asks: 'Why didn't we propose that?' And if you tell him it's a budget gimmick, he asks: 'Is it illegal?' And if you say it's legal and oppose it as unsound, you've got to withstand the Board of Estimate and the City Council, who are saying to you in private, 'Are you crazy? This guy [i.e. Beame] is giving you a way out.' John did as well as he could by opposing indefensible things on pensions, cash flows, payment dates, and shifting costs to the capital budget. But the pressure was huge."

Beyond his acceptance of accounting gimmicks and hidden deficits, of course, is the extent to which the mayor was responsible for presiding over rising costs that went beyond what the city could afford. It would be absurd not to hold Lindsay accountable for these developments, even though they were driven by larger factors. But here most scholars of the period show that though city costs went up in the Lindsay years at an astonishing rate, the rate was not terribly faster than the rate he inherited. As for municipal wages, pension benefits, and fringe benefits, Morris studied comparisons in *The Cost of Good Intentions* [and in his essay in this book] and found that although the city's labor costs were much higher than those in the private sector, the increases were comparable to those in other large cities (though fringe benefits, including health care for workers, grew at an above-average rate). In fact, the cost of police, fire, and sanitation was growing in the suburbs in some cases at an even faster clip than in New York City. A similar conclusion was reached by Shefter in his book.

In the end, the major failing of Lindsay, obvious only in hindsight, may well have been that he did not explain to New Yorkers what subsequent mayors, especially Edward I. Koch, learned to do after the fiscal crisis in 1975 and under the discipline of a state control board: that there was a limit to its resources and that it could not live the way it had when New York City was the bounty it had been.

In preparing this essay, and rethinking a period of history that I covered as a reporter for *The New York Times*, I decided to ask Koch which of his predecessors he would single out for blame. His answer was even-handed.

"Lindsay and Beame were responsible for the 1975 fiscal crisis in that both administrations borrowed money expressly for the purpose of funding operating expenses," Koch wrote me in an e-mail message. "What they did, while known to various auditors and opinion makers, was accepted as not unreasonable—indeed, what had been encouraged by Nelson Rockefeller as governor and begun by Wagner in the last year or years of his third term."

Fred Hayes, the city budget director from 1966 to 1970, has argued that "to believe or hope, as we did in the Lindsay administration, that we could put city finances on a sound long term course seems, in retrospect, an exercise in hubris."

Hubris, ignorance, or arrogance—all are easier to judge in retrospect. Only when the end came in 1975 did what had seemed impossible—a financial meltdown—come to be seen as inevitable. Many people say today that the United States government cannot sustain the budget deficits projected as far as the eye can see, and that China and other foreign governments will not forever finance them by buying Treasury securities. And yet the United States proceeds on its fiscal course, just as New York City did.

"We are in general lousy at predicting points of discontinuity, no matter how smart we are," says Hamilton, now a consultant based in California. "What happened in New York City had the characteristic of an earthquake. We know there is going to be a major earthquake in Los Angeles in 50 years. But we really won't know until the earth starts shaking when it's going to happen."

Mayor Lindsay confers with aides (from left) Barry Gottehrer, Harvey Rothenberg and Jay Kriegel at City Hall.

Kenneth T. Jackson

The Mayoral Matchup

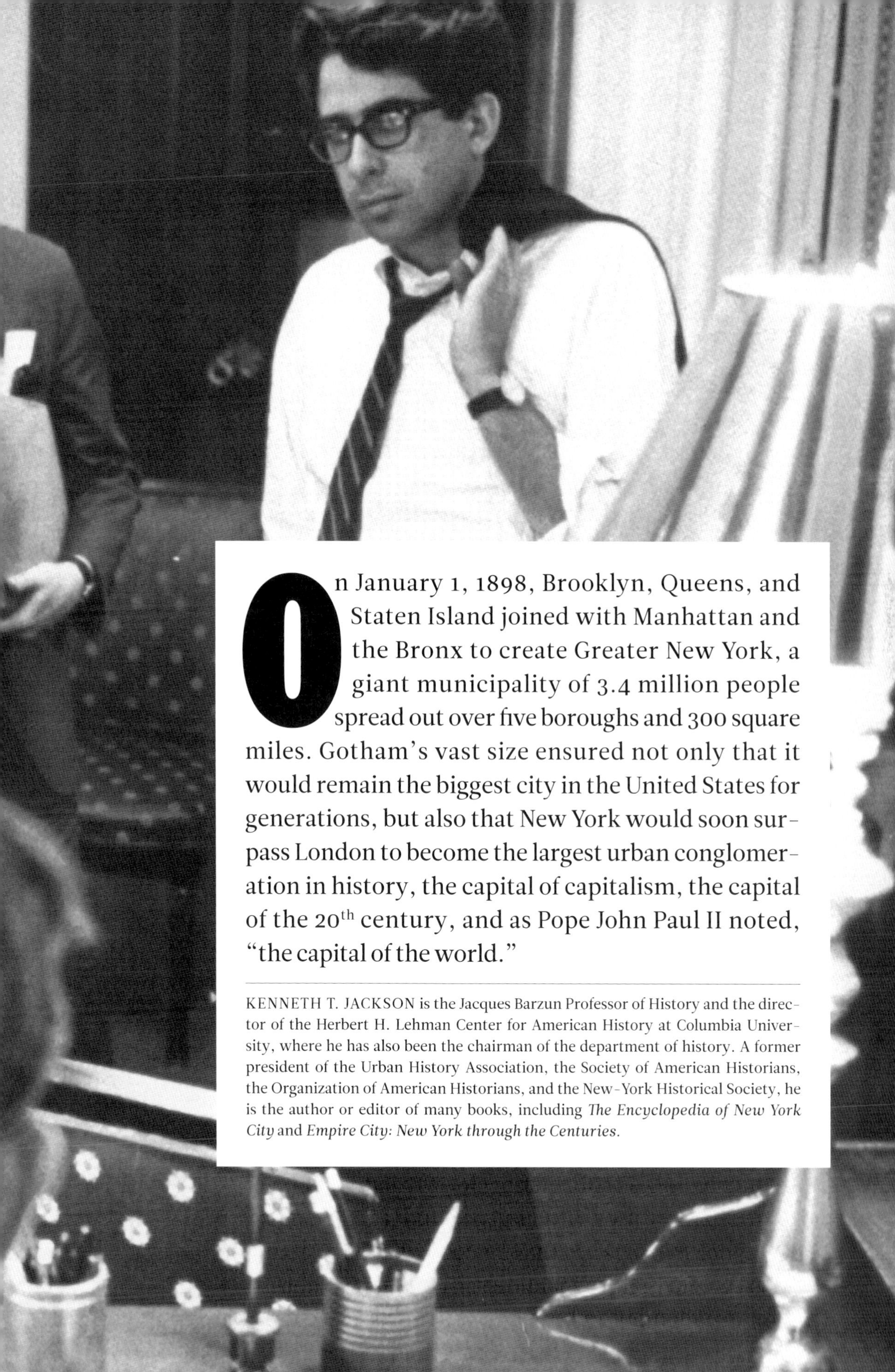

On January 1, 1898, Brooklyn, Queens, and Staten Island joined with Manhattan and the Bronx to create Greater New York, a giant municipality of 3.4 million people spread out over five boroughs and 300 square miles. Gotham's vast size ensured not only that it would remain the biggest city in the United States for generations, but also that New York would soon surpass London to become the largest urban conglomeration in history, the capital of capitalism, the capital of the 20th century, and as Pope John Paul II noted, "the capital of the world."

KENNETH T. JACKSON is the Jacques Barzun Professor of History and the director of the Herbert H. Lehman Center for American History at Columbia University, where he has also been the chairman of the department of history. A former president of the Urban History Association, the Society of American Historians, the Organization of American Historians, and the New-York Historical Society, he is the author or editor of many books, including *The Encyclopedia of New York City* and *Empire City: New York through the Centuries*.

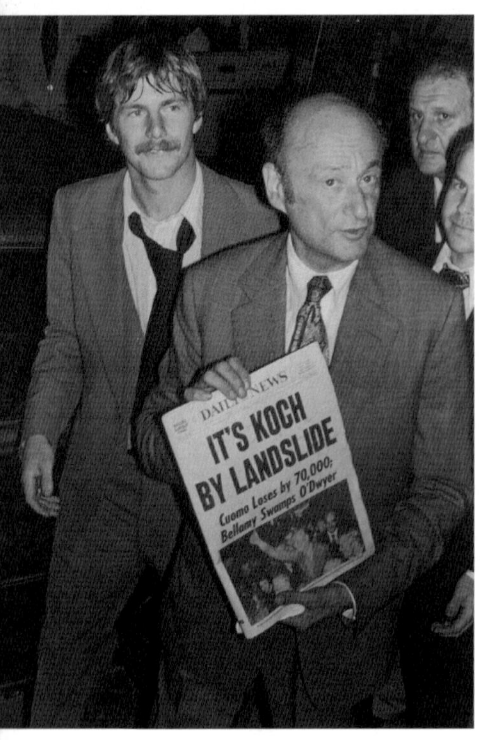

Edward I. Koch, like Lindsay an East Side congressman, would serve three terms as mayor. He gave Lindsay a critical endorsement in 1965, but instead of returning the favor, Lindsay backed a Republican to succeed him in Congress. Koch won the seat nevertheless but never forgave Lindsay.

The creation of the Greater City also meant that the mayor of New York would become the most famous and powerful city official on earth. There are three reasons for this circumstance. First, municipal governments in the United States, unlike those in Europe, Asia, Africa, and Australia, are typically charged with responsibility for basic services like fire, police, sanitation, planning, traffic management, water supply, public health, and transportation. Second, even within the decentralized American framework, New York has always had a strong mayor system with more functions than in places like Los Angeles, where the county, rather than individual municipalities, controls many facets of government. Moreover, New York has never turned to professional "city managers" or a commission-style administration.

New York since 1810 has been bigger than other American places, and from 1920 to 1970 was larger than any other city anywhere. As a result, the mayor of New York has long managed a budget of staggering size. In 1900, for example, the city spent $60 million, or approximately as much as all the states on the Atlantic seaboard from Maine to Florida, *combined*, including New York State itself. Not until the 1960s did any government in the United States, excluding the national administration in Washington, have a larger budget than City Hall in lower Manhattan.

Thus, in weighing the legacy of any single mayor since consolidation, from Robert A. Van Wyck in 1898 to Michael R. Bloomberg in 2010, we must recognize that each of the 18 chief executives (all of them male) have occupied an office both uniquely prestigious and powerful. They have all had an unusual ability to shape the metropolis, to care for its citizens, and to affect its prosperity. The mayor of New York does not simply give speeches, preside at public ceremonies, or cut ribbons at celebrations; he makes decisions. His words, his vision, his appointments, his abilities, and his ambitions have in large measure determined the city's business climate, its tax structure, its credit rating, its crime statistics, and even its physical shape.

Four Great Mayors

Within this rubric, four mayors have left particularly powerful, positive, and enduring legacies. The first, Fiorello H. La Guardia, is often referred to as "the great mayor" because he led New York through the Great Depression of the 1930s, when one fourth of the work force was unemployed, when homeless encampments ("Hoovervilles") were ubiquitous in parks and under bridges, and when once-proud heads of households resorted to peddling apples and pencils on street corners. It was not an easy time to be an elected official, because demands upon government were many and resources few. But the "Little Flower" relished the job. Under La Guardia's stewardship, and with

EDWARD I. KOCH was mayor of New York City for three terms, from 1978 through 1989.

He looked like a great leader, but he was not a great leader. The greatest thing that John Lindsay did was to bring wonderfully able, intelligent civic-minded people into city government. And I brought many of those people back into my government. But that was the greatest thing he did. Now, once again, my feelings about Lindsay relate to my personal feelings of how he, in my judgment, betrayed our relationship based on what I had done for him in helping to elect him. And two, I thought from my civic public point of view that he was a failure.

He was a Boy Scout, not a leader. I hope the Boy Scouts don't feel upset about that. What I was simply trying to convey by Boy Scout, is: "I'm going to do it this way, because this is the way it looks best from a civic point of view," as opposed to getting down and dirty, and running down to the bridge and yelling, "Walk over the bridge! We're not going to let these bastards bring us to our knees."

He believed, and he was quite correct, that he had a special relationship with the African-American community. He did, and it's all to his credit.

I personally, and for public reasons that I've given to you, believe he was vastly overrated in a whole host of areas, and that he was in part responsible, with Bob Wagner to the least extent, Abe Beame to a greater extent, for the city's fiscal condition of near bankruptcy.

Mayor Lindsay cleans piles of trash in Yorkville, near Gracie Mansion, in 1967.

JIM SLEEPER, a lecturer at Yale, is the author of *The Closest of Strangers: Liberalism and the Politics of Race in New York*.

He brought idealism, strength. It was kind of like what John Kennedy brought after Eisenhower. People saw Dwight Eisenhower as having played out, tired, grand, but old. That's how people felt about Wagner, Lindsay's predecessor. John Lindsay came in fresh, young, bold, with a new sense of moral purpose. The city was already beginning to suffer from some real trend lines pointing down. People were getting nervous.

He was one of the only big-city mayors to bring both the civil rights movement and these modern management ideas—good government, clean reform, and modern technocratic management—into the government at that time. These ideas were bubbling around, and no other mayor of a major city embodied that change, so he did.

Also, I think a certain conception of the city as this integrative, absorptive mechanism through which blacks would move just as other previously despised groups had moved, that was what broke. It was that sense of the city about itself as this great heart that draws into itself all these blood streams and processes them. All of a sudden, there was a clot. There was a rupture. There was a group that was saying, "We're not being allowed to come in, and so we're not going to come in. We want you to section us off and give us resources, and to hell with you, and you get out of our neighborhoods." That was a shock to everything that La Guardia and the New Deal and all the liberals had fought for.

(continued on next page)

CLARENCE TAYLOR is a professor at Baruch College and author of *Civil Rights in New York City: From World War II to the Giuliani Era*

I think Lindsay is a person who comes into power at a time when there's this rapid transformation taking place in New York. No one could really have expected the events that Lindsay faced.

Lindsay thought that the previous mayor had capitulated too much to the unions and this is why New York was in this sort of financial crisis and he was going to come in and set these boundaries. And so immediately he is in a confrontation with a powerful union in New York City and he loses that battle.

He is a failure because he wasn't able to deal with the New York City school crisis in the manner that he should've dealt with it. And this, like I said, was one of the worst incidents in modern New York City history. It really poisoned the relationship between blacks and Jews in New York City and Lindsay just allowed this incident to go on too long without showing some real leadership. On the other hand, I think Lindsay should be remembered as a person who attempted to address race relations and show—and he showed I believe—a real sensitivity to black and Latino communities, and attempting to provide social services—to get blacks and Latinos to participate more in government.

VINCENT CANNATO is author of *The Ungovernable City: John Lindsay and His Struggle to Save New York,* in an interview with Michael Epstein for the film *The Lindsay Years,* produced by Thirteen for WNET.org.

The story of John Lindsay is tragic. This is a man who had it all, in many ways, in the early 1960s. He had the looks, he had the charm, he had a wonderful family, he was right on the edge of American politics. He was right there on all the big issues, but then he's also—he's a man who time forgot. He—his politics—the country became more conservative. He became more liberal. The city becomes more conservative. After the fiscal crisis, we get sort of a period of retrenchment, fiscal retrenchment. And people don't look back to Lindsay going, "Oh, let's go back to the Lindsay administration." What did they do? They don't call Lindsay. Mayors don't call Lindsay and say, "How did you handle that problem?" They don't—newspapers don't call on Lindsay, "Can you write an op-ed for us explaining this issue?" People don't call him. People don't ask him to speak that much. He's kind of a forgotten man.

The way I would put it is that when John Lindsay took office in '65, the city was not in good shape. He came into office promising to clean up the city, improve the city, and turn the city around. In '73, the city was worse off, and Lindsay for the most part was not really able to follow through on what he had promised in '65. Could anyone? That's the million-dollar question.

MAJOR OWENS, a Lindsay anti-poverty official, served as a Brooklyn congressman from 1983 through 2007

The greatest expression of John Lindsay's exceptional idealism was his determination to open government and let the under represented participate. Certainly this was the most controversial part of his eight years.

[H]is struggle on behalf of the 'Other America' assumed tragic dimensions. The use of power to advocate on behalf of the powerless is the greatest virtue of any leader.

Lindsay belongs within the ranks of Lincoln, Franklin Roosevelt, Lyndon Johnson, Robert and Ted Kennedy. These men never asked: 'How am I doing?' But instead, in the spirit of Martin Luther King asked: 'Who are we helping?'

the help of his legendary parks commissioner and construction czar, Robert Moses, the metropolis not only survived the economic crisis, but also witnessed the building of an enormous array of public improvements, including the Triborough and Whitestone Bridges, the West Side Highway, the Northern State and Grand Central Parkways, Orchard Beach, the 1939–40 World's Fair, and hundreds of small parks. Although himself a Republican, La Guardia managed to make common cause with President Franklin D. Roosevelt, a Democrat, and remarkably, for the only time in its long history, New York seemed to get back almost as much from Washington as it had collectively paid to the federal tax man.

Edward I. Koch also saw New York through depression, but it was a depression of the spirit as much as of the economy. When Koch, the former Greenwich Village congressman, took over City Hall in 1978, New York seemed to be going the way of every other city in the Northeast and Middle West. Its transit system was in shambles, its corporate headquarters were departing for the suburbs or the Sunbelt, and its citizens were heading out of town. In the 1970s, New York's population declined by more than 700,000. In that single decade, the Bronx alone lost 300,000 middle-class residents, as it became in the public mind a dispiriting collection of burned-out buildings, pockmarked streets, and graffiti-scarred subways. The urban theorist Roger Starr suggested a new term, "planned shrinkage," as a logical economic and political path to bulldozing large swaths of empty urban real estate.

By the end of Koch's third term, New York was growing again, and the city had reclaimed its swagger and luster. Koch's famous query, "How am I doing?" put to passersby and colleagues alike, was based on the assumption that he was doing a good job. Particularly important was his commitment to improving conditions for the homeless. As he left office at the end of 1989, New York was spending more of its own funds on providing permanent housing for the homeless than the next 50 American cities combined.

A third mayor with an overwhelmingly positive legacy, Rudolph W. Giuliani, will always be associated with the decline in crime. In 1992, the year before he took office, there were more than 2,200 homicides in the five boroughs; in 2001, the last year of his second term, the number had dropped by 70 percent, to 649. While other cities around the country also experienced a decline in violent crime, New York became so much the poster child of the safe city that when Giuliani left office, public concern had shifted from the fading danger on the streets to a feeling that the police were being too hard on potential lawbreakers.

Michael R. Bloomberg, who became mayor in 2002, faced perhaps the greatest challenge of all. A sharp economic downturn began in late 2000 and became worse over the succeeding 18 months. By September 2001, a powerful recession was in full swing. Meanwhile, Giuliani had left the incoming Bloomberg administration with a budget deficit of $5 billion. The first mayor of the new century thus had to begin his term with a sharp tax increase. The terrorist attack on the World Trade Center made a bad situation worse. It not only cost thousands of lives, but also wiped out 15 million square feet of office space, caused the loss of perhaps 100,000 jobs, and destroyed hundreds

Reflections

JOYCE PURNICK covered Lindsay for the *New York Post* on his last day at City Hall

I always felt that he was teary [on his final day in office] because he had seen the promise of his leadership fail, and in his gut he knew that what he wanted to do, what he had hoped to do—the dream of bringing new, modern, progressive, liberal urban leadership to New York City to change it, to make it a better place, to make it a kinder place, to make it better for the poor, to change the schools, to make them work, which is what he promised at the beginning—he had failed to do. A lot of it failed, and maybe it all came together in his mind at that point.

He was a victim of a changing society, and he was mired in an earlier era, in idealism that was no longer valid, or was becoming less valid.

JAY L. KRIEGEL was Lindsay's chief of staff and special counsel. He later served as senior vice president of CBS, founding publisher of The American Lawyer, and President of NYC 2012

It has been fashionable for the neo-cons to dismiss much of the Lindsay era based on simplistic ideology and artificial retroactive calculations, decades later, based on their own economic models. But we know what those days and nights were really like. We...actually felt society being torn apart. We saw others resort to cheap rhetoric or simplistic solutions. J. Edgar Hoover blamed the communists. Nixon blamed the kids. Whites blamed blacks. Blacks blamed the cops. And the cops were out there along—except for J.V.L. He literally gave himself day after day, night after night, as tangible evidence that someone cared, that someone would listen, that someone would make every possible effort to hold us together. And he did.

John Lindsay was in his time a national figure. He taught all Americans what our cities meant to this country at a time when national politicians were bent on forgetting them and national policies were based on ignoring them.

PETER C. GOLDMARK JR. served as Lindsay's chief of staff, and later became executive director of the Port Authority and president of the Rockefeller Foundation

He had things to say to those who lived at the most desperate margins of our society that no mayor had ever said before, and to say them he went places to which no mayor before or since has gone. During a time when every city in the country was troubled and divided, and many of them were in flames, New York City was led by the clearest voice of all.

of small businesses in lower Manhattan, and it threatened the very idea of the city. Respected urbanists predicted that the age of the skyscraper was over. After all, if ordinary workers were afraid of elevators, tall buildings, or subways, the dense urban fabric of Manhattan would become obsolete and untenable.

Miraculously, though, New York prospered. Even as the metropolis mourned the loss of an unprecedented 343 firefighters and thousands of men and women just entering the prime of life, young families with children, resources, and options poured into Manhattan. The price of real estate rose to new heights (until the Great Recession), all but one of the city's 450 neighborhoods began to improve (lower Manhattan, early on, being the exception), 200 building cranes started pushing new structures into the sky, and more than 40 million tourists visited the city annually. Perhaps most important, crime continued to fall so that 2009 set new records for safety.

"John Lindsay was a visionary leader for our city at a time when belief in our city's future had waned. He was unafraid to act on his positive vision of the city. His personal courage and ability to see people for what they were—rather than how they looked or where they lived—guided us safely through times of great tension and explosiveness in our city and across our nation."

—Franklin A. Thomas *was a deputy police commissioner and later president of the Ford Foundation*

The Lindsay Record

As the years pass and as more scholarly work on municipal politics appears and as the city gains in prestige and livability, another mayor, John V. Lindsay is beginning to look better. The negative assessments of his mayoralty have been overstated. Taking office at a time of disillusionment with the Vietnam War, of frustration on all sides of the civil rights issue, and of unhappiness with rampant inflation, Lindsay brought the idealism and the hopes of a new generation of residents to the steps of City Hall itself. He was energetic, smart, idealistic, and young, and he became a beacon of liberalism during an era of growing Republican hegemony. He brought glamour and sophistication to an office that had long lacked both. And garbage piles and protestors notwithstanding, New York City was not the scene of a major riot, as were Los Angeles, Detroit, and Newark. Arguably, New York survived the racial upheavals that doomed other cities in the late 1960s because of Lindsay. His personal courage and commitment, founded on a heartfelt compassion for the poor, were his greatest legacy.

The Lindsay administration was also particularly effective in terms of the quality of people that it attracted to public service—idealistic college graduates, ambitious lawyers, and others who shared his vision of a shining city accessible to all. And while crime increased, the increase was modest compared to the surge during the crack epidemic in Edward Koch's administration. Similarly, white flight was a common phenomenon in many older American cities between 1950 and 1980, and, if anything, New York fared much better than other Northeastern and Midwestern municipalities in the postwar years. Revealingly, Lindsay was re-elected in 1969 without the support of either the Democratic or Republican parties. Like Nelson A. Rockefeller before him, Lindsay's blue-blood appearance belied his populist sentiment. Rockefeller, who has been criticized and remembered for his punitive drug laws, was on other policies a consummate liberal, one who believed

How New York Changed Under Lindsay

Median Age

1960

31.4

1970

28.4

SOURCE

U.S. Department of Commerce, Bureau of the Census, *County and City Data Book*. Washington, D.C. Bureau of the Census, 1960, 1970. http://www2.lib.virginia.edu/ccdb

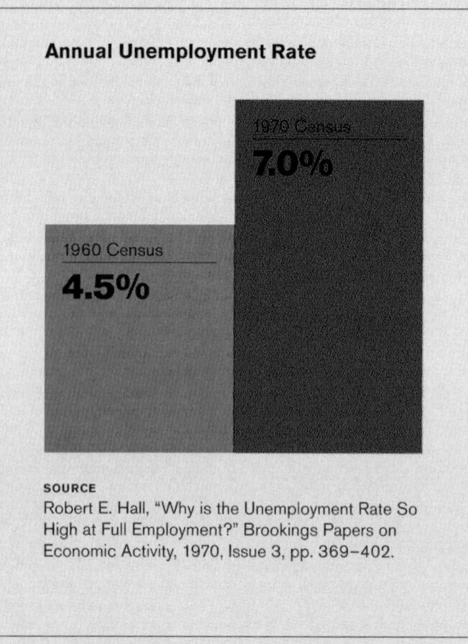

SOURCE

Robert E. Hall, "Why is the Unemployment Rate So High at Full Employment?" Brookings Papers on Economic Activity, 1970, Issue 3, pp. 369–402.

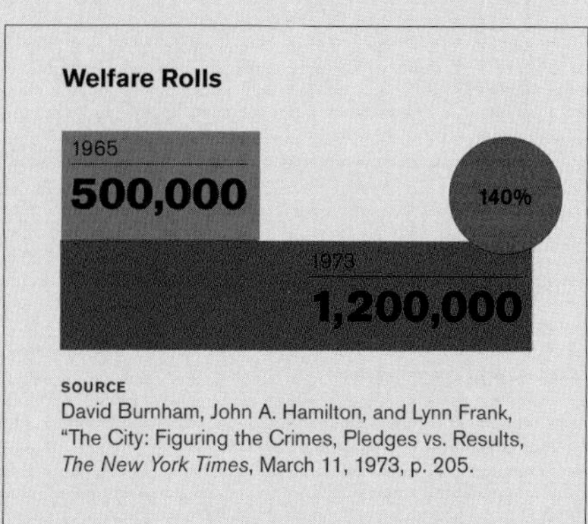

SOURCE

David Burnham, John A. Hamilton, and Lynn Frank, "The City: Figuring the Crimes, Pledges vs. Results, *The New York Times*, March 11, 1973, p. 205.

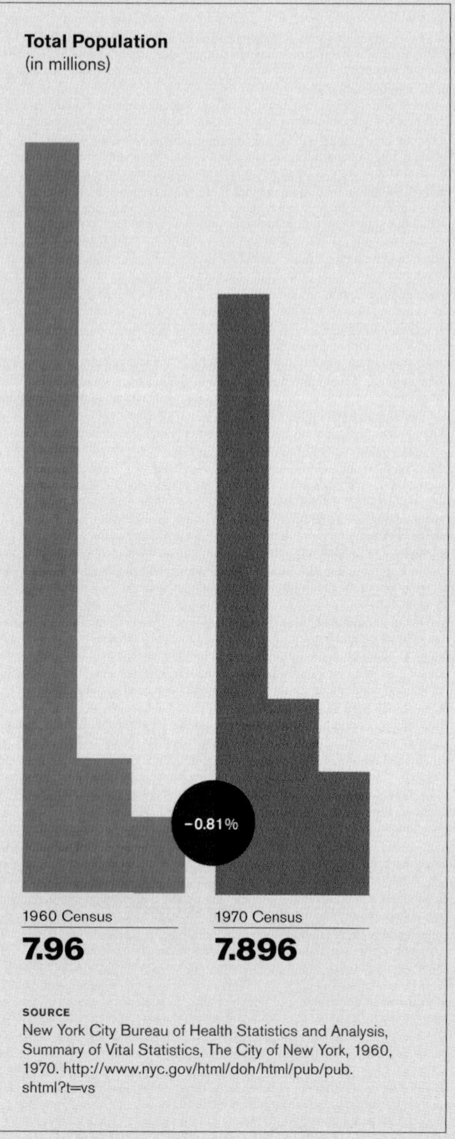

SOURCE

New York City Bureau of Health Statistics and Analysis, Summary of Vital Statistics, The City of New York, 1960, 1970. http://www.nyc.gov/html/doh/html/pub/pub.shtml?t=vs

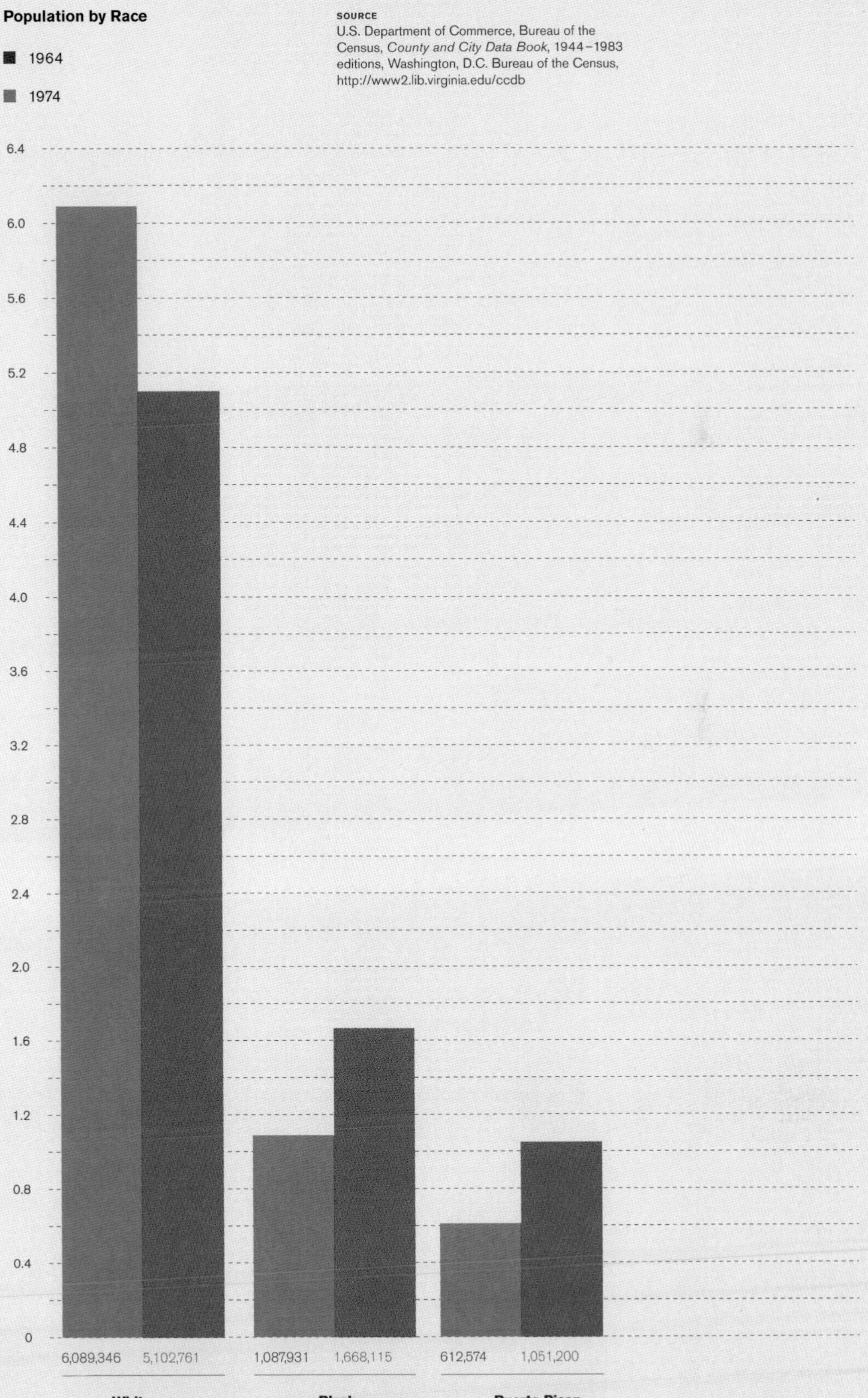

(continued on next page)

How New York Changed Under Lindsay (continued from previous page)

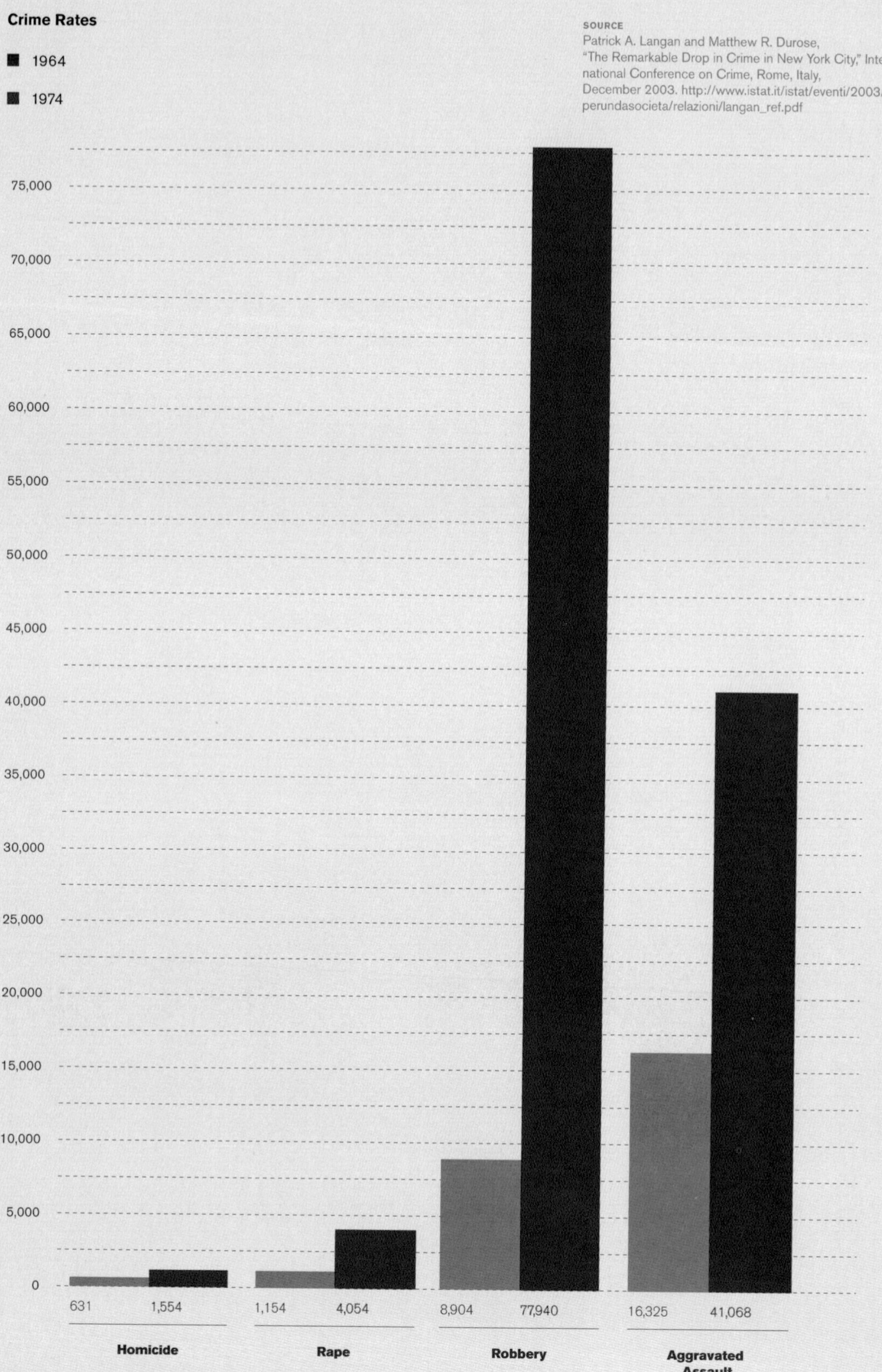

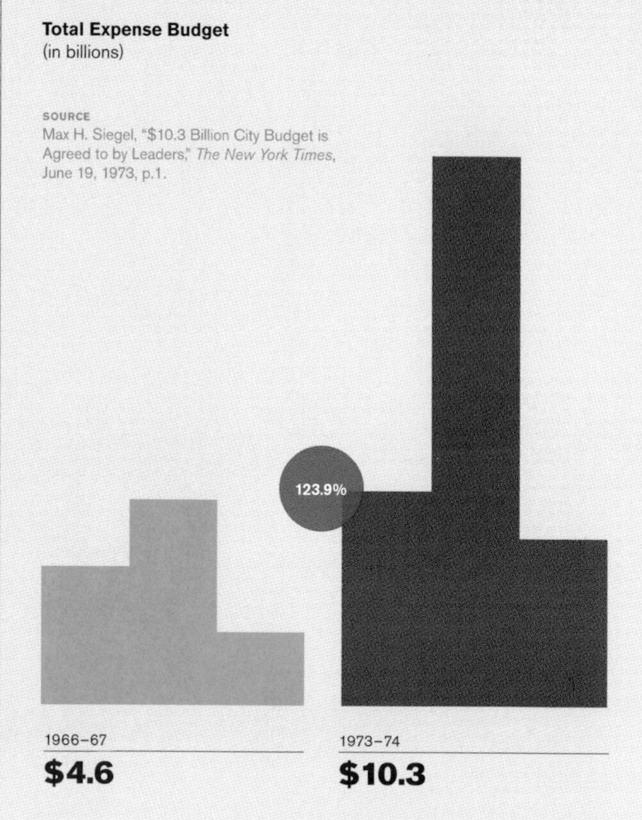

Number of Fortune 500 Companies

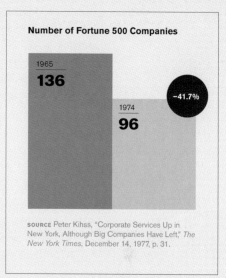

1965
136

1974
96

−41.7%

SOURCE Peter Kihss, "Corporate Services Up in New York, Although Big Companies Have Left," *The New York Times*, December 14, 1977, p. 31.

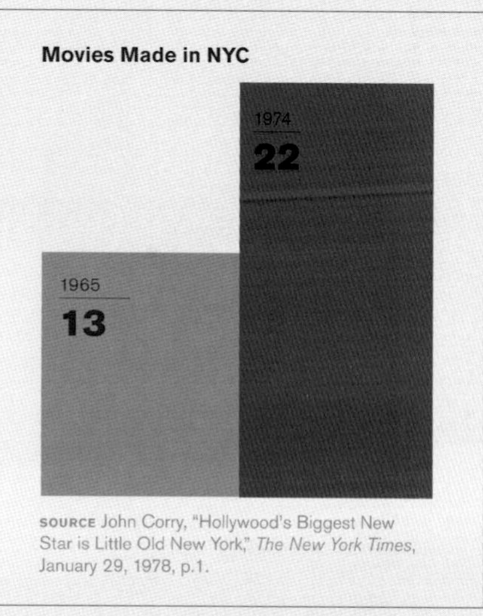

Prices

SOURCE
Isadore Barmashi, "Food Price Rise is No Surprise," *The New York Times*, July 23, 1975, p. 62; "Distant Rumble in the Subways," *The New York Times*, July 27, 1965, p. 32; Linda Greenhouse, "Upstarters are Won Over on Saving 35-cent Fare, *The New York Times*, January 16, 1974, p.115.

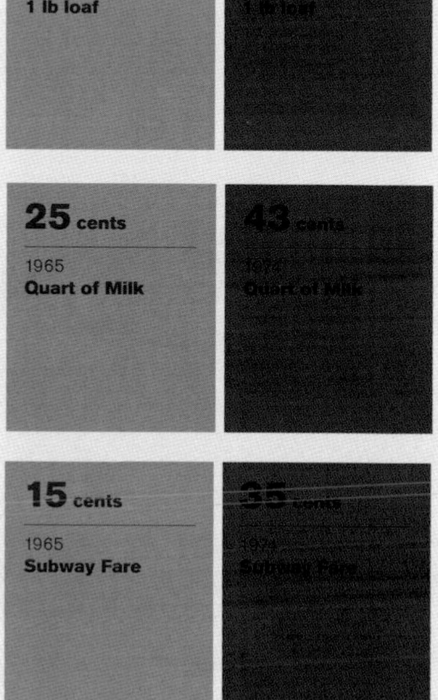

that education, arts, social welfare, and opportunity should be accessible to all. He believed in the greatness of New York State.

Lindsay picked up on Rockefeller's progressive mantle and applied it to New York City. A generation that sought leaders who would break with the past saw in him only the ideals, not his lack of administrative experience. Nor did they see what a behemoth the city was in terms of governance. Ordinarily, Lindsay's personal role in avoiding devastating racially inspired violence might, in itself, be enough to catapult him into the pantheon of great New York mayors. Yet too much other baggage dragged him down.

September 14, 1966: (from left) Mayor Lindsay and Senators Jacob K. Javits and Robert F. Kennedy announce that they will campaign for the mayor's Civilian Complaint Review Board, which went on to be defeated in a referendum in November 1966 by almost 3 to 1.

Why is Lindsay generally not regarded as among the great mayors of the consolidated city? There are a number of reasons—fair or not—for this judgment. Most obviously, the first significant economic and demographic decline in the four century-long history of the metropolis coincided with the eight years of Lindsay's term of office. Between 1966 and 1974, at least 800,000 middle-class residents left the city. The departing families were only partially replaced, and the newcomers were less able to pay taxes than those who left.

Second, municipal expenditures grew at an unsustainable pace during the Lindsay years. Over the eight years between 1966 and the beginning of 1974, city spending increased 124 percent (60 percent, taking inflation into account), from $4 billion a year to $10 billion. As a percentage of personal income, the increase in city spending during the Lindsay years was from 9.5 percent to 15.4 percent. Most ominously, the city increasingly resorted to short-term borrowing to pay ordinary operating expenses. This, of course, led to near-bankruptcy by 1975. And Lindsay appeared to be out of touch with fiscal reality. For example, in Senate testimony in 1966, he remarked that New York City needed $5 billion a year in federal assistance over the next 10 years to remain livable. That sum, over 10 years, would have represented 38 percent of the revenue of the entire United States government for a year.

Third, by spending disproportionately more money on hospitals and welfare, which were more significant to needy families, Lindsay, in effect, redirected spending away from police, fire, transportation, and sanitation, all of which were services important to the middle class. In fact, the number of New Yorkers on the welfare rolls more than doubled during his administration, in

Striking Transport Workers Union members picket in January 1966 as Lindsay faces his first crisis as mayor.

part because caseworkers were instructed specifically to find people who were eligible for welfare but not yet on the rolls. Meanwhile, Lindsay denounced the idea of asking welfare recipients to do some work as reminiscent of the Dark Ages.

Fourth, labor relations during the Lindsay years were contentious and in the long run disastrous to the city's fiscal stability. In Lindsay's first term alone, in addition to the devastating transit workers' walkout in the first days of his administration, there were two major teacher strikes, as well as a sanitation strike, a strike by welfare caseworkers, and a strike by municipal hospital doctors and nurses. Taken together, they created the impression of a city out of control, or of a city run for the benefit of its employees rather than its citizens. The long-run implications of union settlements would not become apparent for several more decades, when pension benefits and early retirements created a growing burden for the budget.

"A Mayor of Vision"

The New York Times, Editorial, December 31, 1973

John V. Lindsay, a mayor of vision who dared to raise the sights of his fellow citizens, leaves office tonight after an unprecedented eight-year effort to reinvigorate and reshape this great metropolis. Despite all the setbacks and difficulties, this leader of verve and imagination achieved far more than he was generally given credit for. We are confident that in the perspective of time his record of accomplishment will place him securely among the outstanding mayors of New York.

At a time when cities everywhere have been subject to crushing pressures from forces that are often beyond their control, Mayor Lindsay has been exceptional in his perception of the urban problem and its causes. Although his innovative responses to the challenge of change have often provoked sharp controversy in his home city, Mr. Lindsay has earned wide recognition, in the words of Mayor Kevin White of Boston, as "probably the most significant politician in the history of municipal government in doing something for the cities."

John Lindsay would be the first to admit that New York today still falls far short of the vision of a civilized, efficiently managed, livable city that he carried into City Hall eight years ago. He has made serious mistakes both in style and substance, and has suffered innumerable disappointments and frustrations in the struggle against formidable social, economic, and political forces.

Nevertheless, the outgoing mayor leaves a city which in many ways, small and large, has become more civil, more manageable, more livable than it was when he took office; above all, a city that has reversed course and is moving forward after an era of morbid decline. He leaves a city government which, while still far from ideal, is better equipped organizationally and physically to deal with the excruciating problems that still threaten to overwhelm it.

Mayor Lindsay's most striking achievement lies in one of the most critical areas of modern American urban life—race relations. Who can forget his courageous sorties into the streets of troubled neighborhoods during the long hot summers of the late 1960s, "cooling" New York while other urban centers across the nation exploded in racial violence? His proud assertion that "we have given leadership to a city that didn't burn down" was no idle boast, especially in view of what happened in other cities and what could have happened here.

Ironically, his strenuous and sensitive efforts to respond to the grievances of dispossessed minorities became the cause of John Lindsay's most serious alienation from another large body of citizens—"blue collar" and middle class—who felt, sometimes with justice, that their own interests had been neglected. In the end, however, the Lindsay Administration's effort to engage disaffected minorities in the governmental process through decentralized school boards and "little city halls" has given all citizens a better opportunity to participate in the decisions that affect their lives.

The Lindsay record is full of ironies. While the mayor was criticized as an indifferent administrator, many of his appointments have been outstandingly good, and he and some of his able aides have substantially strengthened the cumbersome administrative structure they inherited: through the consolidation of more than 50 overlapping agencies into 10 new "superagencies"; through the introduction of systems analysis, computerization and other modern management techniques; and through the vigorous recruitment of able young top- and middle-management personnel.

Although he has been the nation's leading exponent of increased federal and state aid for the cities, Mayor Lindsay showed realism and courage in meeting the city's own fiscal responsibilities by introducing the first city income tax and by forcing through other unpopular but necessary fiscal measures. He shares credit with his successor, Mayor-elect Beame, for the "A" status the city has gained from the nation's two major credit-rating agencies.

Mayor Lindsay's most conspicuous failure—at least in his first term—but one that by no means was entirely his own fault was in the field of labor relations. From his first day in office when the subwaymen went on strike, his administration was plagued by bruising confrontations with organized municipal employees which provoked serious and sometimes perilous interruptions in vital services and which invariably led to costly settlements. In view of the growing power and militancy of the unions and internal problems that provoked their leaders to press extreme demands, it is questionable how much of this might have been avoided even if the mayor had enjoyed from the start the kind of rapport with labor that he later developed.

In any event, he is bequeathing to his successor a relatively effective organization for collective bargaining, the nation's first binding arbitration law for a major city and a tough and imaginative productivity program, tied to bargaining, that is beginning to offset the damage done by earlier extravagant wage settlements.

While crime in the streets and the accompanying threat to the personal security of every individual have undoubtedly done more to blacken the reputation of New York City than any other single factor in recent years, Mr. Lindsay is leaving the Police Department in better shape in every respect—leadership, standards, equipment,

(continued)

personnel, organization—than it was when he found it. And while the crime problem, like the narcotics problem, has certainly not been mastered, there are unmistakable signs of increased efficiency in meeting it.

It is quite possible that Mayor Lindsay's most-lasting contribution to the city has stemmed from his deep personal commitment to improving the urban environment. His administration has enforced tough new anti-pollution laws. It has expanded, improved, and opened the park system. It has energized the housing program. Above all, it has achieved pioneering breakthroughs in urban design, strengthening and broadening the planning process and using zoning creatively to preserve and enrich the diverse physical characteristics of a unique metropolis.

John Lindsay's lofty vision of what this city could and should be leaves a lasting challenge to his successors in City Hall and to the entire citizenry to carry on the fight. After a deserved vacation with Mrs. Lindsay—who has herself proved to be a great asset to the city—it is inconceivable that Mr. Lindsay himself will not resume the battle, taking to other levels of government the perception, energy, and hard-won experience that for the last eight years have served this city well.

From "He Refreshed 'Fun City' with Heart and Mind"

JACK NEWFIELD

The New York Post, December 21, 2000

John Lindsay was an idealist who didn't have a mean bone in his body and tried to do good during a tough time in this city and country.

He was an eloquent urbanist—more advocate than manager—who should have become a senator in 1968 after R.F.K. was assassinated. But he wouldn't grovel to Nelson Rockefeller for the appointment, so it went to Charlie Goodell, who no one remembers.

Lindsay became New York's first civil-rights mayor. He made minorities feel like full citizens of this city. He made himself visible in all the minority communities. He opened vest pocket parks, showed movies in the street.

Lindsay recruited into city government a generation of young aides who eventually matured into civic wise men—Gordon Davis, Peter Goldmark, Steve Isenberg, Nat Leventhal, Lance Liebman.

Lindsay was great on race, but not so great on class. He lacked a certain empathy for the white ethnic communities of the city.

Lindsay didn't know how to communicate with old-fashioned ethnic union leaders like Mike Quill and John DeLury, so there were bitter strikes.

He built up the city's short-term debt to do good things, but that contributed to the fiscal crisis of 1975.

The mayor who wanted reconciliation so deeply accidentally created contention and white backlash.

On balance, history will judge Lindsay favorably. He had real philosophical convictions and the courage to advocate them.

Lindsay rides the subway on his last day in office.

Fifth, in order to pay for new policy initiatives, Lindsay persuaded Albany to approve a city income tax, which ultimately drove more families from the city (although his commuter tax regionalized the burden). By 1972, New Yorkers paid 8.9 percent of their total income in various city taxes, by far the largest proportion in the United States.

Sixth, Lindsay's experiment to decentralize decision-making and to empower neighborhoods met strong resistance. The creation of a local community school board in the Ocean Hill-Brownsville section of Brooklyn led to a bitter conflict between the heavily Jewish teachers' union and black parents. Similarly, the mayor's desire to scatter public housing from ghetto areas to a more dispersed profile around the city, while itself a laudable objective, backfired when Forest Hills, a relatively affluent Queens neighborhood, rose up in opposition to a plan to build high-rise, low-income housing in their backyard.

Seventh, the Lindsay proposal to add civilians to a review board that investigated complaints against the police not only was defeated in a referendum, but also allowed opponents to point out that the crime rate was already increasing and it exacerbated racial tensions.

Eighth, during the Lindsay administration there was more police corruption than at other times in 20th-century New York, although a commission he appointed imposed institutional reforms. Also damaging were revelations of widespread fraud in the Human Resources Administration in 1968. *The New York Times* published a lengthy exposé in January 1969, including the astonishing charge that one in five checks issued by the Neighborhood Youth Corps was fraudulent.

Ninth, as evidence of the mayor's unpopularity outside his liberal, Jewish, and black power base, Lindsay never won even a plurality in any mayoral election outside of Manhattan. Cynics would even claim that he declared war on the other four boroughs, and especially on Irish Catholics, to placate his own constituents. Revealingly, the mayor appointed a school advisory committee without a single representative of white middle-class families outside of Manhattan.

Finally, Lindsay's decision in 1971 to run for the Democratic presidential nomination meant that he would not opt for the drastic retrenchment that the looming fiscal crisis seemed to require. Instead, he resorted to sophisticated accounting tricks to at least temporarily put off the financial day of reckoning that finally appeared in 1974.

Taken together, these charges against Lindsay represent a strong indictment of an administration that never fulfilled its promise. The young reformer rode into office on a wave of hope and inspiration; when he left eight years later, in many respects the city was a wreck.

Maybe it was timing; maybe no one could have done better than Lindsay given the cards that he was dealt. But the budget fiasco and the general notion of maximizing the number of people receiving welfare payments are not likely to be forgiven. "Being mayor is like being a bitch in heat," Lindsay famously wrote in his novel *The Edge*. "You stand still and you get screwed, you start running and you get bit in the ass." The extensive photographic record reveals

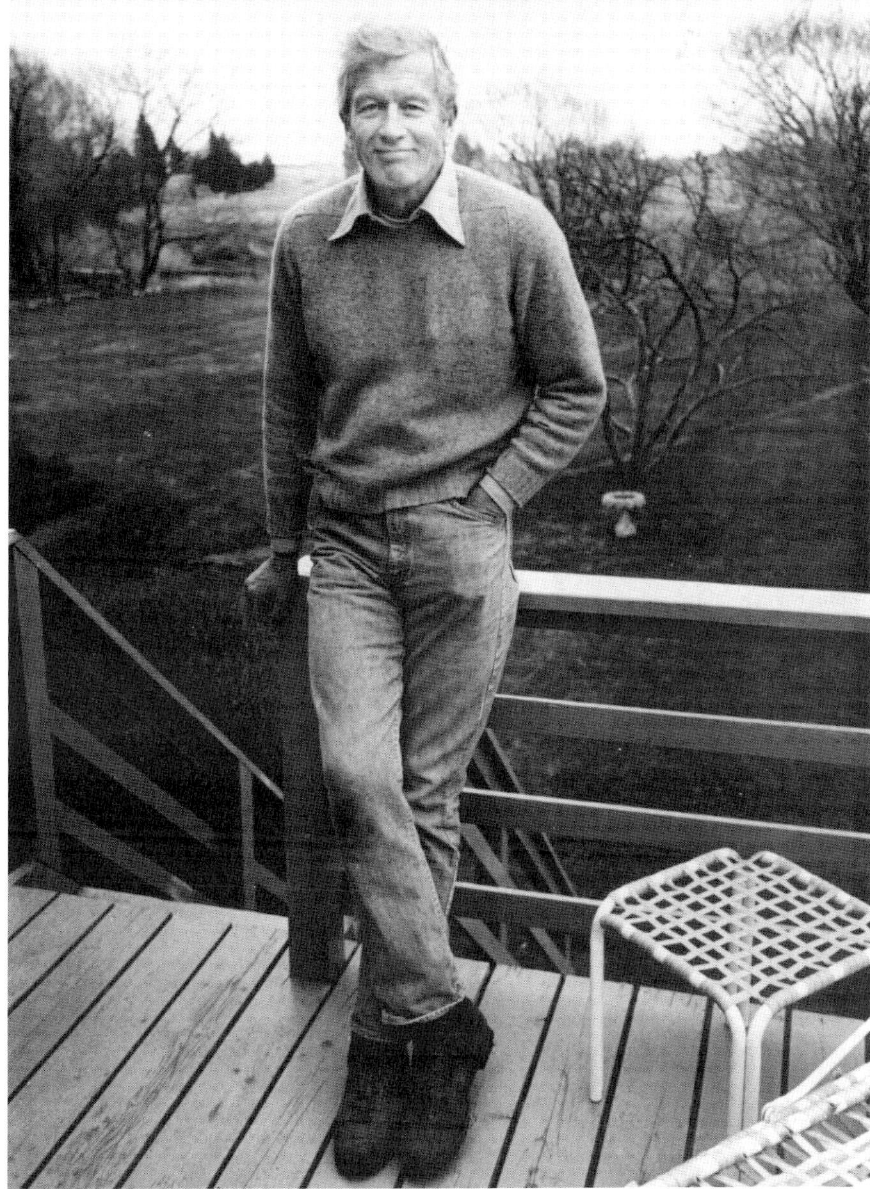

No longer fresh, Lindsay manages a wan smile at the beach in Bridgehampton, Long Island.

a handsome face increasingly marked by sadness and weariness: Lindsay's personal defeat mirrored the city's.

The city rebounded in time, but Lindsay did not. Once he left office, he was largely out of the limelight before his death in 2000. If the city recovered from the doldrums of the 1970s, it was not just because of Koch, Giuliani, or Bloomberg. New York City could not have survived, let alone thrived, without the enduring legacy of John Lindsay's vision of a shining city. The generation that came of age during his mayoralty benefited from Lindsay's insistence on justice, fairness, and an open voice. His ideals may not have been realized in his own time, but became foundational for later administrations. A low crime rate, more-orderly schools, and cleaner streets are desirable goals, but hollow victories without assurances of civil liberties, racial justice, and equal access to the benefits of the city. Revisiting the turbulent years of Mayor Lindsay reminds us that a great city is built not only of bricks and mortar but also of generosity, hope, courage, and commitment.

The Solid Estimate of Lindsay

JIMMY BRESLIN

Always, I shall see him in the times when we didn't know what was going on, what was causing these sudden riots, but he knew to follow his instincts, which were pure. The streets of Harlem and Bedford Stuyvesant carried the sound of broken glass in the night and police firing blanks in an attempt to frighten shouting crowds. It couldn't be done.

When it started, John Lindsay was out in shirtsleeves, talking to crowds, telling them that they weren't alone in life, he was there, representing the city. It was supposed to be dangerous, but what does this mean to him? He knew where he should be, and he was there. He had to be the only white you saw for blocks. The black politicians came running to walk with him. They were telling him to go home; they could take it from here. This man was messing with what belonged to them. You saw them as a mob. They knew it was a white guy taking their place.

It wasn't just here. Detroit looked like an air raid victim. In Chicago they fired real bullets. The fabled mayor, Daley, called for the police to "shoot to maim." In New York, Lindsay walked the streets. Lyndon Johnson asked Lindsay to move into the White House. He didn't. He stayed on the streets. White guy crossing over. Could it ever happen the other way?

I thought of the nights of John Lindsay the other night when there was this shout and applause in the polling place across the street from the public housing on Bedford Avenue in Brooklyn and the television was announcing that Barrack Obama was the next president of the United States.

Know ye that nowhere in the history of the world has such a thing happened.

In telling of other things here, municipal matters, I mention things that occurred forty and forty five years ago and of course I shouldn't be old enough to have been near them, but when pressed, I must say that I can see Michael Quill, the transit union head, and Robert Price, deputy mayor to John V. Lindsay, going into the office of Dr. Hyman Zuckerman, cardiologist, on 34th Street in Manhattan.

The occasion was one of those highly secret meetings about a transit strike. The year was 1965 and a strike could be heard in the air and on the rails. Lindsay had just been elected and the city's transit system, the wonder of the world, was about to be stopped. Quill met secretly with Price at the doctor's and Lindsay at the Williams Club, a Quill favorite, although his alma mater was the IRT. When Quill looked at him, he saw the Church of England. Both secret meetings produced nothing. "There is going to be a strike and you can't do anything about it," Quill told both of them.

That was because the emotion that the city still was unable to handle was race. The blacks, the people of color, whatever the name, these citizens, were reaching for a future in the transit union and the old Irish, represented by Quill, thought it was theirs and they should hang on.

There were groups in places like Rosedale, in Queens, who started organizations like ROAR–Respect Our American Rights. All Right is White.

Right away when the strike started, the women of the city reached down and put on sneakers for the walking in front of them. That brought relief to the female feet and changed the fashion in New York, and America, forever.

The rest was complicated to a point where Lindsay made a statement that came out of the befuddlement of trying to run a city of over eight million with no transit system. During this, he made my employment delightful one day when he called for people to stay home from work unless they were absolutely indispensable at their jobs. "I know we all think of ourselves as essential, but at a time like this we all have to look at ourselves in the mirror and tell the truth."

"I am indispensible!" my friend, the late Robert J. Allen called out to the morning air as he hitch hiked to work.

The strike turned for the worse when a court order calling for Quill to go to jail for contempt, of which he had a body full, was handed to him by two police officers in City Hall. His heart was causing him to shake. The paper rattled in his hands. He said in a trembling voice, "The judge...can drop dead in his black robes."

He was off to the Civil Jail, then in the West 30's. It happened that the warden had a wife who wanted to be a writer and one day he asked me to look at her work. Now I had a better reason to help him. I called him and said that Quill was coming down in desperate shape and that he better be at the front door and make sure that a doctor was with him because Quill could drop dead right there. The warden would be called a murderer. He had an acute understanding of survival. The warden stood at the prison front entrance and as Quill came up the steps with the police, he collapsed. He was taken to Bellevue. The warden could see how close he was to losing all. He called me and thanked me. I seized the moment and told him that "You have a Mr. Red High in your place. He is a friend of mine from Queens. He refused to talk to a grand jury about something, gambling I imagine. and he is in your jail on contempt. He must see Frank Sinatra at Jilly's tonight. He promises to return." And that night, here is Sinatra at Jilly's, with a song and a party and drinking. Snapping his fingers to the music is Mr. Red

High. "Lindsay let me out," Red High announced. "That is our man," said Sinatra.

Sinatra subsequently made a big singing appearance at a Lindsay affair. Red High made an enthusiastic vote for him. At least he said he did; I don't now if he was legally allowed to vote. Lindsay was reelected. He had to overcome deep unpopularity coming out of a deep snow in the Fresh Meadows neighborhood in Queens. The sanitation trucks were out there, all right, but they were going around with their plows up in the air, well over the snow. This was their labor dispute with the city and it was perfectly reasonable to them because it was also against this mayor who was too tall and from the Ivy League and, by the way, was too close to the blacks.

In my personal time in this, I am at a bar with Norman Mailer one night in 1969 and Jack Newfield came on the radio and announced that we both were running for mayor. We had a drink on that. We went in the Democratic primary. We had a campaign organization that consisted of detectives from Connecticut looking for pretty and very young volunteers who were in the big city for a glamorous literary-politico experience. But one which caused parents to reach for the 911. My own organization consisted of an angry wife. I forget who won the primary. I sure didn't. But I know I had a book out called "The Gang That Couldn't Shoot Straight" and it was a best seller for half a year and no publicity came between my book and success. Good boy yourself, Breslin.

There was some question about Paul O'Dwyer's neice, Joan O'Dwyer, being reappointed as a judge. It had to do with which side people were on in the cluttered election. One afternoon Lindsay came into Toots Shor's and had a drink with me and I mentioned her problem and Lindsay said, "Don't worry about it. There are ways to jigger that appointment around."

Later, I told this to Paul O'Dwyer and he gave what I think is the solid estimate on Lindsay.

"Did he say that?" Paul asked.

"Yes, he did," I said.

"I'll take his word over anybody's." Paul said.

Of course the word stood up as straight as the guy who gave.

In Memoriam, John V. Lindsay

Representative Charles B. Rangel of Harlem delivered a eulogy at Lindsay's memorial service on January 26, 2001, at the Cathedral of St. John the Divine. These are excerpts:

To know that we celebrate a man that Broadway could call their own, and Harlem thought he belonged to them; a man that could walk all of the streets of this city, and whether you agreed or didn't agree with him, you would know that his heart was making New Yorkers truly believe that they were the tops. A part of the great legacy he leaves is that perhaps today we do have more self-confidence, and more self-esteem than we need as New Yorkers, but by God, everybody knew wherever we were that John Lindsay was our Mayor.

All over the world, I see people that I don't know that come and tell me, "You must remember me. I used to work for John Lindsay." But as I saw this crowd building up in this great cathedral, and see so many faces of so many people that continue to give their service in government, and not-for-profits, and working for the community, and being in the private sector, and providing leadership in all of these levels, and find out that in this great sorority, this great fraternity, how deeply they feel that no matter how much they succeed, or no matter how much they do, that they feel the proudest of saying they're part of the Lindsay family.

He has brought what we call a lot of class to our profession of politics. I had never met in my life, being born and raised in Harlem, a white Protestant Republican. I'd heard that they were around. But we'd never seen them. But maybe that's why he was so special, because he didn't act like he was white; he certainly didn't act like he was Republican. And he did act as though he wanted all of the people to feel like he did, that we were the tops.

Sam Roberts

The Legacy

The mayor was depicted as a young student activist (middle) and an African American (bottom) in these illustrations by Paul Giovanopoulos that accompanied a Gloria Steinham article on Lindsay's urban strategy for *New York* magazine, May 11, 1970.

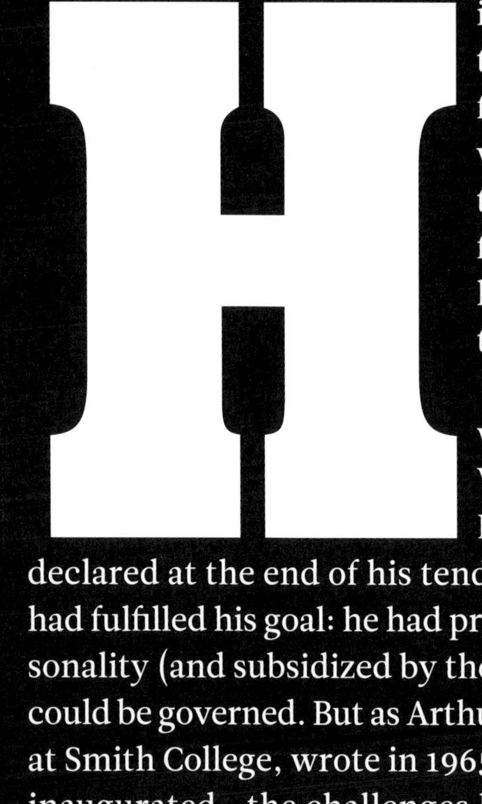

istory judges mayors by the challenges they confronted, the resources they were able to muster to meet them, and whether, in fulfilling their agenda, they left their constituents and their successor a better city.

Fiorello H. La Guardia, whose portrait faced John V. Lindsay's desk in his City Hall office for eight years, declared at the end of his tendentious third term that he had fulfilled his goal: he had proved, by sheer force of personality (and subsidized by the New Deal), that New York could be governed. But as Arthur Mann, a history professor at Smith College, wrote in 1965—even before Lindsay was inaugurated—the challenges he was inheriting could be considered more formidable than those facing La Guardia. "The narcotics racket is not quite the same thing as the slot-machine racket," Mann wrote. "Nor can we equate, except superficially, today's welfare rolls with yesteryear's relief rolls." Moreover, Mann concluded, "Lindsay is the first New York mayor really to have to care about incorporating the Negro into the American dream."

It was no coincidence that Lindsay—an unabashedly magnetic figure who could deliberately inspire and polarize people with the same policy ("He is fresh and everyone else is polite," was just one paraphrase of Murray Kempton)—was sandwiched between two relatively lackluster mayors. In the last half-century, New Yorkers have had an uncanny knack for electing the right *candidate* at the right time. The deliberative Wagner was succeeded by the charismatic Lindsay, who was followed by Beame, the taciturn bean counter, who was beaten by the irrepressible Koch. Koch lost to Dinkins, who insisted he didn't have to be loud to be strong, but was later defeated by Giuliani, who was loud *and* strong. When term limits prevented Giuliani from running again, he was succeeded by Bloomberg, who was also strong, but less loud.

It is impossible, of course, to say definitively how any of the others would have fared as mayor from 1966 through 1973. None had a free ride during his own tenure, nor were any without flaws that, like Lindsay's, detracted from their records. Beame faced a fiscal crisis. Koch's challenge was to revive the city, and he succeeded. Dinkins inherited a city that was racially polarized and plagued by crack-induced crime. Giuliani took over a city that had been judged ungovernable and tamed it, Bloomberg a vastly improved city and made it even better.

In 1965, Lindsay was elected because, as a candidate, he had promised change—change for the better. If history has held him, fairly or not, to a higher standard since then, it was, in part, because he had dared New Yorkers to buy into his dream. Given the alternatives, they gambled that he would deliver. Ironically, two of his greatest legacies, the talent he would attract to government and the pivotal role he would play in saving the city from the ravages of rioting, had barely been contemplated during his first mayoral campaign.

In the last half-century in New York, two elected officials—Governor Hugh L. Carey and John V. Lindsay—deserve disproportionate credit for attracting a cadre of dedicated public servants to their administrations (Koch did too, many of them Carey and Lindsay alumni). For decades, they would serve with distinction in government and in civic institutions. Some still do. Lindsay recruited to his administration his own version of the best and the brightest. Many actually were. Others compensated with energy and earnestness for what they lacked in experience (even if, in the beginning, his administration was short on wise, pragmatic grown-ups—not to dampen the exuberance of his youthful crusaders, but to temper it). All of them shared a commitment to throwing open the gates of a calcified government to estranged New Yorkers—blacks, Puerto Ricans, women, gays, the poor, and younger people—who had been largely disregarded or even scorned. They helped Lindsay keep New York from burning.

In 1965, despite simmering unrest that had produced a minor race riot in Harlem the summer before, who would have imagined that three years later a century of repression would be ignited in more than three dozen American cities by the assassination of the nation's foremost advocate for civil rights? Many cities never recovered. New York was generally spared, not just because of Lindsay's personal courage in walking the streets of Harlem that night, but because he did not walk those streets as a stranger. He had already demonstrated his good will. His strategy of police restraint in the face of civil unrest, a strategy that was sorely tested and politically costly, would be validated by the president's commission on civil disorder, of which he was vice chairman. Before Bill Clinton was embraced as the First Black President, as Charlayne Hunter-Gault recalled, Lindsay was the Black Mayor. At least in the short term, he succeeded more effectively than any other big-city mayor in the nation in demonstrating concern to poor blacks and, in the long term, that remains perhaps his greatest legacy

"I will never forget the night Martin Luther King was killed—because of what John Lindsay did that night," Gordon J. Davis, a mayoral special assistant, recalled. "While other cities across America went up in flames, New York did not." David Garth, Lindsay's media consultant, who was with him that night, remembered: "There was a wall of people coming across 125th Street, going from west to east. I thought we were dead. John raised his hands, said he was sorry. It was very quiet. My feeling was, his appearance there was very reassuring to people because it wasn't the first time they had seen him. He had gone there on a regular basis."

Today, perhaps, the supposition that anybody "kept New York from burning" seems almost quaint. Lindsay did, though. And, if that had been his sole accomplishment—and it was not—wouldn't it, arguably, have been enough to celebrate his mayoralty? If he had failed, there would have been no city—or, surely, a diminished one—for Koch to salvage or for Giuliani and Bloomberg to revive.

New York survived, but, like much of urban America, the city became even more riven by race. Lindsay's personal commitment to civil rights and to the plight of the poor appeared to come at the expense of other New Yorkers (and contributed, along with generous labor contracts, to the 1975 fiscal crisis, although beyond vetoing budgets it is questionable what more legally Lindsay could really have done to impose fiscal restraint). That preferential treatment for the poor—not just any poor, but the black and Puerto Rican poor—produced an enduring backlash, a quiet riot. With America splitting into two societies, one black and one white, the chief challenge facing every public figure was to reconcile the demands of both groups and to ameliorate their estrangement from government and its remote processes. Lindsay overlooked the *other* other half, a snub that would recalibrate the city's political alignment for decades.

Murray Kempton once summed up the dynamic that would lead to the mayor's undoing: "Mr. Lindsay loses when he represents a lower social order against a higher one and he wins when he comes forward for a higher against a lower. The debate over the Civilian Review Board was won by the police, a superior class once it is cast against the Negroes and the young. The teachers beat the mayor on school decentralization and thus preserved an order where, if teachers sometimes need to defer to the parents of the rich, the parents of the poor must always defer to teachers. But the mayor beat the sanitation workers, on style at least, because he made the issue of whether the city should bow its head to garbage collectors, having, in this case, arrayed snobbery on his side."

Roger Starr, an urban planner, would describe the process in profoundly personal terms that smacked of elitism. Lindsay, he once said, was comfortable with only two kinds of people: those who had so little money that they needed more to get by, and those who had so much that they needed to give some of it away. Years later, Lindsay himself would admit that his neglect, benign or not, of white ethnic New York was a mistake. "It is true, I think," he told me, "that in recognizing the demands of deprived neighborhoods for a sign of concern, we did not realize how much the vast bulk of city people—hard-working white middle-class citizens—felt estranged, too, from the process of government."

Still, there were achievements that produced substantial and enduring benefits for all New Yorkers, achievements that seem all the more remarkable in the context of those troubled times (times that, in truth, the administration sometimes made even more turbulent). Lindsay, said Art Buchwald, the columnist with whom he used to play touch football in Washington on weekends, is "not fast, and he's not what you'd call agile, but he thinks up some devilishly clever plays." As a result of those intuitive tactics, subway cars were finally air-conditioned (they probably would have been eventually, but who knows when; Lindsay refused to spend city money on cars that weren't). The 911 emergency system was established and police commanders were granted more latitude to deploy officers when and where crime rates were highest. The police force grew (though the number of officers on patrol barely budged because the cops got more generous vacations and days off). The rival jurisdictions within the criminal justice system were being coordinated and infused with innovations from City Hall. Strategic urban planning included efforts to embellish the city's aesthetic and to spur economic development in several central business districts. Pedestrian-friendly happenings made the city more fun and vest-pocket parks made recreation and respite more available to everyone. Earth Day celebrations were just one gesture in championing the environment. City Hall inspired a resurgence of film-making. Collective bargaining with organized labor was rationalized and modern management polices were initiated citywide. Open admissions at the City University enabled any high school graduate to attend, free. Yankee Stadium was rebuilt (at high cost), a passenger-ship terminal was constructed, Shakespeare in the Park got a permanent home, and Gateway, the first national urban park, was established.

In 1968, Lindsay could have gracefully escaped the mayoralty by succeeding Robert F. Kennedy in the United States Senate, but he refused to pander to Governor Nelson A. Rockefeller, who would appoint a successor after Kennedy was assassinated, and also, perhaps, he felt guilty about jumping a sinking ship. In 1969, he sought re-election, spared from ignominious defeat when Norman Mailer's bizarre mayoral candidacy cost Lindsay's most liberal potential challenger, Herman Badillo, the Democratic nomination. Lindsay turned the race against two conservative rivals from a referendum on himself to one on the war in Vietnam. To woo wavering voters, he also reversed course on more than one unpopular policy and project, including Linear City, a modernistic development that would have bisected Brooklyn (leading Murray Kempton to quip: "In that one, the mayor played St. George *and* the dragon").

"Fighting a thousand dragons to keep the city alive," was the way the journalist Marquis Childs once described Lindsay's job. The fighting took its toll. "When we ask Sir Lancelot to feed the horses and do the washing," Jeff Greenfield, Lindsay's speechwriter, observed, "the armor tends to tarnish." The dragon-slaying analogies also recalled Don Quixote and his windmills and the final scene of *Man of La Mancha,* when the battered knight sings:

And the world will be better for this
That one man, scorned and covered with scars
Still strove with his last ounce of courage
To reach the unreachable star.

Was the world better for Lindsay's reaching? Or, had the Man of Manhattan overreached? "We feel mean-spirited when we make fun of John Lindsay," Murray Kempton once wrote. "One does not mock the innocent and the brave."

Lindsay never recovered politically from his ill-conceived presidential campaign in 1972. He lost a Democratic primary for the United States Senate in 1980, began to falter physically and financially (the Giuliani administration graciously placed him on the municipal payroll as general counsel to the United Nations Development Corp. so he would be eligible for health insurance) and faded from view. At a Lindsay administration reunion in 1993, someone, paraphrasing Kempton's famous aphorism from 1965, yelled, "You still look fresh, Mr. Mayor."

"Not true," Lindsay replied. "We're tired and everyone else is dead."

Lindsay died in 2000. He was 79. Tributes flowed from his former staff, many of whom had gone on to do good in other incarnations, and from dignitaries and contemporaries. But the average New Yorker, those, at least, who had lived in the city through the 60s and 70s, still associated Lindsay largely with the economically disastrous 1965 subway strike or the politically calamitous 1969 snowstorm and perhaps the racially charged combat over school decentralization and low-income housing. And those events, events that everyone would agree could have been better quarterbacked, would eclipse Lindsay's quixotic quest, which began with high hopes for what may never have been a possible dream amid the last gasps of New Deal liberalism, and ultimately his record of accomplishment. William F. Buckley Jr., Lindsay's erstwhile rival, offered the outgoing mayor one word of advice: "Repent."

December 31, 1973, was John Lindsay's last day as mayor of New York. He was teary as he walked down City Hall's granite steps as mayor for the last time. The Lindsay team, the aging Kiddie Korps that had vigorously charged into City Hall eight years earlier, was not necessarily tired, but they were no longer fresh, "Remember those good old days in New York City," one of the mayor's young wise men, Barry Gottehrer, would later recall, not without irony, to others who had worked for Lindsay, "when we all were young, beautiful, invincible and we all really cared?" Gottehrer left the administration early, after concluding that, "the best kind of power, your power for constructive change, is very limited." He added: "I gave myself pep talks more frequently that were based less on our achievements than on the belief that other administrations, on the whole, did a lot worse."

Which, in the end, is how Lindsay should be judged. Would anyone else have done better in dreaming a dream and delivering on it in those tumultuous times when, it seemed, every day was, to one faction or another, a Day of Outrage? In eight years, the city had changed. The ground had shifted from under the mayor. And the mayoralty, the job itself, had changed, too. Lindsay's one-time deputy, Robert Price, would advise the next mayor, Abraham D. Beame: "Keep alert even when you're sleeping. Walk with your back to the wall. Be optimistic. Carry a Bible. Pray and punt."

For those who stuck with Lindsay to the bitter end, the transition to Beame was more constructive than that from Wagner to Lindsay. But, like it had been eight years before, the contrast between the two administrations could not have been more stark: The young, if a little weary, Lindsay staff, some of whom had not been old enough to vote during the first campaign, and the incoming graybeards in their 60s, some of whom were veterans of several prior administrations. Seated with the Lindsays in the front row at Beame's inauguration were three battered New York fixtures from the past—former Mayor Wagner, the boxer Jack Dempsey, and the New Deal Democratic boss James A. Farley—placed there, perhaps, as props to make Beame seem more vital.

A few days before, as the Beame team left a transition meeting in the Blue Room of City Hall, the Lindsay staffers, with just hours left to effect the constructive change they had hoped would create a city of tomorrow, sat there glumly to contemplate all they had accomplished over eight years and what would become of it now under a well-meaning, but conventional mayor. Their turn had come, and gone. Finally, Ed Hamilton, Lindsay's bearded, 34-year-old deputy mayor (he was half Beame's age), broke the spell with some welcome gallows humor. "Face it fellows," he said. "The torch has passed to a new generation."

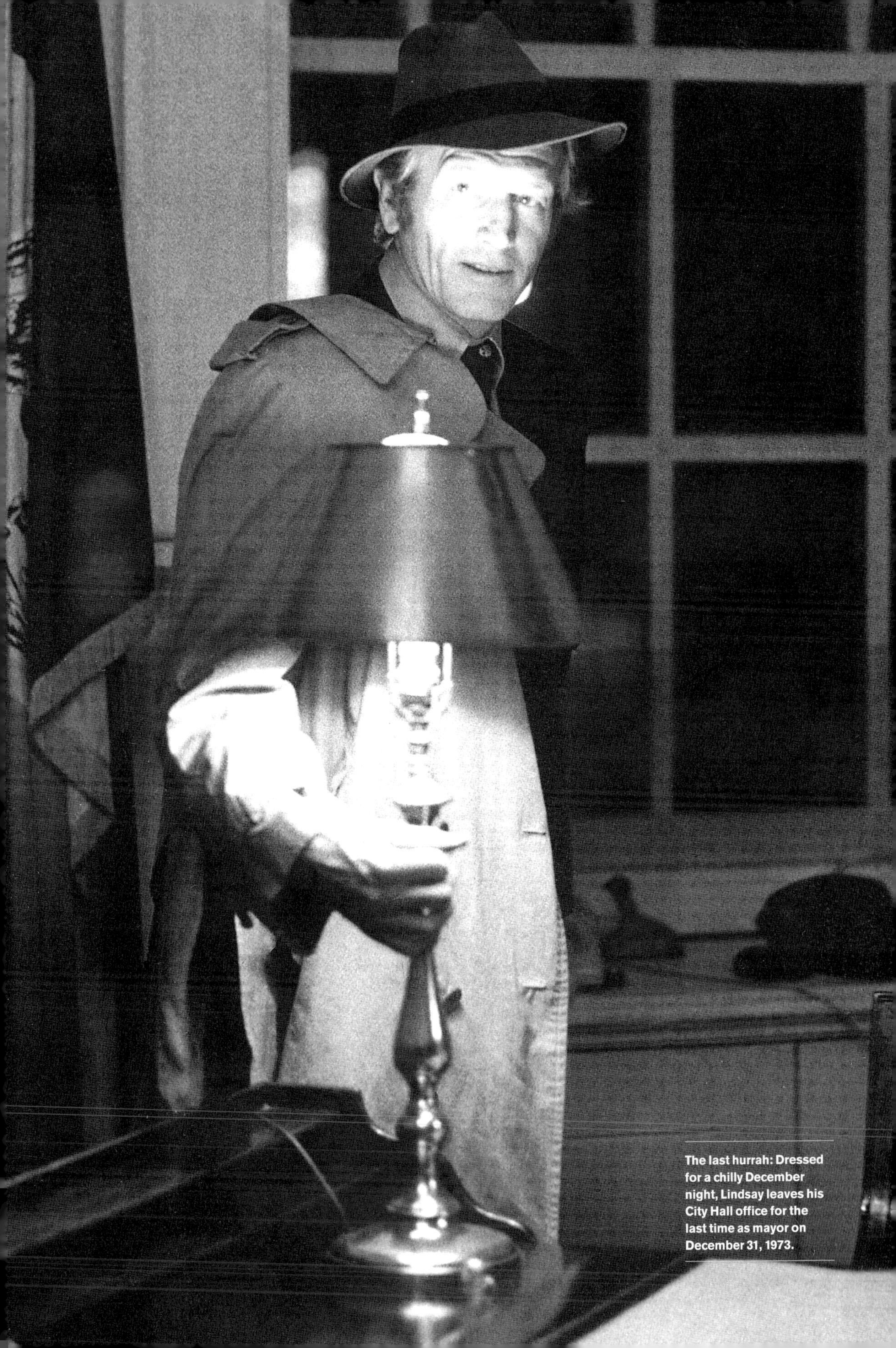

The last hurrah: Dressed for a chilly December night, Lindsay leaves his City Hall office for the last time as mayor on December 31, 1973.

PHOTO CREDITS

Front Cover Photograph by Henri Dauman. © 2001 Henri Dauman/ Dauman Pictures NYC
Back Cover Photo by John Dominis/Time Life Pictures/Getty Images
Title Page Neal Boenzi/The New York Times
Page 6 From *Newsweek*, May 31 © 1965 Newsweek, Inc. All rights reserved. Used by permission and protected by the Copyright Laws of the United States. The printing, copying, redistribution, or retransmission of the Material without express written permission is prohibited.
Page 8 Photograph by Henri Dauman. © 2001 Henri Dauman/ Dauman Pictures NYC
Page 9 From TIME, November 12 © 1965 TIME, Inc. All rights reserved. Used by permission and protected by the Copyright Laws of the United States. The printing, copying, redistribution, or retransmission of the Material without express written permission is prohibited.
Page 10–11 Photo by Central Press/ Getty Images
Page 12 Photo by Greg Villet/Time Life Pictures/Getty Images
Page 14 (top) Courtesy of Steven Jaffe
Page 14 (bottom) Photograph by Katrina Thomas. Courtesy of the Lindsay family
Page 15 Photo by Fred W. McDarrah/ Getty Images
Page 17 Library of Congress, Prints & Photographs Division, NYWT&S Collection, [LC-USZ62-136894]
Page 18 © New York Daily News, L.P. Used with permission.
Page 20 Courtesy of Steven Isenberg
Page 24 © New York Daily News, L.P. Used with permission.
Page 26–27 Photograph by Katrina Thomas. Courtesy of the Lindsay family
Page 28 (all) Courtesy of the collection of Katharine Lindsay Lake
Page 29 Courtesy of the Lindsay family
Page 30–31 Still images from campaign commercials courtesy of The Garth Group.
Page 32 Courtesy of the Lindsay family
Page 33 Courtesy of the Lindsay family
Page 34–35 Courtesy of the Lindsay family
Page 36 (all) Photograph by Katrina Thomas, courtesy of the photographer
Page 37 Courtesy of the Lindsay family
Page 38 Edward Hausner/The New York Times
Page 39 © Bettman/Corbis
Page 41 © New York Daily News, L.P. Used with permission. Courtesy of Katharine Lindsay Lake
Page 43–44 Photo by John Dominis/Time Life Pictures/Getty Images
Page 45 © Bettman/Corbis
Page 46 Don Hogan Charles/The New York Times
Page 48 © New York Daily News, L.P. Used with permission.
Page 49 John Burns/The New York Times
Page 51 © Bettman/Corbis
Page 52 © Bettman/Corbis
Page 54 Photograph by Katrina Thomas. Courtesy of the Lindsay family
Page 55 © New York Daily News, L.P. Used with permission.
Page 58–59 © Bettman/Corbis
Page 61 Photograph by Norma Holt, courtesy of the photographer
Page 62 United Federation of Teachers Photographs Collection, Tamiment Library, New York University. Photograph by Sam Reiss.
Page 64 © New York Daily News, L.P. Used with permission.
Page 65 Photograph by Diana Davies. Diana Davies photographs, Manuscripts and Archives Division, The New York Public Library, Astor, Lenox and Tilden Foundations
Page 66 Photo by Fred W. McDarrah/Getty Images
Page 67 Photo by Hulton Archive/Getty Images
Page 68 © New York Daily News, L.P. Used with permission.
Page 72–73 Photograph by Horst Schäfer. Museum of the City of New York Prints & Photographs Collection, 02.93.2, Gift of Horst Schäfer
Page 74 Photo by Arthur Schatz/Time Life Pictures/Getty Images
Page 75 Courtesy New York City Municipal Archives
Page 76–77 Meyer Liebowitz/The New York Times
Page 78 Don Hogan Charles/The New York Times
Page 79 Courtesy of The New York Times
Page 80 Photograph by Richard Howard
Page 81 Photograph © Catherine Ursillo. Museum of the City of New York Prints & Photographs Collection, 03.104.5, Gift of the photographer
Page 82 Photo by Fred W. McDarrah/Getty Images
Page 83 Photo by Fred W. McDarrah/Getty Images
Page 84–85 Courtesy of the collection of Katharine Lindsay Lake
Page 86 © [2010] The Associated Press
Page 87 American International Pictures/ Photofest
Page 88–89 United Artists/ Photofest
Page 90 AVCO Embassy/ Photofest
Page 91 New York City Parks Photo Archive
Page 92 New York City Parks Photo Archive
Page 95 New York City Parks Photo Archive
Page 96 (left) Property of the artist Hangford Yang, NY
Page 96 (right) © Peter Mauss/Esto
Page 97 Design by Van Ginkel Associates; Rendering by B. Johnson. Property of the Canadian Center for Architecture
Page 98 Courtesy of Harold Prince
Page 99 © New York Daily News, L.P. Used with permission.
Page 102–103 Michael Evans/The New York Times

Page 105 United Federation of Teachers Photographs Collection, Tamiment Library, New York University. Photograph by Hans Weissenstein.
Page 107
Barton Silverman/The New York Times
Page 108 Barton Silverman/The New York Times
Page 109 Sam Falk/The New York Times
Page 110 © 1984 The Estate of Garry Winogrand, courtesy Fraenkel Gallery, San Francisco
Page 113 Photograph by Tim Kantor
Page 116 © New York Daily News, L.P. Used with permission.
Page 118–119 Ernest Sisto/The New York Times
Page 121 Courtesy Transport Workers Union of America, AFL-CIO
Page 122 © New York Daily News, L.P. Used with permission.
Page 123 © Bettman/Corbis
Page 125 United Federation of Teachers Photographs Collection, Tamiment Library, New York University. Photograph by Hans Weissenstein.
Page 126 © New York Daily News, L.P. Used with permission.
Page 127 © New York Daily News, L.P. Used with permission.
Page 128 © [2010] The Associated Press
Page 129 © New York Daily News, L.P. Used with permission.
Page 130 Courtesy Public Employee Press DC 37
Page 131 Photograph by David Bernstein. Museum of the City of New York Prints & Photographs Collection, 01.51.2, Gift of David M. Bernstein
Page 132–133 © New York Daily News, L.P. Used with permission.
Page 135 From *The Lower Manhattan Plan*, 1966, by the Office of Lower Manhattan Development. Courtesy of John West.
Page 137 Photo by Truman Moore/Time Life Pictures/Getty Images
Page 138 (all) Courtesy of Jonathan Barnett
Page 139 Drawing by John V. Y. Lee for the South Street Seaport Development Plan. Courtesy of John West
Page 140 Courtesy of Jonathan Barnett
Page 141 (top) Courtesy of Terrence Williams
Page 141 (bottom) Courtesy of Jonathan Barnett
Page 143 Photo by John Dominis/Time Life Pictures/Getty Images
Page 144 © Joseph Farris/Condé Nast Publications/www.cartoonbank.com
Page 147 © New York Daily News, L.P. Used with permission.
Page 150–151 © New York Daily News, L.P. Used with permission.
Page 152 Michael Evans/The New York Times
Page 153 Don Hogan Charles/The New York Times
Page 154–155 © Benedict J. Fernandez. Museum of the City of New York Prints & Photographs Collection, Gift of Ben J. Fernandez.
Page 157 © Bettman/Corbis
Page 158 © Bettman/Corbis
Page 159 © New York Daily News, L.P. Used with permission.
Page 160 Still images from campaign commercials courtesy of The Garth Group.
Page 162 © New York Daily News, L.P. Used with permission.
Page 164 © New York Daily News, L.P. Used with permission.
Page 165 (left) Photo by John Dominis/Life Magazine, Copyright Time Inc./Time Life Pictures/Getty Images
Page 165 (right) From TIME, November 1 © 1968 TIME, Inc. All rights reserved. Used by permission and protected by the Copyright Laws of the United States. The printing, copying, redistribution, or retransmission of the Material without express written permission is prohibited
Page 166 Courtesy of the Lindsay family.
Page 167 Photo by Focus On Sport/Getty Images
Page 168 Librado Romero/The New York Times
Page 170–171 Neal Boenzi/The New York Times
Page 172 Courtesy of the Lindsay family.
Page 175 Photo by David Fenton/Getty Images
Page 177 Photograph by John Albok. Museum of the City of New York Prints & Photographs Collection, 82.68.12, Gift of Ilona Albok Parker
Page 178 © Bettman/Corbis
Page 182 Neal Boenzi/The New York Times
Page 184–185 Photograph by Frederick Kelly. Museum of the City of New York Prints & Photographs Collection, 01.59.7, Gift of Rena C. Kelly.
Page 186 Courtesy of Fales Library & Special Collections, New York University, Judson Memorial Church Archives
Page 189 © The Estate of Gib Crockett. Courtesy of the collection of Katharine Lindsay Lake
Page 191 Robert Walker/The New York Times
Page 192–193 Library of Congress, Prints & Photographs Division, NYWT&S Collection, [LC-USZ62-132501]
Page 195 © New York Daily News, L.P. Used with permission.
Page 197 Neal Boenzi/The New York Times
Page 198 © Bettman/Corbis
Page 199 Photo by Arnold Sachs/Consolidated News Pictures/Getty Images
Page 200–201 Photograph by Jon Naar © 1973, 2010
Page 202 Photo by Keystone/Getty Images
Page 209 William Sauro/The New York Times
Page 210–211 © [2010] The Associated Press
Page 212 © Bettman/Corbis
Page 214–215 Photo by John Dominis/Time Life Pictures/Getty Images
Page 216 Photo by Fred W. McDarrah/Getty Images
Page 217 Photo by John Dominis/Time Life Pictures/Getty Images
Page 226 © Bettman/Corbis
Page 227 Courtesy Transport Workers Union of America, AFL-CIO
Page 229 Joyce Dopkeen/The New York Times
Page 236 © 1970 Paul Giovanopoulos/www.giovanopoulos.com
Page 241 © New York Daily News, L.P. Used with permission.

INDEX

Photographs and charts are indicated by *italicized numbers*

ABOUT THE MUSEUM OF THE CITY OF NEW YORK

The Museum of the City of New York celebrates and interprets the city, educating the public about its distinctive character, especially its heritage of diversity, opportunity, and perpetual transformation. Founded in 1923 as a private, non-profit corporation, the Museum connects the past, present, and future of New York City. It serves the people of New York and visitors from around the world through exhibitions, school and public programs, publications, and collections.